Understand
the Cold War
C.B. Jones

For UK order enquiries: please contact Bookpoint Ltd, 130 Milton Park, Abingdon, Oxon OX14 4SB. Telephone: +44 (0) 1235 827720. Fax: +44 (0) 1235 400454. Lines are open 09.00–17.00, Monday to Saturday, with a 24-hour message answering service. Details about our titles and how to order are available at www.teachyourself.com

For USA order enquiries: please contact McGraw-Hill Customer Services, PO Box 545, Blacklick, OH 43004-0545, USA. Telephone: 1-800-722-4726. Fax: 1-614-755-5645.

For Canada order enquiries: please contact McGraw-Hill Ryerson Ltd, 300 Water St, Whitby, Ontario L1N 9B6, Canada. Telephone: 905 430 5000. Fax: 905 430 5020.

Long renowned as the authoritative source for self-guided learning – with more than 50 million copies sold worldwide – the **Teach Yourself** series includes over 500 titles in the fields of languages, crafts, hobbies, business, computing and education.

British Library Cataloguing in Publication Data: a catalogue record for this title is available from the British Library.

Library of Congress Catalog Card Number: on file.

First published in UK 2004 by Hodder Education, part of Hachette UK, 338 Euston Road, London NW1 3BH.

First published in US 2004 by The McGraw-Hill Companies, Inc.

This edition published 2010.

Previously published as *Teach Yourself the Cold War*

The *Teach Yourself* name is a registered trade mark of Hodder Headline.

Typeset by MPS Limited, A Macmillan Company.

Printed in Great Britain for Hodder Education, an Hachette UK Company, 338 Euston Road, London NW1 3BH, by CPI Cox & Wyman, Reading, Berkshire RG1 8EX.

The publisher has used its best endeavours to ensure that the URLs for external websites referred to in this book are correct and active at the time of going to press. However, the publisher and the author have no responsibility for the websites and can make no guarantee that a site will remain live or that the content will remain relevant, decent or appropriate.

Hachette UK's policy is to use papers that are natural, renewable and recyclable products and made from wood grown in sustainable forests. The logging and manufacturing processes are expected to conform to the environmental regulations of the country of origin.

Impression number	10 9 8 7 6 5 4
Year	2016

Contents

Meet the author		ix
Only got a minute?		x
Only got five minutes?		xii
1	**What was the Cold War?**	**1**
	What was the Cold War?	2
	Who were the Great Powers?	3
	Conflicting ideologies	5
	Conflicting aims in Europe	7
2	**Europe at the end of the Second World War**	**10**
	The end of the war in Europe	10
	Yalta	12
	Poland	13
	The Potsdam Conference	15
3	**Containment**	**21**
	Poland	22
	Bulgaria	23
	Hungary	23
	Romania	23
	East Germany	24
	Yugoslavia	24
	Greece	25
	The Truman Doctrine	27
	The Marshall Plan	28
4	**Germany**	**33**
	Germany divided	34
	The formation of NATO	41
	The German question	43
	Crisis in Berlin 1961 – face-off at Checkpoint Charlie	44
	Ich bin ein Berliner	46
5	**The Far East**	**49**
	China 1949–50	50
	Fear of Communist expansion	51
	The Malay Emergency	52

	Korea	54
	The Domino Theory	65
6	**The thaw**	**70**
	Khrushchev	71
	Poland	73
	Hungary	74
7	**The arms race**	**81**
	What was the arms race?	83
	The hydrogen bomb	84
	National prestige	85
	U-2 incident	87
	Rocket science	87
	The missile gap	89
	NASA	90
	Should the West use nuclear weapons?	91
	How safe were nuclear weapons in the hands of the superpowers?	92
	Détente and the arms race	94
	Ronald Reagan and the second Cold War	96
	Reagan and Gorbachev	99
	Gorbachev's bombshell	101
	Public reaction to the arms race	101
8	**Kennedy and Khrushchev**	**106**
	Castro's revolution	108
	American attempts to destabilize Cuba	109
	The Bay of Pigs invasion	110
	Cuba grows closer to the USSR	112
	Khrushchev's bright idea	112
	ExComm hawks and doves	114
	Cuba in quarantine	116
	Cuba's view of the situation	120
	Reaction of the people	121
	Win–win	123
	Result of the crisis	124
9	**A new domino**	**127**
	Russia and China	127
	Sino–Soviet split	129
	A new domino	131

The likelihood of war increases 135
Gulf of Tonkin 136
Operation Rolling Thunder 137
The United States commits to ground involvement 139
Peace initiatives 141
The Tet offensive 141
Vietnamization 142
Peace with honour? 143
Implications of the war 144

10 Czechoslovakia 149
The Prague spring 150
Fear of reform in the Eastern bloc 152
The invasion of Czechoslovakia 153
Were the Soviets invited in to seize control
in Czechoslovakia? 154
Why did the West once again fail to act? 155
Brezhnev Doctrine 156

11 Détente 1971–9 158
Motives of the Great Powers 159
Relations between the USA and China 161
The United States and the USSR 163
Arms limitation discussions 164
Human rights on the agenda but ignored 167
The end of détente 169

12 The Middle East 172
United States interests 174
Conflicts in the Middle East 176
Arab–Israeli conflict – the background 176
The Suez crisis 1957 177
The Six Day War 180
The October War 181
Sadat's 'sacred mission' 184
Iran 186
The Gulf War – Iran v. Iraq 188
Afghanistan: the Soviet Vietnam 189

13 The Cold War in Africa and Latin America 194
Angola 197
The Horn of Africa 201

	Latin America	203
	Chile	204
	Nicaragua	207
14	**The second Cold War**	**213**
	Poland	214
	Confrontations	217
	Mikhail Gorbachev – change in the USSR	218
	Détente	219
15	**The collapse of Soviet influence in Eastern Europe**	**222**
	Hungary 1988	224
	East Germany 1989–90	225
	Czechoslovakia – the Velvet Revolution 1989	227
	Romania	228
	Bulgaria	230
	Yugoslavia	230
16	**Cold War spies**	**234**
	Why spy?	237
	Technology and spying	238
	Spies in literature and the movies	240
	Ordinary people	242
17	**The end of the Cold War**	**246**
	How did the Cold War affect the people?	249
	What was the financial cost of the Cold War?	251
	Glossary	**254**
	Taking it further	**260**
	Index	**263**

Credits

Front cover: © CreativeAct – Objects series/Alamy

Back cover: © Jakub Semeniuk/iStockphoto.com, © Royalty-Free/Corbis, © agencyby/iStockphoto.com, © Andy Cook/iStockphoto.com, © Christopher Ewing/iStockphoto.com, © zebicho – Fotolia.com, © Geoffrey Holman/iStockphoto.com, © Photodisc/Getty Images, © James C. Pruitt/iStockphoto.com, © Mohamed Saber – Fotolia.com

Meet the author

Welcome to *Understand the Cold War*!

'The Cold War' is a term generally used to describe the aggressive relationship that developed between the capitalist USA and the Communist Soviet Union in the late 1940s. For over 50 years these countries built up military forces, engaged in political manoeuvring, and gave secret military assistance to allies and satellite nations.

This book will provide you with a straightforward narrative introduction to these events. The first three chapters deal with the beginning of the conflict and how Stalin, one-time ally of the West, began his bid to spread the Communist system throughout the world following the end of the Second World War.

Then it examines the development of the Cold War across the world, exploring many features associated with the conflict, including nuclear weapons and the arms race, détente, the space race, propaganda and spying.

In my opinion the Cold War is frequently misunderstood by many, and yet it has shaped our society and its institutions, and has repercussions which remain to this day. This conflict led to the development of computers, missiles and space rockets – all things we take for granted. Institutions such as The European Union and North Atlantic Treaty Organization in the West and the Warsaw Pact in the East were created in order to pursue the Cold War. The terrorism evident in our society today has its roots in the tactics employed by both sides during the Cold War as each side tried to undermine and humiliate the other. An understanding of the Cold War legacy is vital to understand the modern world in which we live.

I hope you enjoy this book, and if you find you want to know more about the subject, take a look at some of the websites and books suggested in the Taking It Further section.

Carole Bryan Jones

Only got a minute?

The Cold War is usually defined by historians in the West as the ideological struggle between the democratic West and the Communist Soviet Union as the latter endeavoured to spread Communism across the world. However, there are other interpretations of this conflict. Was it a struggle for the control of Europe? Or was it a protracted Third World War, albeit with little direct fighting between the superpowers?

Diplomats identify three different types of war: a hot war, where fighting between armies is ongoing; a warm war, where armed forces are being mobilized but diplomatic talks continue and the possibility of a peaceful outcome remains; and a cold war, where neither side fights the other directly but rather 'fights' vicariously using client states.

Neither the USA nor the USSR wanted a hot war to break out as the development of atomic weapons had made it increasingly likely that such a war would lead to the destruction of civilization. Therefore, the two sides never actually went to war against each other but often supported each other's enemies, conducted media and propaganda campaigns against each other and even clashed in international sporting events.

The Cold War was more than just posturing. There were many examples of fighting that threatened to bring open war as aggression between the USA and the USSR spilled over into other countries. The Berlin blockade and airlift (1948–9), the Korean War (1950–3), the Cuban Missile Crisis (1962), the Vietnam War (1964–75) and the invasion of Afghanistan (1979–89) were all proxy conflicts between the USA and the USSR. In 1989, the destruction of the Berlin Wall led to the end of the Cold War; by December 1989, US President George Bush and Soviet President Mikhail Gorbachev had officially ended the conflict, but tensions between the two superpowers linger to this day.

5 Only got five minutes?

Historians have found it difficult to agree on many aspects of the Cold War. Generally they agree that the term refers to the political, military and diplomatic relationships that developed between the United States of America and the Soviet Union following the end of the Second World War in 1945. Some believe that the relationship between these countries had been strained since the development of communism in the USSR following the October Revolution in 1917.

The Cold War is usually said to have begun in earnest during the closing days of the Second World War and to have ended between 1990 and 1992, as the Soviet Union's sphere of influence waned and many of the countries which made up the USSR went their separate ways. For nearly half a century these countries vied with each other to gain worldwide power and influence and to extend their political ideologies via political, diplomatic, military and technological means, frequently using spies and espionage to keep their side ahead of the game.

Historians disagree as to which side began the Cold War and why. The orthodox view of the 1950s saw the Cold War as the fault of Soviet aggression in Eastern Europe. By the 1960s a revisionist view blamed the USA's aggressive attempt to expand trade and political influence into Eastern Europe despite Russian interests in that area. These historians argue that Russia merely did what any power would have done – look after its own national interests by dominating Eastern Europe. Post-revisionist historians contend that there was fault on both sides. They accept that Stalin was more interested in preserving a secure buffer zone between Russia and the West than in world domination, but also maintain that Western powers could not be certain of this at the time and therefore perceived Stalin's intentions as a threat to the West.

Whoever was responsible, neither side wanted a 'hot war' to break out. The world was still recovering from the Second World War (1939–45), and the development of atomic weapons by both the USA (1945) and the USSR (1949) had made such a war extremely dangerous; these weapons of mass destruction could result in a MAD war – one of mutually assured destruction. Consequently, open warfare had to be avoided. Instead, both sides dabbled in international conflicts all over the world, used propaganda and 'dirty tricks' to make each other look foolish, provided funding and military might to support or subdue satellite states and tried to prove that their particular political ideology was the one which would ensure eventual victory.

The conflict was more than just posturing and propaganda: there were plenty of examples of real violence and fighting that threatened to bring open war. The Berlin blockade and airlift (1948–9), the Korean War (1950–3), the Cuban Missile Crisis (1962), the Vietnam War (1964–75) and the invasion of Afghanistan (1979–89) all had the potential to develop into 'hot' conflicts. Various attempts were made to bring about détente during the conflict: President Nixon negotiated with both Russia and China; Leonid Brezhnev was eager to forge a better relationship with the USA on certain issues. By the end of the 1970s this thaw in relationships had disappeared with the invasion of Afghanistan by the USSR. The advent to power of President Reagan saw the USA adopting an increasingly hard line with the Soviets and dramatically increasing military spending.

In 1985 Mikhail Gorbachev introduced a series of internal economic reforms known as *perestroika*, while at the same time attempting to improve relations with the West, via *glasnost*. These reforms failed to prevent the collapse of the Soviet system and, in 1989, the destruction of the Berlin Wall saw the beginning of the end of the Cold War. By December 1989, US President George Bush and Soviet President Mikhail Gorbachev had officially ended the conflict.

1

What was the Cold War?

In this chapter you will learn about:
- *the definition of Cold War*
- *the participating Great Powers*
- *the importance of conflicting political ideas in creating an atmosphere of mistrust.*

Picture the scene. It is springtime in Eastern Europe and two groups of young men and women have met at midday on the banks of a river and are busy socializing, drinking and dancing to the wheezing of a concertina, hugging, kissing, shaking hands and vowing to be friends. A charming rural idyll? No. This was the meeting of the American and Soviet troops on the banks of the Elbe near Strehla on 25 April 1945. For the sake of the cameras this meeting was repeated two days later at Torgau but in spite of press intrusion the scene was one of happiness and unity between young comrades-in-arms. True, there were differences between the two groups as one US soldier, Private Jim Kane, recalled later:

> They (the Soviet Red Army) were still using horse-drawn wagons, cavalry pieces, horse-drawn artillery... The soldiers were on horseback. It was like the medieval times...

Who could have imagined on that heady day of peace and goodwill that these two nations would soon become mortal enemies and spend the next 45 years engaged in a frosty stand-off which was to shape the second half of the twentieth century.

If you were to compare a series of maps of Europe during the twentieth century it would immediately be obvious that the frontiers of certain countries have been far from stable. During the second half of the century the changes in frontiers were largely due to developments known as the Cold War between the Great Powers. This strangely named conflict, which began in 1945, was to last until the early 1990s – the dates of its beginning and ending are debatable. The causes of the conflict are equally a matter of contention between historians and, indeed, so complex are the various elements of this conflict that one is forced to make generalizations in order to make sense of the causes and events which developed following the end of the 1939–45 'hot' war.

Insight

Historians disagree as to when the Cold War began. Was it after the Russian revolution in 1917; or in 1945, when the Allies disagreed over how to govern occupied Germany; or following Churchill's speech in Fulton Missouri in 1946, when he used the term 'the iron curtain'? Each case has its merits.

During these years each side had its own interpretation of the other's actions – what one side considered self-defence, the other side interpreted as aggression. The very nature of the 'Cold War', with its climate of mistrust and suspicion, makes it difficult to work out the motives and reasons for the actions of the Great Powers. Indeed, frequently what contemporaries thought had happened was often more important than what actually happened!

What was the Cold War?

Following the Second World War, an increasingly frosty atmosphere developed between the Great Powers, and this grew into a tense rivalry which became known as the 'Cold War'.

This was to last for over 40 years and spread from Europe, where it originated, to the rest of the world during the 1950s and 1960s.

This rivalry had all the features of a traditional 'hot' war with one exception – there was no open, armed conflict. It was a war because there were two opposing sides each equipped with armies, navies and air forces and each had allies. It is called a 'cold' war because there was no direct fighting between the Great Powers, although there were a few instances when the Cold War spilled over into open conflict, often through 'proxies'. All other features of warfare were present – causes, weapons, tactics, events and results, and each side used spies and propaganda to further their aims or to persuade others to join them in their mission against their enemies, whom they believed were trying to destroy their way of life. There was fear, hostility, suspicion, competition, threats and quarrels between the two sides, yet the obvious feature of direct fighting was avoided.

Neither side wished to risk the prospect of a 'hot' war, perhaps because of the existence of nuclear weapons.

Insight

The first nuclear device was exploded by the US Manhattan Project in 1945. Extremely powerful explosive devices, they were originally designed as strategic weapons to destroy entire cities and, during the Second World War, were used against the Japanese cities of Hiroshima and Nagasaki.

Who were the Great Powers?

A Great Power is a country which has a number of important features. It generally has a large land area rich in natural resources and a large population, its economy is prosperous, its industry strong, and foreign trade contributes to its economic wealth. Another aspect of a Great Power is political stability and these features, combined with strong armed forces, give the Great Power worldwide influence.

Great Powers tend to use their extensive resources to influence other powers and world events by persuasion, economic pressure or sometimes by force and this can lead to both direct and indirect conflict.

For centuries the Great Powers were European, but following the twentieth-century world wars, the map of Great Powers was redrawn with the United States, the USSR and later China taking the place of the European Powers as the movers and shakers of world events.

There were many differences between the Great Powers, but it was in the fields of politics and economics that the countries differed the most. In terms of ideology, the USSR and China were (and China still is) based on communism, while the American political system is based on democracy. In economics, the United States followed capitalism, based on private enterprise; the Communist states on the other hand had command economies, where the state owned the means of production.

Insight

Communism is a system of government based on the ideology of Karl Marx. The one-party state owns all property and the means of production, plans and controls the economy and aims to create a classless society.

Capitalism is a free market economic system whereby the means of production is owned mainly by private individuals who are motivated by the opportunity to make a profit. Investors in private companies are known as shareholders.

The Cold War is generally regarded as a conflict between East and West or between communism and capitalism. These two ideologies were personified by the Soviet Union (USSR or Russia – Communist) and the United States of America (capitalist), the two 'superpowers' that had emerged following the eclipse of the leading European Powers in the wake of the Second World War. However, the origins of the Cold War can be seen to date back to the Russian Revolution in 1917 after which Communist Russia seemed to threaten the liberal democracies in Western Europe. The establishment in 1919 of the Comintern, an organization dedicated to the expansion of communist ideals at the expense of capitalism, strengthened this fear and contributed to the decision on the part of many Western powers to aid the opponents of the Bolsheviks during the Russian Civil War of 1918–21. Indeed Churchill, the British Secretary of State for War, summarized his policy during this period as 'Kill the Bolshie. Kiss the Hun', as the Western nations built up a defeated Germany in order to prevent the spread of communism. Germany joined the League of Nations in 1924 but the Soviet Union received no such invitation.

Insight

The League of Nations was an international organization established in 1919, aiming to ensure that a world war was never repeated. It attempted to settle disputes between nations peacefully, taking economic sanctions against any country that resorted to war rather than submit to arbitration. Unfortunately all decisions had to be unanimous, which lessened the League's effectiveness. The League was replaced by the United Nations in 1945 (see page 13).

Conflicting ideologies

The difference in political, social and economic ideas between Russia and the West became apparent during the 1920s. Communist countries were generally classless societies where individual profit-making was prohibited and where industry and agriculture were owned not by private individuals but by the state, which encouraged its citizens to work for the greater good of society rather than for personal gain. In these 'one-party states', the government maintained close control of the lives of the populations through political, social and financial mechanisms including censorship, propaganda and limitations on travel and religious worship.

In contrast, citizens in the capitalist West had a variety of political parties from which to choose their governments, via free elections. These governments had a limited control over their citizens' lives, and freedom of speech and movement were the norm. Most industry and agriculture was in the hands of private companies or individuals who employed others to work for them, and whose aim was to make as much profit as possible.

During the Second World War, out of necessity, these contrasting ideologies had formed an uneasy alliance against Hitler and Nazism, but in spite of their co-operation on the surface, tension had existed between the two sides, a tension which intensified following the defeat of Germany and her allies, the Axis powers, in 1945. Their political ideologies and very different forms of government, economy and society were naturally a point of irritation and had resulted in an increasing atmosphere of mistrust.

From a Western point of view, communism threatened their democratic values and beliefs; Stalin's political purges and agricultural policies had killed many of his own people during the 1920s and 1930s. During the 1930s a young American, George F. Keenan, witnessed events in the Soviet Union and concluded that the country was 'unalterably opposed to our traditional system'. In spite of growing concern as Hitler reasserted German power, no serious attempt was made by Britain and France to cultivate an alliance with Russia, and the world was astonished to hear of the Nazi–Soviet non-aggression pact signed in August 1939. Those in the West would remember Stalin for this cynical signing of the Molotov–Ribbentrop Pact – the Nazi–Soviet agreement which had divided Poland in 1939.

Similarly, communists regarded capitalism as evil – Karl Marx and Friedrich Engels, the authors of *The Communist Manifesto* in 1848, had emphasized how the rich prospered through their exploitation of the 'proletariat' – the working classes. Nor could

Russian Communists forget how the West had helped the 'Whites' (an anti-Communist coalition) fight against the Bolshevik Red Army during the Russian Civil War. Churchill (Britain's wartime leader during the Second World War) had been Secretary of State for War at this time, and had sanctioned the sending of British troops to Russia to aid the 'White Army'. This had followed another humiliation when, in 1919, the Entente powers had distributed Russian territory to other countries including Poland. Small wonder, then, that in 1945 Stalin commented to Milovan Djilas, a fellow Communist:

> *Perhaps you think that, because we are allies of the English, we have forgotten who they are, and who Churchill is. They find nothing sweeter than to trick their allies.*

Further humiliation followed during the inter-war years when Russia was excluded from the League of Nations, and the attempts of the Russian diplomat Litvinov to organize a united front against Hitler's demands on Czechoslovakia in 1938 were ignored.

Still later, in 1942, Britain and the USA had refused to open up a second front against Hitler by invading Europe quickly and thus relieving Russia of some of the pressure upon her.

Conflicting aims in Europe

The two power blocs had conflicting aims for Central and Eastern Europe following the Second World War. The Western powers were anxious to support democratic movements in these areas and were eager to hold free elections. They believed that Poland's Western frontier should remain as it was and Germany should be aided and encouraged to produce her own goods and food in order that she could quickly rejoin world trade. This would avoid a repetition of the economic difficulties that she had faced following the end of the First World War when hyperinflation bred discontent and contributed to the rise of the Nazis.

The Union of Soviet Socialist Republics, as Russia had become in 1922, wanted a 'buffer zone' – an area of friendly states between her and Germany to protect 'Mother Russia' from invasion by the West. These 'friendly' states would, of course, have Soviet-style governments, an unlikely event if free elections were held, as few inhabitants were eager to see Communist-style governments in their countries. To further strengthen Russia's western borders, Stalin was anxious to redefine Poland's western border and to keep Germany weak both economically and politically, since in this way Russia would be protected.

These differences in aims began to become apparent at the two peace conferences held in Yalta in early 1945 and in Potsdam following the end of the war.

10 THINGS TO REMEMBER

1 *American and Soviet troops met each other at Strehla on 25 April 1945.*

2 *The 'Cold War' is so called because there was no open, direct conflict between the great powers – the USA and the USSR.*

3 *Orthodox historians have blamed the USSR for beginning the Cold War. Revisionist historians blame the USA. Post-revisionist historians implicate both sides in the causes of the conflict.*

4 *The Western powers were democratic and capitalist countries. The Eastern powers were Communist and followed a command economy.*

5 *Communist countries generally have only one political party and the state, which decides what and how much to produce – hence 'the command economy'.*

6 *Democratic countries hold free elections for a variety of political parties, and most of industry and agriculture is privately owned and aims to make a profit – hence 'the capitalist economy'.*

7 *The West believed that communism threatened democratic values and beliefs such as freedom of speech.*

8 *The Communists believed that the capitalist system exploited the working classes so that the rich might increase their wealth.*

9 *Relations between East and West had been difficult for many years. In spite of co-operation during the First World War, the situaton worsened following the end of the Second World War in 1945.*

10 *The West wanted democratic governments in Eastern Europe and was keen to reintegrate Germany. The USSR sought protection by creating a buffer zone of friendly states on her western borders.*

2

Europe at the end of the Second World War

In this chapter you will learn about:
- *the peace conferences following the end of the Second World War*
- *the points of post-war tension between the Big Three – Britain, the USA and the USSR*
- *the coming of the iron curtain.*

The end of the war in Europe

The 'Big Three' leaders of the Allied forces – Winston Churchill of Britain, Franklin D. Roosevelt of the USA and Joseph Stalin of the USSR – met at Tehran in 1943. Military issues dominated the meeting with Stalin pressing for the opening of a second front. He was assured that plans were afoot to do just that the next year, provided Russia launched a major offensive in the East at the same time. Stalin agreed.

Insight

Stalin wanted the Western Allies to invade Europe from the west so that the Axis forces would have to split their armed forces and supplies to meet the Allied attack, which would relieve pressure on Russia on the Eastern Front. The D-Day landings of 6 June 1944 created this second front in order to relieve the pressure on Russia.

The future of Germany and Poland was also discussed at this meeting and all three believed they had made progress. Unbeknown to the Western leaders, their suites at Tehran had been bugged and Stalin, not wishing to leave anything to chance, had studied transcripts of their conversations.

On 6 June 1944, D-day, Allied troops landed on the beaches of Normandy. The American, British and Canadian forces began to advance towards the Rhine. Meanwhile, the Red Army launched their offensive advancing westward relentlessly, pausing only near Warsaw. There, the free Polish Resistance rose up and took control of the capital in anticipation of declaring an independent Poland. The Nazis returned and crushed the uprising, while the Red Army waited, in spite of Churchill's pleas to Stalin. The Red Army needed time to regroup, Stalin claimed, and he refused to permit Allied planes to use Soviet airfields to supply the Poles.

Insight

The revolutionary Red Army was founded by Trotsky following the Bolshevik Revolution in October 1917 and developed into the national army of the USSR. The name 'Red Army', which referred to the traditional colour of the workers' movement, was abandoned in 1946 in favour of the title the Soviet Army.

Following 63 days of fighting, the Nazis overcame the Polish resistance; 200,000 Poles (90 per cent of them civilians) were killed and the city was reduced to rubble. Stalin had deliberately allowed the Poles to be massacred in order to place his own men in control. The ruins of Warsaw became a monument to the extinguished hope for democracy in Eastern Europe.

In October 1944 Churchill flew to Moscow to meet Stalin and discuss dividing Europe into spheres of interest. The proposals were written on a scrap of paper and Stalin indicated his approval by a large tick.

These proposals gave the USSR 90 per cent influence in Romania; Britain was to have 10 per cent; 75 per cent of influence in Bulgaria would go to the USSR and the remaining 25 per cent to others. In return, Britain would receive 90 per cent influence in Greece, and in Yugoslavia influence would be shared equally between Britain and the USSR. Following these suggestions there was a long pause. Churchill later remembered that he said, 'Might it not be thought rather cynical if it seemed we had disposed of these issues, so fateful to millions of people, in such an offhand manner? Let us burn the paper.'

'No,' Stalin replied, 'you keep it.'

This cavalier attitude towards the fate of millions of people in several countries was hardly in accordance with the terms of the Atlantic Charter of 1941 or the Anglo–Soviet Treaty of 1942. The Atlantic Charter had agreed that there would not be any territorial adjustments without the 'freely expressed wishes of the peoples concerned' while the Anglo–Soviet Treaty read:

> **The High Contracting Parties agree to act according to the principles of not seeking territorial aggrandisement for themselves, and of non-interference in the internal affairs of other States.**

There was no mention of the USA in this document and Churchill told an adviser that there was nothing he could do for Poland.

Yalta

In February of 1945 the Big Three met in Yalta, home of the old summer palace of the Tsars, to discuss how Europe was to be structured after the war. Although this represented the 'high tide of Allied collaboration and understanding', tensions were already apparent. Stalin distrusted both Churchill and Roosevelt, while Churchill feared a lack of US support in post-war Europe and was constantly being blocked by Roosevelt who distrusted his 'imperialist adventurism'. In spite of these differences, the three leaders managed to decide that, once Germany had been defeated, she should be disarmed and split into four zones which the Big Three, together with France, would occupy. Eastern European countries including Poland were to be allowed to hold free elections in order to decide how they would be governed in the post-war world. The USSR agreed to join the war against Japan a month after Germany had been defeated and all agreed that a United Nations organization would be set up, in spite of Stalin's reservations that it might be controlled by the USA and Britain.

Insight

The United Nations was established in 1945 and aims to promote world peace and develop international co-operation in such areas as law, security, economic development, social progress and human rights. Today it has a membership of 192 nations and has its headquarters in New York.

Poland

There were disagreements about how Poland would be governed. The British wanted to install the Polish government in exile in London, while the Soviets wanted the pro-Soviet government that had been set up in Lublin. While Churchill tried to explain that Poland's freedom and sovereignty had been the reason for Britain declaring war on Germany in 1939, Stalin emphasized the USSR's need for security since it was through the Polish Corridor that the Soviet Union had been invaded twice in the previous 30 years.

Insight

The Treaty of Versailles of 1919 gave a strip of German land to Poland so that the newly independent country could have

(Contd)

The USSR was eager to move her frontier with Poland westwards, compensating Poland in turn by moving her Western frontier into German territory and removing the German population from that area. In addition, Stalin wanted massive reparations (money to repair the damage done during the war) from Germany, at a far higher level than the other two powers thought realistic. This was opposed because of the confusion the question of reparations had caused following the First World War and the fear that these payments would hinder Germany's recovery following the end of the Second World War. The Soviets saw high reparations as imperative as compensation for the destruction caused by the Nazis, as a way to punish the Nazis and as a symbol of the victory of Communism over Nazism. A figure of $20 billion to be paid in goods and equipment over a period of years was the final compromise.

Yalta was a controversial meeting and was immediately criticized. The Western leaders appeared to have ignored the fact that Eastern Europe would be liberated by the Red Army thus giving the Soviet government the decisive influence in what was to happen in those countries. Even if the Western leaders were aware of the implications of liberation by the Red Army, they certainly appeared to have been ignorant of the ideological differences between East and West.

Some believe that Stalin skilfully manipulated Roosevelt into agreeing to what amounted to a betrayal of Poland and its handing over to the USSR, in return for Stalin agreeing to 'free elections' in Poland. Stalin had no personal experience of 'free elections' in the Western sense and it is likely that his interpretation of this concept was completely different to that of the Western powers. He was acting pragmatically. Poland was an important part of Stalin's plans for the future and for the construction of a buffer zone between Russia and the West.

The meeting also exposed the cracks in the Grand Alliance. Once the unifying ambition to defeat Hitler had been removed, only the trust between the three leaders could hold it together.

The Potsdam Conference

In July 1945, the Allies met again at Potsdam near Berlin. However, this time things were different. There was a change among the leading players and with it came a change of attitude. President Roosevelt had died in April and he had been replaced by Harry S. Truman. Although Truman had played a leading role in the USA's war effort, his knowledge of foreign affairs, particularly the situation in Europe, was superficial. Unlike Roosevelt, he was unwilling to compromise with 'Uncle Jo' Stalin, who he believed was little more than a bully.

Churchill was present in the early stages of the conference, but lost the British General Election and was replaced by Clement Atlee, leader of the new Labour government.

Stalin remained as secretive and as determined as ever. Some decisions were made but there was little agreement and it was clear that tensions and divisions between the East and West were increasing.

In Germany, the Powers finalized details regarding the zones of occupation. The Nazi party was to be banned and the Nazi leaders were to be put on trial as war criminals.

Each Power was to collect industrial equipment from their zone as reparations, but since the USSR's zone was predominantly agricultural, the other zones would contribute additional reparations.

Poland's western border was to be along a line defined by the Oder and Neisse rivers, and Germans living in Poland, Hungary and Czechoslovakia were to be returned to Germany.

Although the conference ended amicably enough, there had been areas of disagreement. The USSR's request for the Ruhr to be opened to international influence, for access to the Straits (Dardanelles) and for control of Libya were rejected. Similarly, Western requests for Europe's main waterways to be accessible to all and for a greater say in Eastern and South-East Europe were also refused.

The divisions between East and West were growing. The West was increasingly concerned about Stalin's intentions in Eastern Europe. In March, the non-Communist Polish leaders had been invited to Moscow, where they were promptly arrested. Communists were now in control of the key positions in the Polish government.

It became apparent that far more Germans were to be expelled from Eastern Europe than the Western Allies had anticipated.

Truman became convinced that Stalin was planning world conquest and that the only thing the Soviets would understand was force. The United States' 'trump card', the atomic bomb, became a vital factor.

On 16 July 1945, the eve of the Potsdam Conference, the first atomic bomb was tested at Alamogordo in the New Mexico desert. Truman was informed immediately of its success and, five days later, learned that it was far more destructive than previously thought and would be ready for combat use soon. Churchill noted that Truman was a changed man – he was delighted with the United States' new power. Stalin was informed of this new weapon on 24 July, but if Truman had been hoping for a reaction, he was disappointed. Stalin already knew of the bomb's existence thanks to his spies, including Klaus Fuchs, a German physicist working on the bomb in England. Fuchs had passed detailed notes on the bomb to his contact Harry Gold in June 1945.

Insight

Harry Gold was a US laboratory chemist who was a courier for Klaus Fuchs. Gold was arrested in 1950 and his

16

information led to the arrest and trials of several other active Soviet spies, including Julius and Ethel Rosenberg.

When Truman informed Stalin of the United States' big new weapon Stalin merely replied, 'Good, I hope the United States will use it.' Privately Stalin ordered Molotov to speed up the Soviet bomb project.

Truman lost no time in putting the atomic bomb to work. On 6 August 1945 a B-29 Superfortress aircraft named 'Enola Gay' dropped an atom bomb on Hiroshima, a city in Japan. The explosion, which had a force equivalent to that of 13,000 tons of TNT, created heat and blast that destroyed the city in minutes. The exact figures are uncertain, but approximately 100,000 civilians were killed immediately and thousands more died of radiation poisoning over the next few years. On 9 August 1945 a different type of bomb, a plutonium implosion bomb, was dropped on Nagasaki. The city was destroyed and thousands killed.

Insight

A 'plutonium implosion' – the generic name for early nuclear devices used by the USA against Japan in 1945 – is the opposite of an explosion: the blast converges inwards towards a point instead of travelling outwards from it, thus attaining critical mass and triggering the nuclear explosion.

Truman hoped to avoid an invasion of Japan and prevent huge numbers of US casualties by dropping the atomic bombs on these cities. On 10 August the Emperor of Japan announced his decision to surrender and terms were agreed on 14 August. The Second World War was over. Truman must have been aware of the immense strength the possession of such a bomb gave the United States, especially in dealings with the Soviets. He was becoming increasingly suspicious of Stalin's motives. The Red Army was the biggest in the world, there were no signs of it being disbanded and it seemed likely that Stalin was building a buffer zone along his country's western borders. This was a natural response to being invaded from Europe three times in the last century and a half.

As the Red Army liberated territories in Eastern Europe, Stalin's henchmen established friendly pro-Soviet regimes.

Stalin's tactics in Eastern Europe risked confrontation with the West and, less than six months after the end of the war, the United States increasingly viewed its wartime ally as a possible enemy. This U-turn was exacerbated by Stalin's speech to the Supreme Soviet in February 1946 where he insisted that the very existence of capitalism made war inevitable since that was how capitalism developed and increased its strength.

Insight

The Supreme Soviet, the highest legislative body in the USSR, was a bicameral body, i.e. it had two chambers: the Soviet of the Union, with members elected from the population, and the Soviet of the Nationalities, whose members were elected along national or ethnic lines.

Washington was alarmed and asked its Embassy in Moscow for details and explanations of Stalin's foreign policy. The reply came to be known as the Long Telegram – and no wonder, it was 5,500 words long! The author was George Kennan, who was all too aware of how Russia's past influenced present thinking. His telegram predicted nothing less than a fight to the death between communism and democracy. This shocked Washington and Kennan's warning seemed to have come true when Stalin refused to withdraw Soviet troops from northern Iran, thus threatening oil supplies to the West.

These fears of Communist influence infiltrating Iran, Turkey, Greece and Italy and aiming at world domination echoed Winston Churchill's speech in Fulton, Missouri: 'From Stettin in the Baltic to Trieste in the Adriatic, an iron curtain has descended across the continent.' This speech declared that Europe was divided by Soviet policy into two separate halves: in the West were free democratic states, while in the East, behind an iron curtain, were countries under the control of Communist parties directly controlled by the Soviet Union.

The American public was horrified and Truman, in public, denied all prior knowledge of the content of the speech. In private it was just what Truman and his advisers wanted to hear. It warned of the spreading influence of the Soviets and of the need to stop this expansion westwards. Stalin accused Churchill of being a warmonger; the Soviet press accused him of being a racist and even compared him to Hitler. Churchill may have been out of office with no control over British policy, but his speech in Fulton proved that even as a private citizen he could influence the United States' policy and push it in what he believed was the right direction.

10 THINGS TO REMEMBER

1 The 'Big Three' were the leaders of the Allied forces –
   Churchill (Britain), Roosevelt (USA) and Stalin (USSR).

2 The leaders met in Tehran (1943) to discuss how best to defeat
   Hitler – suspicion and mistrust were present even then.

3 The Soviet Army's inaction during the Warsaw rising showed
   that Stalin was determined to achieve Soviet dominance in the
   area.

4 Churchill and Stalin both ignored the non-intervention terms
   of the Atlantic Charter and the Anglo–Soviet Treaty.

5 The meeting of the Big Three in Yalta in February 1945
   discussed how best to deal with Germany and reshape Europe
   after the war.

6 Churchill and Stalin disagreed about the type of government
   to be established in Poland; Roosevelt agreed to Stalin's
   demands so long as he later held 'free elections' – a concept
   which was alien to Stalin.

7 At Potsdam, divisions became obvious as President Truman
   proved to be more suspicious about Stalin's motives than his
   predecessor had been.

8 Truman believed that the nuclear weapons held by the USA
   would give America the advantage, but Stalin had already
   accelerated the Soviet nuclear programme.

9 George Kennan sent Washington the 'Long Telegram'
   predicting that there would be a fight to the death between
   communism and democracy.

10 Following Stalin's speech claiming that capitalism profited by
   war, and Churchill's 'iron curtain' speech in Fulton Missouri
   in March 1946, the stage was set for the Cold War.

3

Containment

In this chapter you will learn about:
- *the Soviet expansion in Eastern Europe*
- *the Greek Civil War*
- *Yugoslavia's stand against Stalin in 1948*
- *the Truman Doctrine and the Marshall Plan.*

> *They drive today... as the Tartars used to drive centuries ago;*
> *in crowds and hosts, uncounted and uncountable, infinitely foreign*
> *and lost in all these Western countries of which they have never*
> *heard and which they are utterly unable to understand; a flood*
> *from the steppes, spreading across Europe.*
>
> Stransky, J., *East Wind Over Prague*, Hollis and Carter, 1950, pp. 22–3

These were the Soviet forces as they marched across Eastern Europe.

The Soviet Red Army freed Poland, Czechoslovakia, Bulgaria and Hungary, Romania and Eastern Germany from German occupation and established themselves in occupation creating Communist governments that were closely controlled from Moscow. Stalin wanted a *cordon sanitaire* in Eastern Europe, a buffer zone of countries controlled by the Soviets which could protect mother Russia's western frontier from the threat of invasion.

The Soviet takeover followed the same pattern in each country that they occupied. First, coalition governments were set up in which the Communists shared power with other parties. Gradually, with backing from Stalin, the Communist parties took over elements vital to the running of the state – the civil service, the police, newspapers and the armed forces. Opposition leaders in these states were arrested, exiled or just disappeared. Elections were held as promised but were fixed to ensure support for the Communists. Finally 'people's democracies' were set up and the states became mere satellites to Moscow.

There were home-grown Communists in these countries who welcomed the Soviet 'liberators', but people such as Gomulka (Poland), Rajk and Kadar (Hungary) and Tito (Yugoslavia) were considered suspect by Stalin. He preferred leaders who had been educated in Communism in Moscow and who then returned to their countries with the Red Army. These leaders had been educated in the need for absolute loyalty to the worldwide Communist movement where there was no room for national loyalties. Dimitrov (Bulgaria), Rakosi (Hungary), Ulbricht (Germany) and Gottwald (Czechoslovakia) were all quite prepared to be Stalin's puppets.

Poland

The immense problems of reconstruction were overshadowed by the internal struggle for power where violence and intimidation were used by the Communists against the other political parties. Political meetings were broken up by mobs; non-communist politicians and party members were arrested, kidnapped and murdered. By the time the elections came in January 1947, thousands of political activists were in prison.

The rigged elections returned 80 per cent of the vote for the Communists and the leader of the Peasant Party, Mikolajczyk, fearing for his life, fled from Poland to the West after his party had been disrupted, harassed and finally banned.

Bulgaria

In Bulgaria, the Red Army's political advisers helped set up a provisional government, abolished the monarchy in September 1946 and made Georgi Dimitrov Prime Minister. He proceeded to run Bulgaria as 'a suburb of Moscow'.

Hungary

In Hungary, free elections held in November 1945 led to the Smallholders' Party winning four times as many seats as the Communists. In an attempt to gain popularity with all sections of the community and promote national unity, the Smallholders invited Matyas Rakosi to join the government. Their only condition was that they hold the post of Minister of the Interior, which would give the Smallholders control over the police and the media. Once in power Rakosi refused the Smallholders' request and piece by piece the Communists, subsequently appointed by Rakosi, disposed of the opposition 'like slicing salami'. They organized the dismissal of independent-minded ministers; non-communist parties were taken over in a series of mergers; the police were used to harass opposition politicians, breaking up and closing down their meetings and even arresting and imprisoning some without trial. Eventually all political parties were banned and Rakosi led a Stalinist hardline government equipped with a ruthless secret police.

Romania

Romania retained King Michael as head of state but he was forced to make concessions to the Communist-dominated Democratic Front which was in power after March 1945. In December 1947, the king was forced to abdicate and Romania became a People's Republic under a Communist hardline government.

East Germany

On the very day that Hitler committed suicide in his Berlin bunker, Walter Ulbricht was flown to the city in a Russian plane to take control of the Russian zone of occupation. He had been a Communist deputy in the German Reichstag until expelled by Hitler in 1933.

Insight

Following the Reichstag fire in February 1933, which the Nazis blamed on the Communists, the Nazis consolidated their lead over the Communist Party by using the Presidential Decree to undermine the Communists in the Reichstag. By July 1933 the party had been officially banned.

Ulbricht had fled to Russia where he became a Soviet citizen and was prepared by his political masters to take over Germany after the war. Once in Berlin, he approved the Oder-Neisse frontiers with Poland and allowed the Soviets a free hand as they stripped the Russian zone of anything which might be of use in rebuilding the Russian economy. These unpopular acts resulted in the Communists winning only 20 per cent of the vote in the free elections held in East Berlin in October 1946 – less than they had won before Hitler came to power in 1933. Ulbricht ignored the result and, with the help of the Soviet Army, imposed a Stalinist government on East Germany and East Berlin.

Yugoslavia

The liberation of Yugoslavia owed nothing to the Red Army; Josip Broz, better known as Tito, the leader of one of the resistance movements in Yugoslavia, had blended his brand of communism with anti-German nationalism in the struggle for liberation from German forces. Following liberation in October 1944 his supporters wiped out the opposition to Communism, and in the

elections of November 1945 Tito's National Front Party won
90 per cent of the votes. Yugoslavia was proclaimed a republic
and a 'People's Democracy'.

Four people governed Yugoslavia – Tito, Kardelj, Rankovic and
Djilas – very different to most Stalinist-style governments. Tito was
too independent-minded to please Stalin and his security at home
in Yugoslavia and fame internationally made it unlikely that he
would be totally obedient to Stalin. Although he was a 'graduate'
of Moscow training, Tito was less malleable than other Russian
'puppets'; he believed that Yugoslavia had earned the right to
determine its own destiny. This independence manifested itself
when Tito gave aid to the Greek Communists, in spite of Stalin's
reluctance to get involved, yet he could also be a faithful follower
of the Moscow line, such as when he firmly rejected the Marshall
Plan (see page 28). Such independence of thought displeased Stalin
and at the first meeting of the Cominform (which was meant to
co-ordinate party activities throughout Europe) Tito rejected
Russian control and insisted that each country had the right to
choose its own 'road to socialism'.

Stalin, who had intended to use Cominform to dictate policy to
his Balkan satellites, was furious and ordered the conference to
expel Yugoslavia – he even considered military action against
Tito, but wisely decided against it. An economic blockade against
Yugoslavia was organized and Tito had no choice but to turn to
the West for aid. Although not technically part of the Marshall
Plan, Yugoslavia received over a million dollars' worth of aid from
the West, yet it remained an independent Communist state.

Greece

In 1940 Greece had been invaded by both Italy and Germany
but resistance fighters, many of them Communists, continued a
guerrilla war against the invaders. Stalin had promised Churchill
that Greece was within the British sphere of influence and that he

would not support the Greek Communists in their attempt to seize power. Greece had suffered greatly under the Nazi occupation and much of the country's infrastructure had been ruined: roads, railways, bridges and factories had been destroyed and the Corinth Canal had been blocked by the retreating Germans. Greece was finally liberated in 1944 by which time the resistance fighters, the ELAS (the National Popular Liberation Army), controlled much of the country.

Churchill was determined to restore the monarchy in Greece as he believed this would ensure a pro-Western government in the Eastern Mediterranean. He sent British troops to aid in the restoration and this resulted in a bloody civil war between Royalist and Communist extremists. Stalin honoured his agreement with Churchill regarding spheres of influence but the Americans believed, wrongly, that Stalin was secretly supplying the Greek Communists. In fact Marshal Tito, the Yugoslav leader, was sending arms across the Macedonian border and continued to do so for three years until his split with Moscow. Britain supplied the anti-Communist forces but, following the devastating effects of the severe winter of 1946–7, was unable to cope with responsibilities abroad.

Insight

The UK suffered one of its most severe winters at a time of austerity when there was still rationing of basic items such as coal. The coldest period was from 21 January to 16 March and over 4 million workers were idle because of the power cuts caused by deep snow.

In late February 1947 the British government decided to end economic aid to Greece and to withdraw British troops. This would leave Greece open to communism unless the United States could be persuaded to fill the gap. The United States' new Secretary of State, George C. Marshall, soon realized the severity of the situation but was also aware that Congress was solidly Republican and would oppose giving aid to Greece. President Truman and

Marshall presented their point of view to the congressional leaders, but it was Dean Acheson's (the Undersecretary of State) compelling report which swung things. He drew the analogy of a barrel of apples being infected by one rotten one – if Greece fell to Communism so too would other countries in the Eastern Mediterranean. After a long silence, the congressional leaders pledged their support for President Truman when he asked Congress for $400 million to aid Greece and Turkey.

The Truman Doctrine

On 12 March 1947, Truman presented his request to Congress in a speech which was to become known as the Truman Doctrine. He spelled out the realities of the world in the aftermath of the Second World War, and, although it was prompted by the Greek crisis, he clearly intended it to have wider implications.

His speech began by explaining that he believed the United States should help any country that was threatened by communism and made it clear that he thought the only choice was between 'democracy' and 'totalitarianism'. He asked Congress to approve $400 million to assist Greece and Turkey and also to approve the use of US civilian and military personnel to help in the reconstruction of both countries and to supervise the aid provided. Congress was unusually quiet during Truman's speech – there was no doubt in anyone's mind that this was an important moment in history.

Insight

Friedrich and Brzezinski contend that a totalitarian state has absolute control over its people and would have certain key features: a single political party and charismatic leader; a compulsory ideology; governmental control over the armed forces and the mass media, a secret police and an economy under central control. (See 'Taking it further' at the back of the book.)

The idea of holding back the spread of communism was known as 'containment' and had been elaborated long before the speech to Congress but had not been made known to the American public. The public in 1947 were not keen to embark on an anti-communist crusade. In order to get the economic and military resources needed to carry out an active foreign policy, Truman had to convince the majority of the American people that the Soviet threat was real and increasing, which was why he described the Greek situation in terms of 'good' versus 'evil'. He was brilliantly successful. Truman's words would echo down the decades of the twentieth century. His speech meant that the United States was ready to take a major part in world affairs and send money, weapons and advisers to any country in the world that felt threatened by communism. The United States was prepared to draw a line and say to the Soviets 'no further'.

Truman had no intention of sending troops to Europe to fight communism; instead he planned to attack it at its roots. He saw misery, poverty and want nurturing the seeds of communism and allowing them to grow and spread. Governments in Europe were still struggling against the effects of the Second World War. Two years after the defeat of Hitler, much of Europe still lay in ruins, farms and factories produced less than they had in 1939 and even the weather hindered recovery with a severe winter in 1946–7 followed by floods and drought. In Britain, rationing had been extended to include that basic necessity, bread, something which had not even been rationed during the war years. Truman believed that if the United States used its wealth to help Europe recover and regain prosperity, fewer countries would be tempted by communism. In addition, America's own economy would benefit by encouraging the revival of trade. His objective was economic reconstruction with a political purpose.

The Marshall Plan

In June 1947, General George Marshall announced what was to be known as the Marshall Plan – a programme of aid to help war-torn Europe to re-equip its factories and revive agriculture and trade. Marshall insisted that the policy was not directed against any country or doctrine but against the chaos brought about by poverty and hunger and he emphasized that the offer of aid was open to all countries. This aid took the form of money, equipment, food and technical assistance to countries willing to co-operate to create economic recovery. These countries would then agree to buy American goods and allow American companies to invest in their industries. This move would stimulate the American economy and consolidate American influence in Western Europe.

The European leaders, confronted with economic problems and no resources to solve them, were not in any position to question America's motives. They swiftly accepted the offer. The USSR rejected it. This decision came as no surprise as the United States had made it very difficult for the Soviets to accept help, insisting that Soviet economic records be available for scrutiny and that the markets of Eastern Europe be opened to American businessmen. *Pravda*, a Soviet newspaper, described Marshall Aid as 'a plan for political pressure with the help of dollars… for interference in the affairs of other countries'. Stalin refused to allow any Eastern European countries to share in Marshall Aid, though some, like Czechoslovakia, had been keen to take part.

It soon became a tactical weapon of the Cold War. Truman saw it as one of America's greatest contributions to world peace while the Soviets saw it as aiming to unite countries against communism. Russia's reply was to create the Cominform, an attempt to consolidate control over the Soviet satellites and bring conformity to Eastern bloc strategy in the face of the Marshall Plan. However, the West saw the Cominform as an instrument to further extend Soviet influence in Europe and subordinate all Communist parties to the interests of the Soviet Union. This interpretation was strengthened when Czechoslovakia was taken over by the Czech Communist Party in a bloodless coup in 1948.

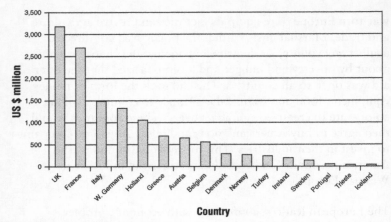

Figure 3.1 Chart showing distribution of Marshall Aid.

THE MARSHALL PLAN IN ACTION

In April 1948 the US Congress allocated $5.3 billion to implement the Marshall Plan, and 16 non-communist European countries drew up the Organization for European Economic Co-operation (OEEC) to distribute US aid and to ensure a secure European economy through the economic co-operation of the 16 members. The Marshall Plan enabled Europe to import supplies essential to the reconstruction of Europe. Raw material, machinery and fuel bought by this means were used to develop agriculture, industry and transport. By the time the Plan had come to an end in 1951, over $13 billion had been spent and this had enabled European countries to develop their economies and improve their standards of living at a rate that, without US aid, would have been impossible.

There is little doubt that the Marshall Plan aided the economic recovery of Europe and it began a period of prosperity in Europe which lasted into the 1970s. Churchill saw it as the 'most unselfish act by any great power in history', but it should be remembered that it also protected US interests and enabled the United States to dominate Europe economically.

Insight

After the First World War, American farmers found their
foreign markets shrinking. The long-lasting agricultural
depression that followed had a profound effect on the
economy. The USA was determined to avoid this in 1945;
aid to Europe helped Europe to recover economically and
enabled the US economy to prosper.

The aid was not distributed as charity and only 20 per cent of
it was in the form of loans. Instead the aid was given as grants
in order to lessen Europe's financial obligations in the future.
Often the aid was given in the form of goods – grain or industrial
machinery – and this enabled the United States to control its end
use rather more easily than giving dollars. Some aid was given in
'counterpart funds'. Often a European manufacturer would want
to buy US goods but, because the dollar was in short supply, would
find this to be impossible. Each European country therefore set up
a fund which the ECA (the European Co-operation Administration)
would match in dollars. A French company could then pay
francs into its government fund in order to buy equipment; from
counterpart funds the correct number of dollars would be used
to pay the American producers of that equipment. It was not just
industrial areas which benefited. In predominantly agricultural
Greece, aid came in a variety of forms, including Missouri mules
to work the land. Although these eventually proved extremely
useful, at first they created mayhem as they were twice the size
of indigenous Greek mules!

10 THINGS TO REMEMBER

1 *As the Red Army liberated Eastern Europe from Nazi control they established Communist governments in order to protect Russia from potential invasion from the West.*

2 *Bulgaria, Hungary and Romania saw hardline Communist governments established following the end of the war.*

3 *The 'free elections' that Roosevelt had wanted in Poland were set against a backdrop of Communist violence and intimidation and resulted in an 80 per cent vote for the Communists in January 1947.*

4 *In East Germany, although the Communists gained fewer votes in the election of October 1946 than they had in 1933, Walter Ulbricht, a Stalinist puppet, imposed a Communist government on East Germany and East Berlin.*

5 *Yugoslavia under Josip Broz (Marshal Tito) chose its own 'road to socialism' and refused to bow to Russian control.*

6 *As an independent Communist state, Yugoslavia received over a million dollars in Western aid when it was expelled from Cominform and blockaded economically by Stalin.*

7 *The Truman Doctrine resulted in the United States sending military and economic aid to any country perceived to be under threat from communism.*

8 *Containment was the policy of restraining the spread of communism by both military and economic means.*

9 *The Marshall Plan gave monetary aid ($5.3 billion) to help European countries to reconstruct their economies and prevent the spread of communism.*

10 *The aid was not completely altruistic as it also ensured prosperity for US industries and allowed the USA to dominate European economies.*

4

Germany

In this chapter you will learn about:
- *the effects of the Second World War on Germany*
- *the Nuremberg Trials of Nazi war criminals*
- *the Berlin blockade and airlift*
- *the formation of NATO and the Warsaw Pact*.

In 1945, police found a butcher's shop in the Ruhr, Germany, stocked with human meat. This was a defeated country of ruins and refugees and an increasingly desperate population. Factories were closed in this once great industrial nation and agriculture could not produce enough food to feed the population which continued to increase as 16 million more Germans arrived from Eastern Europe. There was nothing to buy in the shops except the most meagre rations and little comfort in the bombed-out ruins many called home. The old currency was valueless and most deals were made using American cigarettes.

Areas of land in the east of Germany had been handed over to the Poles and Russians and the rest of the country was divided into four zones each controlled by one of the victorious Allies – the United States, Britain, France and the USSR. Berlin was divided in the same way. Originally it was decided that an Allied Control Council comprising army leaders would run Germany. The country would be run as an economic and political unit and joint elections would be held simultaneously in the four zones. It was hoped that the country would eventually be reunited as a democratic entity.

Unfortunately, disagreements between the Allies about how the German state would be run in future became so intense that it soon became clear that a unified Germany was impossible.

Germany divided

The four zones were very different from each other. The American zone was a mixture of rural and industrial areas of approximately 17.2 million inhabitants and was totally dependent on the Ruhr for coal and steel; the British zone included the Ruhr, thus controlling 87 per cent of coal production and 70 per cent of steel production, and 22.3 million people, but was dependent on other areas for food; the French zone was fairly self-sufficient in the short term, having coal, timber, food and a small population of just 5.9 million; the Soviet zone, with its population of 17.3 million, was largely agricultural and dependent on coal from the Ruhr.

The four Commanders in Chief put into practice the 4 Ds – denazification, democratization, demilitarization and decartelization.

Insight

By getting rid of all the features of Nazi government, making German society less military-orientated and weakening the monopoly of big businesses, the Allies hoped to move Germany in the direction of democracy and a free market economy.

Denazification in each of the four zones was carried out to varying degrees. In the American zone Nazis were arrested with great thoroughness. In the Soviet zone not only were Nazis removed from their posts but also the whole economic structure was changed as the Soviets believed it was the fault of capitalism that Nazism had flourished. Large estates were broken up into smaller entities and industry was nationalized. It soon became clear that many key administrators had been Nazis and without their help and expertise the Allies could not run the country. Both the British

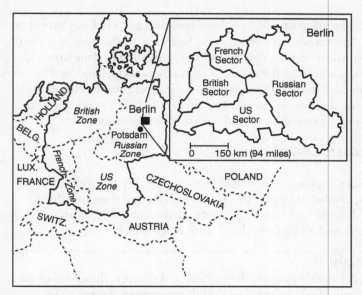

Figure 4.1 How Germany was divided after the Second World War.

and the Soviets tolerated former Nazis in key economic positions provided they were effective. It soon became apparent that the Allies did not have the time or the resources to denazify millions of minor Nazis and this job was increasingly handed over to German tribunals.

The Allies did, however, put 22 surviving Nazi leaders on trial in Nuremberg in November 1945. The setting for the trials was symbolic. Nuremberg was the very epitome of Nazism and it was here that the major rallies had taken place before the war. The accused were brought before the International Military Tribunal and the trials lasted 11 months. They were inevitably controversial, some seeing them as mere show trials and acts of revenge based on very dubious legal arguments. Of the 22 accused, 12 were sentenced to death, seven were sentenced to varying terms of imprisonment and three were acquitted. The trials did have the effect of ridding Germany of the Nazi political leadership, and the publicity and detailed documentation and evidence did much to publicize the Nazi atrocities to the German people.

Re-education should have been part and parcel of any programme of denazification in order to rid Germany of the Nazi ideas and militarism and to provide a sound grounding in democratic ideas. Textbooks were rewritten, Nazi teachers sacked and new teachers trained. The Soviets introduced radical reforms in schools and universities while the Western powers failed to make any real changes to the educational structure of Germany.

DEMOCRATIZATION

West Germany became a federal country. By the end of 1947 the Länder (states) in the Western zones had their own local parliaments, or Landtage. In the Soviet zone federalism was distrusted and a centralized state was formed.

Insight

A federal system is democratic and protects the rights of the individual against a powerful government. Power to govern is not based on strong central institutions but distributed to low-level political institutions such as states or provinces and is shared between national and state governments. For example, the Prussian State, which had dominated two-thirds of pre-war Germany, was broken up to liberate the smaller states and create new states, such as Westphalia.

It may seem surprising, but political parties first appeared in the Soviet zone. The four main political groups which were apparent in both East and West Germany were the Christian Democrats (CDU), the Communists (KPD), the Socialists (SPD) and the Liberals (LDPD). The Soviets were determined to dominate these parties and use them to spread communism throughout Germany, but they had reckoned without the political skills of the CDU leader in the British zone, Konrad Adenauer. At the age of 70 he took over the leadership of the whole Christian Democrat Party. In spite of Stalin's efforts, the amalgamation of the KPD and the SPD failed to win people's votes. In contrast the CDU had a wide appeal. It appeared to be all things to all men and it was Adenauer who kept these disparate elements together. In the Eastern zone, the USSR imposed communism but in the Western zone elections the Communists never gained more than 8 per cent support.

THE ALLIES FALL OUT

In 1946 the Allies clashed over reparations: the Soviets were determined that Germany should pay $10 million for the deaths of millions of Russians and war damage. It had been agreed at Potsdam that the USSR could take a portion of the reparations from the Soviet zone as it was unclear how long it would be before reparations could be paid. It was also agreed that a quarter of the industrial goods made in the Western sectors would be given to the USSR in exchange for food and coal from the Soviet zone.

Both the French and the Soviets began to take advantage of surpluses in their zones to exact the maximum reparations payments. Britain and the United States had to import food into their zones at their own expense and naturally felt very annoyed watching France taking machinery and goods and the Soviets removing whole industrial plants to Russia. It was impossible to demand that the Soviets stop extracting reparations from Germany as this might result in the USSR being crippled economically. In 1945 the Soviets had asked for a $1 billion loan to rebuild their shattered infrastructure but this request had been 'lost' by the US government. When it was finally found some months later the United States offered to discuss the loan if the Soviets would allow US investment and goods in areas of Russian influence. Stalin refused.

In May 1946 the Americans announced that no further reparations would be sent from the American zone to the Soviet zone because the Soviets had refused to supply foodstuffs from their zone as previously agreed. They demanded that Germany be treated as a single economic unit. This naturally alarmed the Soviets as they feared that the United States would dominate a revived German capitalist economy and this would be a direct economic and political threat to them. France too was upset by the American stance, but the United States remained unrepentant. By making

West Germany self-sufficient they could lift their financial burden and gain West Germany as a political ally. Germany held no military threat for the United States: after all, the latter had the atomic bomb. General Clay, the military governor of the American zone, rejected the idea of reunifying Germany and accepted its division into East and West. He did, however, support the merging of the Western zones which he believed would bring immediate economic and political benefits and possibly military advantages.

The unification of the American and British zones to form Bizonia in 1947 began the process of economic reconstruction and handing back to the Germans the responsibility for their own affairs. This had been encouraged by the British Foreign Secretary, Ernest Bevin, who was fearful that a united Germany would be accepted by the Soviets only if it was Communist. He believed that a Western economic recovery was only possible with the establishment of an independent West German state and pushed the United States in this direction at the Moscow and London conferences in 1947 and 1948. The French zone joined Bizonia in June 1948 and a new currency, the Deutsche Mark, was introduced to this new federal German state. Germany had been in effect partitioned.

Stalin watched these developments with mistrust and countered the Anglo-American moves with his own initiatives. In response to Bizonia came the German Economic Commission. He established Cominform – a Communist co-ordinating agency and information bureau to fight back against the Marshall Plan – viewed by many as Comintern (a vehicle for worldwide revolution) in another guise.

Insight

The Communist International (Comintern) was formed in 1919 with the purpose of promoting world revolution, overthrowing the bourgeoisie or middle classes, and establishing worldwide communism. It was an instrument for establishing Soviet control over the international communist movement.

The final *coup de théâtre* in response to the new currency was the introduction of the East Mark, which the Western governments refused to allow to be circulated in their zones in Berlin since they had no control over it. Instead they introduced the Deutsche Mark into West Berlin. Stalin's response was the Berlin blockade.

THE BERLIN BLOCKADE AND AIRLIFT

> **Insight**
> Berlin is regarded as the centrepiece of the Cold War. It became a symbol of freedom, an oasis of democracy amid a Communist desert. Its position, 100 miles inside Soviet-controlled East Germany, meant both sides could spy on each other and it became the espionage capital in the 1950s.

Berlin was 160 kilometres (100 miles) inside the Soviet zone of Germany but it had been divided into four zones, one for each of the Allied powers. Britain, the United States and France relied on free access through the Soviet zone for road, rail and canal links with the city. On 23 June 1948, a message from the Soviet news agency was sent to the main newspaper in Berlin.

The Soviet administration is compelled to halt all traffic to and from Berlin tomorrow at 0600 hours because of technical difficulties.

These technical difficulties closed the roads, canals and railways from West Germany to Berlin. The city had only enough food and fuel to last six weeks and it was clearly the aim of the Soviets to force the West to withdraw from West Berlin by reducing the population to starvation. General Clay was convinced that if Berlin fell to the Soviets, West Germany would be the next to fall and communism would triumph.

However, the air corridors remained open and the British and Americans organized a round-the-clock airlift into the city. At the peak of the airlift, 13,000 tons of goods a day were provided and aircraft were landing in Berlin every three minutes, day and night. To stop the airlift the USSR would have to shoot down Western planes. As a warning to the Soviets, B-29 aircraft capable of

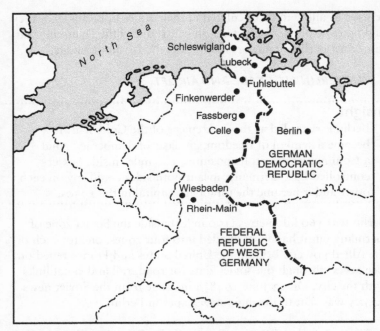

Figure 4.2 Some of the airfields in the Western zone that supplied Berlin during the airlift.

carrying atomic bombs were stationed in Britain within easy reach of Berlin. The West Berliners kept faith with the Western Allies in spite of the shortages and hardships. They ignored Soviet pressure to become part of one city under a Communist council, and on 12 May 1949 the blockade was lifted.

The conventional Western view of the blockade was that Stalin was following an expansionist policy and this was a major bid to take over Europe. However, the USSR was under pressure on a number of fronts – Yugoslavia, Berlin and the growing cohesion of the Western powers. It may have been that the blockade was a desperate attempt to delay the emergence of a Western-dominated West German state. In the West the blockade was presented as a plan to probe the soft spots in the Western Allies' positions. In the USSR it was presented as a Western plot to drag the USSR into war: because the Soviet Union was so moderate this plot came to nothing and the West was forced to abandon its blockade.

Public opinion in the West was outraged by Stalin's actions and a new anti-Soviet bloc was born. On 4 April 1949 the North Atlantic Treaty was signed in Washington. In its determination to halt the expansion of communism the USA had committed itself to close military collaboration.

Insight

The Western Allies formed NATO as an alliance of 12 countries to protect themselves from potential Communist aggression. An armed attack on one member was considered an attack against them all. As Soviet satellite states joined the Warsaw Pact, Europe and the United States felt NATO to be vital in protecting their freedom.

In West Germany, on 19 August 1949, Konrad Adenauer had been elected as the first Chancellor of the new Federal Republic; within a month Willian Pieck had become President of the German Democratic Republic in East Germany. A solution of sorts had been found to the German problem: there now existed two German states, each created in their own image by the two main protagonists of the Cold War.

Germany divided

Hans Hossfield's home in Phillipstal became a victim of the East–West divide. His home was in the Western zone while his printing business was in the Russian zone. He solved this by smuggling bricks into his house and constructing a wall dividing the building in two. Needless to say his family lived in the half of the house in West Germany!

The formation of NATO

The North Atlantic Treaty which was signed on 4 April 1949 was based on Article 51 of the United Nations Charter. This permits individual countries, or several working together, to use force for the purpose of self-defence against armed attack. It was clearly a military alliance as the members agreed to regard an attack on any one of them in Europe or North America as an attack against them all. If such an event took place the members agreed to assist each other 'by taking such action as it deems necessary... to restore and maintain the security of the North Atlantic area'. The necessary action included the use of armed force.

The 12 original members comprised Britain, France, Belgium, Holland, Luxembourg, Portugal, Denmark, Ireland, Italy, Norway, Canada and the USA. All agreed to place their defence forces under a joint NATO command, which would co-ordinate the defence of the West. NATO was meant to be something more than a defensive alliance: there were hints at economic collaboration and some idealists hoped the organization would be the basis for a close-knit Atlantic community. This was not to be. NATO remained first and foremost a military alliance.

At one level NATO was a sign that the USA was determined to make European defence a priority. At another level it marked a significant militarization of Cold War conflict. At yet another level it was clear that national sovereignty was no longer the primary concern it once had been: NATO had a close political structure and members had agreed that part of their national armed forces would serve under its international command.

In May 1955 West Germany became a member of NATO and this reawakened Soviet fear of German rearmament and the emergence of a militarist Germany hell bent on reunification. As Russia had already suffered two invasions by Germany in the twentieth century (1914 and 1941) it seems understandable that the Soviets would fear a third. In response to this perceived threat the Soviet government organized the Warsaw Defence Treaty (1955) with her seven European satellites. It was a military alliance in which the Communist countries of Eastern Europe all agreed to help each other and the Soviet Union in the event of armed attack from the West. In many respects the treaty was unnecessary, since each of the states had their individual security treaties with the Soviet Union, but it did indicate the division of Europe into two armed camps.

The German question

In 1955 West Germany had joined NATO and later that year Adenauer visited Moscow. The purpose of his visit was to examine the possibilities of German unification and the return of the prisoners of war still held in the USSR. Diplomatic relations were established but were hampered by the Hallstein Doctrine, a statement in December 1955 made by the West German Foreign Minister. This stated that West Germany would regard diplomatic recognition of East Germany as an unfriendly act as it would be tantamount to acceptance of the division of the country. Adenauer further claimed that only West Germany had the right to represent 'Germany'. Small wonder that Khrushchev had vowed to 'never, never, never change our minds about the German problem'.

At the heart of the 'German problem' lay Berlin – a divided city in a divided nation. Berliners crossed sector boundaries every day for work and pleasure, some crossed from East to West never to return. These defections were of great concern as over 4 million citizens fled from East Germany between 1951 and 1961; some left because the state discouraged private business; farmers left to avoid being forced to join collective farms; some just disliked the Communist system or wanted to share in the economic prosperity and higher standard of living in the West.

In 1958 Khrushchev had tried to create a crisis over Berlin by threatening to hand over the Western access routes into West Berlin to East Berlin, and told the occupying armies to withdraw from patrolling Berlin. A war of nerves followed, and although Khrushchev backed down, Berliners remained tense and defections continued.

Crisis in Berlin 1961 – face-off at Checkpoint Charlie

Secret documents released in the United States in 2001 revealed that US President Kennedy considered a limited nuclear 'first strike' against Soviet military targets during the Berlin Crisis of 1961.

The crisis came to a head because of Soviet anger over the increasing tides of East German refugees moving West through Berlin, seeking a better standard of living in the West. Between 1949 and 1961, 2.8 million Germans crossed to the West. This mass exodus of mainly young, skilled workers was a serious and embarrassing problem – they were just the type of people needed to build the Communist state. The entire law faculty of Leipzig University defected; 17 key engineers in an industrial plant left, taking their factory's blueprints with them; somehow the hole in the iron curtain had to be filled. In 1958 Khrushchev had set a time limit of six months for Berlin to become a 'free city' under Communist control, but the United States had refused to give up its share of control of the former German capital – the six-month ultimatum passed quietly. The Berlin question was to have been settled in the Geneva Conference in 1960 but the U-2 incident put paid to that.

Insight

A U-2 reconnaissance plane collecting intelligence data was shot down by the Soviets who called the flight an aggressive act and recovered all the photography equipment and the pilot. The United States initially denied it was a spy plane but in the face of the evidence admitted it was. No apology was forthcoming. (For more, see Chapter 7.)

Khrushchev was still smarting from a disastrous visit to China where the Soviet leadership of the Communist world was questioned, and the Gary Powers U-2 incident only served to make him more determined to exert Soviet influence. The election of Kennedy as President in 1960 closely followed by the Bay of Pigs debacle convinced Khrushchev that he could put pressure on Kennedy regarding Berlin.

At a meeting between the two in Vienna, Khrushchev insisted that
the United States withdraw from Berlin by the end of the year.
Kennedy was astounded and declared that the national security of
the United States was directly linked to that of Berlin. Khrushchev
lost his temper, banged on the table and exploded, 'I want peace
but if you want war that is your problem.' Confrontation loomed
as Kennedy addressed the nation on 25 July: 'We cannot and will
not permit the Communists to drive us out of Berlin.' Equally
Khrushchev could not permit the flood of refugees to continue but
realized after careful consideration that 'only a madman would
start a war over Berlin', a phrase he had used to describe Kennedy
but which, by now, applied equally to him.

On 13 August 1961 barriers were erected to prevent free movement
between the Western sectors of Berlin and the Soviet sector. On
17 August the barbed wire began to be replaced with stone – the
Berlin Wall had begun. Kennedy began to contemplate the use of
nuclear weapons and one of his advisers, Carl Kaysen, produced
a report proposing a limited first strike, which he believed would
encourage the Soviets to avoid attacks on American urban and
industrial targets and 'minimize the force of the irrational urge
for revenge'. His 'Strategic Air Planning and Berlin' report dated
6 September 1961 was seriously considered by Kennedy but as it
became clear that there was no direct threat to West Berlin itself
the Western powers felt they had been reprieved. Kennedy sent
General Lucius Clay to Berlin as his special representative, in spite
of a warning from one of his advisers that to send the bullish
commander of the American sector during the airlift of 1948
into such a delicate situation might inflame matters. Indeed Clay
believed he was being sent to Berlin for the purpose of 'taking on'
the Soviets and even went so far as to build a replica 'Berlin Wall'

at a military training school so that his soldiers might practise knocking it down!

In October, Clay overreacted to a seemingly trivial incident when a US diplomat and his wife were denied admission to East Berlin because they refused to show their passports. This was in contravention of the four-power agreement which permitted free passage without passports for Allied and Soviet personnel. Clay sent armed troops to accompany the diplomat into East Berlin and over the next few days, to press home his point, Clay sent American jeeps manned by armed soldiers to accompany American citizens into East Berlin. American tanks were parked near to Checkpoint Charlie, the main crossing point from East to West Berlin, and on 27 October 33 Soviet tanks entered East Berlin, 23 of them parked next to the Brandenburg Gate and ten drove to Checkpoint Charlie where they lined up to face the American tanks.

The tense atmosphere increased as the hours ticked by. The US garrison in Berlin, NATO and Strategic Air Command were all placed on alert; Khrushchev issued instructions that if the Americans started to fire the Soviet commander should reply in kind; the situation had escalated beyond all reason. Kennedy contacted Khrushchev directly and assured him that if the Soviet tanks withdrew, the American tanks would also – here was the get-out clause both sides had been seeking. Sixteen hours of 'stand-off' were broken when a Soviet tank started its engine and pulled back five yards; minutes later an American tank did the same, pulling back just five yards, and gradually the tanks withdrew, one by one. Clay remained in Berlin for only a few months before being recalled.

Ich bin ein Berliner

The wall remained, a visible sign of East–West hostility, a symbol of the Cold War which as Kennedy said was 'not a very nice solution, but a wall is a hell of a lot better than a war'. The President visited Berlin in June 1963, inspected the Wall and looked over it into East Berlin. In his address to a huge crowd of Berliners he made a speech which summed up the gist of the Cold War and ended with the words, 'All free men, wherever they may live, are citizens of Berlin, and therefore as a free man, I can take pride in the words *Ich bin ein Berliner*.' The crowd cheered, and some privately wondered if the President was aware that *ein Berliner* was also the term for a doughnut!

The existence of the wall succeeded in stopping the flood of defectors to the West but did not prevent some from trying to escape. In Berlin today there is a museum dedicated to Checkpoint Charlie where the tales of escapees are told. Some managed to escape by tunnelling; some by swimming where the border ran along the Tetlow canal. Some managed to climb the wall, hoping the East German guards would deliberately take poor aim when ordered to fire at them.

Insight

One famous photograph by Peter Leibing caught the escape of a 19-year-old East German soldier, Conrad Schumann, as he jumped over the barbed wire while the Berlin Wall was being constructed. He was driven away by a West German police car and later settled in Bavaria.

Not all were lucky enough to escape. In the first year 41 Germans were killed attempting to cross to the West, among them Peter Fechter, an 18-year-old bricklayer. He was hit as he attempted to climb over the wall and fell at the base of the wall wounded in the chest and stomach. His agonized cries were heard by West Berliners who attempted to reach him first by ladder, but were warned off by shots from the East German guards, and then by cutting a hole from the Western side to no avail. After an hour, four East German police came and carried the young man away; it was later reported that he had died from his wounds. Among these tragic stories are some rather more light-hearted accounts of people who escaped in hot-air balloons, in specially adapted Trabant cars, dressed as nuns or even disguised in a flock of sheep! As East Germany became more prosperous in the 1960s the number of escape attempts became fewer; as living standards in East Berlin became the best in Eastern Europe, the 'German problem' eased.

10 THINGS TO REMEMBER

1 *Germany was divided into four zones, each of which was controlled by one of the four allies. Berlin was symbolically divided and controlled in the same way.*

2 *The International Military Tribunal tried high-ranking Nazis as war criminals.*

3 *Four main political parties appeared in both East and West Germany – the Christian Democrats (CDV), the Communists (KPD), the Socialists (SPD) and the Liberals (LDPD).*

4 *By 1948 the American, British and French zones had been united, effectively splitting Germany into East and West.*

5 *On 23 June 1948, Stalin blockaded Berlin. The aim was to starve the city and compel the Western powers to withdraw. The Western airlift supplied the city with goods for 11 months.*

6 *Twelve countries formed a military alliance – The North Atlantic Treaty Organization – on 4 April 1949.*

7 *Germany joined NATO in 1955 causing the Soviets to form their own military alliance – the Warsaw Pact.*

8 *In August 1961 the Berlin Wall was raised in order to prevent the loss of millions of skilled East German refugees and to prevent freedom of movement between East and West Berlin.*

9 *October 1961 saw a tense 16-hour stand-off between American and Soviet tanks at Checkpoint Charlie, the main crossing point from East to West Berlin.*

10 *The American President John F. Kennedy showed his commitment to the freedom of Berlin and the containment of the Soviets when he made his famous* Ich Bin ein Berliner *speech on a visit to the city in June 1963.*

5

The Far East

In this chapter you will learn about:
- **the changes in China 1949–50**
- **the Malay Emergency – the only war the West won against communism**
- **the Korean War**
- **the Domino Theory.**

On 27 May 1949 the Communist soldiers of the People's Liberation Army reached the city of Shanghai and the factory workers rushed to greet them. Bands played military music and people danced in the streets. After years of fighting, the three 'mountains' of feudalism, imperialism and capitalism had been toppled. The people felt that they had been liberated from the repression and exploitation of the feudal landlords in the country, and the suppression by capitalists and foremen in the factories. Who had liberated them? The Communist Party, led by Mao Zedong. On 1 October 1949, in Tiananmen Square, Beijing (Peking), before hundreds of thousands of ecstatic people, Mao proclaimed, 'The People's Republic of China is now established. The Chinese People are now standing up.'

Insight

Feudalism is a contract sealed by oaths between a lord and vassal. Historically, the vassal provided the lord with military service, labour and financial support, while the lord protected the vassal and gave him land.

(Contd)

> Imperialism is a means whereby one country gains political and economic control of another, usually by force, and exploits that country for its own purposes. The term is usually used in a derogatory fashion to denounce a country's foreign policy.

China 1949–50

No study of the Cold War or the Korean War can be complete without an understanding of China's role.

This vast nation with a land area of over 10 million square kilometres and a population of over 1,000 million had been an important power in the Far East, but by the first half of the twentieth century it was facing serious problems.

The massive population was mostly illiterate and primitive farming methods could barely produce enough to feed the people, especially during frequent famines which occurred following droughts or floods. Industry was sparse and what existed was largely unmechanized. China had been exploited and invaded by foreign powers including Britain and Japan, the latter in 1931 and 1937. Internally, Chinese politics were volatile and during the 1920s and 1930s there was bitter fighting between Nationalists led by Chiang Kai-shek and Communists led by Mao Zedong. Chiang Kai-shek was supported by the USA who kept him in power with American money, weapons and advisers in order to prevent Mao's Communists from capturing power. During the Second World War, China had fought on the side of the Allies against Japan, but when the war ended, fighting between the Nationalists and Communists began again. The United States poured hundreds of millions of dollars of aid into Chiang Kai-shek's campaign, and almost all of his equipment had been provided by the US government. This was not enough against the enmity of the Chinese masses. Chiang Kai-shek's Kuomintang Party had made little attempt to tackle China's problems; inflation was high and US aid often went into the pockets of Chiang and his family; the Kuomintang had been unwilling to reduce the powers of the landlords thus alienating the millions of peasants in the country – a force which Mao and his Chinese Communist Party successfully harnessed.

Mao naturally looked to the Soviets for aid, but while Stalin believed the Chinese Revolution should be based on support from the industrial workers (as in the 1917 Revolution in Russia), Mao was only too aware of China's primitive industrial development and instead gathered his support from the millions of peasants in rural China.

Civil war had recommenced after the Second World War, but the Communists had emerged from that war far stronger. In 1945 they controlled 777,000 square kilometres (300,000 square miles) and 95 million people. Japan's defeat in 1945 was the signal for the start of a race to control those areas of China previously controlled by Japan. In December 1945, General Marshall had negotiated a truce between the Kuomintang and the Communists, but this collapsed in July 1946. At first the Kuomintang made impressive advances into North China and Manchuria, but the Communist counter-attack in 1947 forced the Kuomintang onto the defensive. By the end of 1948 the Communists had taken Manchuria and won decisive battles in the North. Chaos reigned in the areas controlled by the Kuomintang and food shortages, corruption and hyperinflation turned the people against them. From the beginning of 1949 the major cities fell one by one to the Communists and on 1 October 1949 Mao announced the establishment of the People's Republic of China. This Communist victory surprised even Stalin who privately thought that Mao's Communists had little chance of winning the civil war. Chiang Kai-shek fled to Formosa (Taiwan) where he railed against the paucity of US support for his government, described Mao as a Soviet puppet and a traitor to China and generally predicted that a Third World War would soon result.

Fear of Communist expansion

In the United States, events in China revived the fear of worldwide Communist expansion and that other poor countries in the area might follow China's example and set up Communist governments. In the face of such a scenario, 'containment' once designed to prevent the expansion of communism in Europe now seemed necessary on a worldwide scale. The United States refused to recognize the Communists as the legal government of China and vetoed the Russian-backed claim to have Communist China installed in the Chinese seat in the United Nations, a seat which was still occupied by the Nationalists. When a Chinese invasion of Formosa was threatened, the US Seventh Fleet quickly moved to protect Chiang Kai-shek. In 1950 all trade and travel links with China were banned in the United States and for the next 20 years the United States tried its utmost to exclude Communist China from world affairs.

Russia welcomed Mao in Moscow and praised China's success in establishing communism as a victory for 'world communism'. These words were backed by a Treaty of Friendship to last for 30 years and promises of loans, military aid and technical expertise in order to develop China's industrial strength. It was clear that Stalin saw Mao as a 'junior partner' and that he failed to appreciate China's potential power; however, the very nature of the Chinese revolution gave hope to millions of poverty-stricken people in Third World countries. It was to Mao and his new brand of communism, not Stalin, that they turned their eyes for leadership. A new Red Star was rising in the East and a new 'bamboo curtain' was about to fall.

The first indication of this was to be seen in the conflict which developed in Malaya in 1947.

The Malay Emergency

The Malay Emergency took place as the Cold War was sweeping across Europe and as communism seemed to be seeping inexorably over the world. The word 'emergency' implies a fairly innocuous event, but this hides the savage nature of the full-scale war fought for 12 years between the Malayan Communist Party (MCP) and the British and Malayan authorities. The MCP comprised mostly Chinese members and had tried, unsuccessfully, to lead a revolution in the country in the 1930s. During the Second World War the MCP, under the leadership of Lai Tek, had helped fight the Japanese, and the military wing of the party, the Malayan People's Anti-Japanese Army (MPAJA), received British training and equipment. These carried out guerrilla attacks on the Japanese following the defeat of the British in Malaya and Singapore in 1942. This guerrilla warfare gave the MPAJA experience and weapons which they would later use against the British.

Although they were hailed as heroes by the Malay people, and with gratitude by the British when they emerged from the jungles, the MCP began to subvert the process of independence, determined to see the establishment of a Communist state in Malaya. A violent war began in June 1948 when Chinese communists murdered three British rubber planters. The MCP then began a reign of terror, murdering, maiming and torturing British and Malay men, women and children. They sabotaged installations, derailed trains and staged a deliberate campaign to intimidate the civilian population with the aim of creating a Communist state under the aegis of China. The British were caught unprepared for the ferocity of the experienced guerrillas, but they soon developed new techniques for fighting in the jungle which eventually brought the Communists to heel. Half a million jungle dwellers were resettled to new villages in other regions where there were high living standards and where they received money and the ownership of the land on which they lived. This deprived the Communists of supplies and support from the general population and was probably a major factor in the British success. The British campaign to win the 'hearts and minds' of the general population was also a success: medical help, mutual respect and the prospect of national independence was preferable to the terror inflicted by the Communist guerrillas. Malaya gained independence in August 1957. By 1960 the guerrilla army had been reduced to a few hundred and the emergency was declared at an end in July 1960.

It is unclear why this event was called an 'emergency': was it to hide the real nature of the conflict and the serious political implications behind it, or was it done so that insurance could be collected on damaged and destroyed property?

Korea

> Mistaking the position of British troops, US planes yesterday
> swooped down on them with firebombs and machine guns.
> About 150 men, all believed to be Argyll and Sutherland
> Highlanders, were killed or wounded.
>
> Many of the British were angry, but Private Arthur Holmes of
> Claypool Place, Liverpool, said, 'This is just something that
> could not be helped; up to now the Yank air had given us very
> good support.'
>
> Private Stanley Williamson of Birmingham was overheard
> telling an officer, 'It was hell up there, Sir.'
>
> When half an hour later the enemy themselves attacked the
> Argylls, the British called for artillery support but none was
> available. The Americans had already withdrawn their guns.

Is this a newspaper report of friendly fire during some recent
conflagration in the twenty-first century? No, this incident took
place during the Korean War (1950–3), a struggle between
democracy and communism which has been dubbed by many
'the forgotten war'. How could this obviously 'hot' conflict be
considered part of the 'Cold War'?

Korea had been ruled by Japan since 1910, but following the
Second World War, it was decided by the Allies that Korea would
receive independence. Japan surrendered to Russian forces in the
North of Korea and to American forces in the South of the country.
The dividing line between North and South was fixed on the 38th
parallel of latitude – a temporary measure until free elections
could be held and Korea reunited. The development of the Cold
War in Europe complicated matters in Korea, where the divisions
between North and South became more pronounced. Both Russia
and the United States had withdrawn their forces from the country,
but both continued to give aid and provide support to the areas

previously under their control. All attempts to unite the country failed and in 1948 two separate countries were established. North Korea established a Communist government, led by Kim Il Sung, while South Korea was a non-communist state led by Syngman Rhee. Each government claimed to rule the whole of Korea.

The Communist Revolution in China in 1949 gave North Korea two friendly Communist countries on its borders and this no doubt increased confidence in its dealings with the South. Clashes between the armed forces of North and South intensified along the 38th parallel but it still came as a surprise when, on 25 June 1950, North Korean forces invaded South Korea. Within three days these forces, armed with Russian weapons, had taken Seoul, the capital of South Korea, and had overrun much of the country. With hindsight, it seems likely that the war started because neither Rhee nor Kim Il Sung were prepared to continue with the current state of affairs and that they baited each other until one of them launched an all-out attack. If this is the case, the Korean War had its origins in a civil war.

In the United States in 1950 the situation was viewed differently. Truman believed that the North Koreans were in no position to begin an invasion without first consulting and obtaining support from Stalin. To Truman it seemed obvious that the war had been instigated by Stalin for a number of reasons: Stalin, having lost the initiative in Europe, was looking for another sphere of interest in Asia and was keen to show the 'new kid on the block', Mao, that he was boss; by taking control of the whole of Korea Stalin could directly threaten American control of Japan and thus the USA's position in the Pacific; success in Korea might spur on the Communists in Indochina. In effect, Truman saw the invasion of South Korea as a Communist conspiracy perpetrated by Stalin, yet another step on the road to Russian expansionism.

Of course, Marxist historians have argued that the conspiracy lay with Syngman Rhee who, together with Chiang Kai-shek, General MacArthur and other US officials, forced an attack from the North in order to pressurize the United States into extending its policy of containment to Asia.

25 June – 14 September 1950

CHINA

Yalu River

NORTH KOREA

● Pyongyang

38th
Parallel

25 June 1950

● Seoul

SOUTH
KOREA

14 September 1950

● Pusan

0   200 km
         (125 miles)

Figure 5.1 Invasion of South Korea by North Korean forces.

Insight

Marxist historians tend to interpret historical events in terms
of class struggle and emphasize the role of the proletariat or
working classes in those events.

Without US protection, both South Korea and Formosa (Taiwan)
were open to Communist attack, and by threatening the balance
of power in the area this cabal could ensure American support.
Evidence to support these theories on the origins of the war is
largely circumstantial.

The military evidence supports the thesis that North Korea initiated
the attack: seven North Korean divisions were ready for combat
by June 1950, three divisions had been newly activated, and there
were two independent regiments, an armoured brigade and also
five brigades of a paramilitary border constabulary. The troops

were well prepared and supported by artillery, T-34 tanks and air coverage provided by Yak fighters and Ilyushin ground attack bombers. In stark contrast to this, the South Korean armed forces were not only inadequately trained, but also lacking in tanks, aircraft and artillery. Even their American allies were ill-prepared, having only four infantry divisions of the US Eighth Army, at 70 per cent of their strength, in Japan. This suggests that Kim Il Sung had concentrated his forces deliberately in preparation for an attack.

Whatever the truth about the origins of the war, Truman believed the United States had to act quickly to prevent the fall of South Korea and promptly sent the US Seventh Fleet to Formosa (Taiwan), where he feared China might attack. In addition to this precautionary measure, Truman also made use of diplomatic pressure. An American motion demanding that the North Koreans should withdraw from South Korea was passed in the United Nations. This was followed by a second motion in the United Nations Security Council which agreed to give assistance to South Korea to resist and repel the armed attack and restore equilibrium. The UN gave the United States unlimited authority to direct the military operation. The passing of this motion happened by sheer chance: Russia had been boycotting the Security Council in protest at the United States' refusal to recognize Communist China, the US support of Chiang Kai-shek and the US embargo on all trade and travel links with China. Had the USSR been present in the Security Council, the American motion would have been vetoed by them.

Insight

The Security Council is the most important body in the United Nations, responsible for keeping international peace and security. It has five permanent members which have the power to veto any decisions made by the Security Council and six non-permanent members appointed by the General Assembly.

These actions were a complete change in US policy in this area; the new policy marked an extension of the Truman Doctrine to the whole of Asia.

The United States also called upon her allies in NATO to provide military forces in Korea. NATO members felt obliged to aid the United States in the Far East since the United States had been supporting them in Europe, but US troops formed the greater part of the UN forces (50 per cent of land forces, 93 per cent of air forces and 86 per cent of naval forces) with General MacArthur as the overall Commander in Chief of the whole operation. MacArthur reported to the President and took orders only from him – a *carte blanche* which was to have disastrous effects.

Task Force Smith, comprising American units stationed in Japan, had been flown into Korea at only a few hours' notice and was unprepared for what was to follow. A small unit, part of the American 24th Division stationed in the hills near to Osan, was overcome by Korean T-34 tanks and infantry. Surrounded by the enemy, with few anti-tank weapons and running short of ammunition and blood supplies with which to treat the increasing numbers of wounded, they were forced to flee. Five days later only half of these troops had made it back to American lines further south. Worse was to come. An entire US regiment was ambushed and wiped out; Major General William Dean was captured and paraded in a Korean propaganda film; US forces became caught up in the thousands of refugees fleeing south and the situation became chaotic. This tiny Asian country using Soviet weapons had humiliated a powerful military force.

The few American successes during this early period came in the air where US planes from the Seventh Fleet decimated Korea's Yak fighters and attacked supply lines, while B-29 bombers from Pacific island bases dropped thousands of tons of high explosives on the North.

As the North Korean forces pushed southwards towards the Pusan perimeter, a defensive line along the Nakdong River, MacArthur's forces attacked the over-extended North Korean supply routes from the rear by a seaborne landing in Inchon on 15 September 1950. The invasion fleet was the largest since D-day and consisted of 269 ships. Following a massive bombardment which flattened Inchon, huge numbers of American soldiers

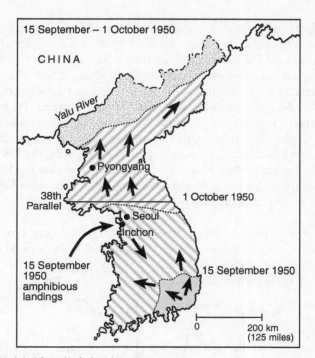

Figure 5.2 MacArthur's forces drive back North Korean troops.

streamed ashore. Among them was General MacArthur, accompanied by photographers and journalists. He had ignored advice not to launch an attack here, as the geography was too exposed and the tides too great, but his gamble had paid off.

The military tide began to turn in favour of the UN/US forces and intense fighting forced the North Koreans back behind the 38th parallel by October; the objectives of the UN resolution had been achieved. The fact that neither Russia nor China had intervened in the first three months of the war suggests that both powers would have been happy to return to the pre-war situation. However, rather than being satisfied with containing the spread of communism, the United States saw this as a chance to reunite Korea and expel communism from North Korea. The Chinese government regarded these plans as a direct threat to their security: North Korea could be used as a base from which to bomb Chinese industrial areas or from which to attack the border with China. After all, how would the United States react were a hostile power to invade Mexico and advance towards the border with the USA? The Chinese issued an official warning: were the Americans to cross the 38th parallel into North Korea, China would intervene. Truman called their bluff. Not only did the American-led forces cross into North Korea, they did so with UN support, albeit six days after the invasion had begun. Having captured Pyongyang, the UN force advanced towards the Chinese border; it was clear that the UN troops were no longer in North Korea to check aggression but to destroy the North Korean government.

In October 1950, 300,000 'Chinese People's Volunteers' crossed the Yalu River (the border between China and North Korea) to

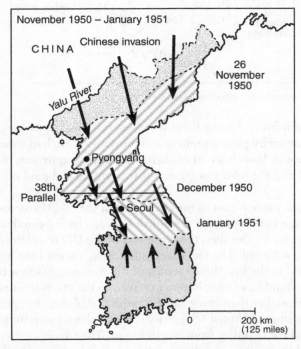

Figure 5.3 Chinese involvement.

fight alongside the North Koreans. The use of the title 'Volunteers' avoided the necessity to declare war on the UN forces and emphasized the civil war aspect of the fighting. In reality, the fighting had developed into a Great Power conflict between the United States, supported by its allies, and the Chinese Communist Government, aided by Russian weapons and advisers.

Sheer weight of numbers was on the side of the North Koreans and Chinese, and their massed armies pushed the UN troops behind the 38th parallel within two weeks. A period of bitter fighting followed with heavy losses on both sides but little difference in the territorial situation. MacArthur ignored President Truman's wishes to establish a ceasefire along the 38th parallel, and pushed on into North Korea, his ultimate aim being to extend war into China itself and defeat Mao Zedong using nuclear weapons if need be. Only the determination of Truman and the Chinese leaders prevented a full-scale conflict developing between the two powers. Following a series of confidential meetings in the White House, MacArthur was removed from his command on 10 April 1951. Unfortunately, the decision was leaked to the press before the White House had informed MacArthur and made an official announcement. Truman was forced to call a press conference to announce his decision at one o'clock in the morning in order to pre-empt an article due to be published in the *Chicago Tribune* the next day. Naturally MacArthur and many Americans were furious at his treatment, and on his return to the USA he was greeted by enthusiastic parades showing the American people's support for him.

Although 'containment' in Korea was unpopular with the American public, Truman stuck to his policy. The war reached a stalemate, with both sides digging into a maze of trenches either side of the 38th parallel, conducting dog fights in the air and heavy bombardment of military targets. On the suggestion of the Russians, peace talks began at a tea house in Panmanjom in June 1951; meanwhile the war dragged on and developed into a war of words as well as direct fighting. Peace talks were complex and frequently broke down, and in spite of pressure on the Chinese

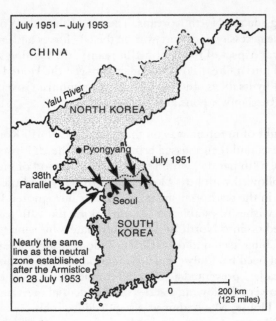

July 1951 – July 1953

CHINA

Yalu River

NORTH KOREA

● Pyongyang

July 1951

38th Parallel

Seoul

SOUTH KOREA

Nearly the same line as the neutral zone established after the Armistice on 28 July 1953

0   200 km (125 miles)

Figure 5.4 Status quo restored.

from General Dwight Eisenhower, who had become President in November 1952, the fighting continued.

It was only the death of Stalin in 1953 that brought about a change of attitude. The confusion in the Kremlin following his death led the new Soviet leadership to decide that the war must be ended. China could no longer be confident of receiving arms and supplies from Russia and had reached the same conclusion. Eisenhower, unaware of these decisions, attempted to coerce the Communists into a negotiated peace by threatening to use nuclear weapons against Beijing and by bombing dams in North Korea which would lead to extensive flooding. Only Syngman Rhee remained stubbornly against peace. Talks continued without him and finally an armistice was agreed on 27 July 1953. There followed a complicated exchange of prisoners. Of more than 12,000 UN prisoners, only 21 Americans and one Scot decided to stay on

in Communist China; 50,000 Communist prisoners of war were
released of whom two-thirds wanted to go to Formosa. Some of
the prisoners returning to the North cast off their US-made POW
uniforms, before crossing the border naked and carrying flags they
had made out of rags and dyed red with their own blood. No peace
treaty could be agreed upon, and peace talks continued for over
40 years.

Insight

The peace talks stalled in 2009 when North Korea withdrew
following international criticism of its launching of a long-
range rocket followed closely by a second atomic test.

WHAT WAS THE SIGNIFICANCE OF THE KOREAN WAR?

The war intensified the Cold War generally and the USA, self-
appointed Sheriff of Europe, became a well-armed sheriff for the
whole world. Truman took a series of steps to ensure American
military preparedness for any emergency that should arise. These
included increasing the army to 3.5 million men, submitting a
$50 billion defence budget to Congress, extending US military
bases to Spain, Morocco, Saudi Arabia and Libya and increasing
the American presence in Europe. The American military
establishment had been enormously expanded and as a result
a huge armaments industry wholly dependent on government
contracts developed. The United States' Secretary of State, John
Foster Dulles, believed that the Korean War had taught America a
valuable lesson. Next time the USA would use massive retaliation
including nuclear missiles to deal with communism.

Insight

Massive retaliation is a military principle which argues that,
should a country be attacked, it must retaliate immediately
using force out of proportion to the initial attack. The aim
is to deter other states from launching an initial attack. The
existence of nuclear weapons made this an effective threat
during the Cold War.

The effect on China was tremendous. In trying to act in self-defence it had been branded an aggressor by the UN. This public humiliation forced China to turn in upon itself behind the so-called bamboo curtain, isolating itself from the rest of the world. This isolation was not merely based on China's ideology but had been forced upon it to a large extent by the United States; its exclusion from the UN and its encirclement by a ring of American bases resulted in a feeling of being under siege. The Chinese response was to adopt an uncompromisingly hostile attitude towards the capitalist world and this in turn seemed to justify the West's fear of a Communist bloc stretching from the River Elbe to the China Sea.

There was little to celebrate at the end of the Korean War – the cost had been tremendous. The United States had lost more than 54,000 men and had 100,000 wounded; the UN forces had lost more than 3,000 men with nearly 12,000 wounded; the South Korean army lost 415,000 men and the North Koreans nearly a million; China officially claimed to have lost 112,000 men but military sources estimate the losses as being at least double that figure and possibly nearer to half a million. The Korean people suffered the most with horrendous civilian casualties and losses due to American bombing in the North, and at least 5 million homeless refugees in the South. Most of the major cities had been flattened but within a generation after the war, South Korea had emerged as one of the foremost growth economies of the region.

WHY IS THE KOREAN WAR KNOWN AS THE 'FORGOTTEN WAR'?

The role of the ordinary soldiers on both sides in the Korean War remains largely unpublicized, perhaps as is to be expected in a 'forgotten' war. In Britain the details of the events on Hill 282 described at the beginning of this section must be kept secret until the year 2025 by decree of the British government. Troops were told to keep quiet, newspaper reports were censored and the British files on the tragedy have been stamped 'Top Secret'. One battle

which is remembered is the stand of the 'Glorious Glosters' and
their heroic efforts to retain control of 'Gloster Hill' from 24 to
25 April 1950. Fewer than 40 effective fighting men held off wave
after wave of Korean attacks, answering the braying of the Korean
bugles with a variety of tunes on their one remaining bugle –
not once was retreat sounded. Only a handful escaped capture.
On 8 May the 1st Battalion, the Gloucestershire Regiment, and C
troop, 170 Independent Mortar Battery, were honoured with a US
Presidential Citation. Lieutenant Colonel James Carne of the 1st
Battalion, the Gloustershire Regiment was awarded the Victoria
Cross for his 'courage, coolness and leadership'.

Many people know of the Korean War through the success of
M*A*S*H (1969), a fictional account of Dr Richard Hornberger's
experiences in his years at the 8055 Mobile Army Surgical Hospital
in Korea which became a very successful film and a cult television
series which lasted for 11 years. The film was released in the
autumn of 1970 when anti-Vietnam sentiment was high – it was
an instant success.

The Domino Theory

In April 1954, Eisenhower announced publicly the 'falling domino'
theory which had influenced the United States' actions in Asia. The
theory had first emerged in February 1950 in the National Security
Council. It compared the countries of South-East Asia to a row
of dominoes – if one fell to communism it would knock down the
next in the line and so on until every one of them had fallen under
the control of Communist governments. This theory was developed
over the next few years and by 1954 Eisenhower was predicting

that the loss of a single country in South-East Asia would not only lead to the loss of all of South-East Asia but also of India and Japan, and finally the security of Europe would be compromised and its stability threatened.

Spurred on by this theory, the United States took over from France the task of giving military, economic and political backing to the non-communist government of South Vietnam. By 1955 the United States was firmly supporting Ngo Dinh Diem, who had refused to take part in elections which were due to take place in Vietnam and which would decide whether Ho Chi Minh, leader of the Vietminh Communists, or his non-communist opponents would control the whole of Vietnam once it was reunited.

In March 1955 the Chinese Communists attacked the islands of Quemoy and Matsu (part of Formosa) which were occupied at the time by Chiang Kai-shek's troops. In line with Dulles's ideas of massive retaliation the use of tactical atomic bombs was threatened. The United States was closer than at any other time during the Cold War to launching a preventative war. In the face of this brinkmanship (going to the brink of war to force the enemy to retreat), China backed down but the prospect of nuclear conflict had been real.

Insight

Brinkmanship presumes the other side will back down and make concessions rather than risk conflagration. This policy was particularly dangerous during the Cold War when the existence of nuclear weapons could have led to mutual destruction.

Winston Churchill had been urging the Americans and Soviets to meet to discuss their differences, a suggestion which had been consistently rejected by the United States. The confrontation over Formosa together with the fact that the Soviets were developing and improving their nuclear weapons made the USA more amenable to discussion. Russia too was open to the idea of détente and during the summer of 1955 there seemed to be developing a mood of disenchantment with the Cold War.

Insight

Détente describes an easing of tension in the relationship between East and West, symbolized by more frequent diplomatic and cultural contact, an increase in trade and co-operation between the superpowers and a willingness to negotiate about arms and weapons.

10 THINGS TO REMEMBER

1 On 1 October 1949, Mao Zedong led the Communist forces to victory against the Kuomintang forces led by Chiang Kai-shek, and established the People's Republic of China.

2 America treated China with deep suspicion, extending containment to the Far East to prevent other countries following China's lead; Russia welcomed Communist China.

3 In China agricultural peasants supported communism, while communism in Russia was supported by the industrial proletariat.

4 In 1948 the Malayan Communist Party allied with Chinese communists but failed to oust British rule in Malaya and establish a Communist state by force.

5 Korea had been divided along the 38th parallel of latitude into the Communist North and non-communist South, but in 1950 Communist forces invaded the South.

6 This invasion threatened America's control of Japan and the Pacific and could destabilize that area, so President Truman persuaded the UN to authorise America to aid South Korea militarily.

7 America's Task Force Smith forces were initially soundly defeated by North Korea – a tiny Asian country in comparison to the USA.

8 By October 1950 the North Koreans had over-extended themselves and were pushed back behind the 38th parallel as General MacArthur attempted to reunite North and South.

9   *Communist China sent 'volunteers' to help the North Koreans and thwart MacArthur's ambitions, pushing the American and UN forces back to the 38th parallel where each side 'dug in' until an armistice was agreed 27 July 1953.*

10 *Peace talks are still continuing, although at the time of writing they have stalled.*

6

The thaw

In this chapter you will learn about:
- *détente or peaceful coexistence in the 1950s*
- *changes in the USSR – Khrushchev and de-Stalinization*
- *the 1956 Hungarian uprising – why didn't the West implement the roll back theory?*

The 1950s seemed to mark a change in the nature of the Cold War. Each side held atomic weapons capable of destroying not only each other but also a large proportion of the world. Stalin's death in 1953 and the emergence of Nikita Khrushchev as the new Soviet leader two years later ushered in what seemed to be a thaw in the Cold War, a period of coexistence, or détente. A Summit conference took place in July 1955 when the United States, Britain, China, France and Russia met in Geneva, Switzerland. Hopes ran high in Europe, but those who foolishly expected a dramatic solution to international problems were to be disappointed as little was agreed and no major changes took place. Yet Geneva was a turning point, and it seemed that a new era of international relations had begun. After years of trading mutual insults the United States and the Soviet Union had been able to talk to each other again. The Soviet leaders had proved to their country that détente was not a betrayal of Soviet interests as Stalin had warned, and that they were able to hold their own in the international arena.

Khrushchev

For a period of two years the Soviet Union had several leaders, but by 1955 Nikita Khrushchev had emerged as a clear leader. He was totally different to his predecessor; he loved to travel and show off Russia's achievements and was more a man of the people, unlike the reclusive, sinister Stalin. His personality seemed to offer a better chance for an improvement in East–West relations and the Soviet leader even visited Britain in 1956 and the USA in 1959. Yet events in 1956 rocked the status quo in the Soviet bloc.

In a speech to the Twentieth Party Congress held in Moscow in February 1956, Khrushchev attacked Stalin for promoting a cult of personality and for his use of purges and persecution to reinforce his dictatorship and to reduce the Communist Party to a compliant instrument with which to enforce his personal tyranny. Thus was launched the policy of de-Stalinization. Not only did this violent denunciation have a dramatic effect on the domestic affairs of the Soviet Union, it also proved to be a significant event in the development of the Soviet Union's foreign policy.

Three main concepts were employed to persuade the rest of the world that Stalinism had been abandoned: peaceful coexistence was designed to appeal to the West; different roads to socialism appealed to the satellite states in Eastern Europe; the rejection of violent revolution (in theory) attempted to reassure uncommitted countries.

Peaceful coexistence was the most significant concept for the West. It did not mean that the Soviet Union had rejected the Marxist belief that capitalism was doomed and that the final victory would belong to communism, rather it meant a change in how to bring about that victory. The existence of nuclear weapons which could lead to mutual destruction ruled out the use of war but not necessarily the use of force and conventional weapons. However, the main field of struggle was no longer to be in the military sphere but in the field of economics. The Soviets believed that the West's prosperity would eventually be undermined by an economic slump. Its economic support for other countries would thus cease and nations would soon realize that the only answer was communism. Until that disastrous slump Soviet diplomacy must seek to preserve the status quo.

Khrushchev believed that the status quo favoured the Soviet Union and was, paradoxically, revolutionary. For example, Khrushchev believed that Nasser, the Egyptian leader, would continue to resist Western attempts to preserve their colonial influence in Egypt and would be more open to offers of Soviet aid since the Soviet Union did not have the same colonial past as countries in the West. Admittedly the Soviets exercised quasi-imperialistic power in Eastern Europe, but the countries in the Middle East, Africa and Asia did not feel as apprehensive of Soviet aid as they did about taking aid from previous colonial rulers with all the imperialist baggage which that might entail. The United States saw Nasser as a Communist; in fact he was an Arab nationalist and opponent of Egyptian Communists. This misreading of Nasser led the United States to regard any request for economic or social change in Egypt as being initiated by Moscow and consequently refused to fund the building of the Aswan Dam Project in 1956, allowing the Soviets to step in and exert their influence in the region.

As more and more countries became involved in nationalist revolutions, the United States ran the risk of being sidelined by the Soviets with their offers of aid to those countries which feared the extension of American imperialism.

Khrushchev was less enthusiastic when nationalist uprisings, sparked off by his policy of de-Stalinization, appeared in Eastern Europe. Many countries sought to rid themselves of the leaders imposed upon them by Stalin and had also been buoyed up by Khrushchev's ideas suggesting that the Russian view of Communism was not the only path the satellites could take – were there not 'different roads to Socialism' that they could follow? Stalin had treated the satellites almost as 'slave colonies' of Russia. The standard of living in Eastern Europe had steadily declined, food shortages were common, industrial and agricultural workers were working harder for less and even the state propaganda could not cover up the worsening situation. Each satellite had a feared secret police, political prisons and labour camps; in Hungary alone 25,000 people had been executed without trial since 1945. Stalin's style of communism had left the people of Eastern Europe downtrodden, exploited and resentful. With Khrushchev's speech the hope of a higher standard of living, less economic direction from Moscow and more political freedom seemed possible.

Poland

Riots in Poland sparked off by economic grievances soon developed into demands for political changes. The Poles succeeded in ridding themselves of Boleslaw Bierut, the 'Stalin' of Poland, through natural causes (he died while on a visit to Moscow in 1956), avoiding the appointment of Moscow's candidate Edward Ochab and returning instead a former victim of Stalinism, Wladyslaw Gomulka, as First Secretary. This sent shock waves through Moscow; Khrushchev flew to Warsaw having first closed the Polish border and stationed Russian troops in Poland. He arrived too late to prevent the appointment of Gomulka and was told of the

Poles' intention to follow their own road to socialism. Gomulka introduced a number of major reforms: political prisoners were released and victims of past purges rehabilitated; collective farms were broken up into private holdings and private shops were allowed to open; factory managers were given more freedom; Cardinal Wyszynski, the Archbishop of Warsaw who had been arrested and imprisoned in 1953 was allowed to return to his cathedral; finally in 1957 parliamentary elections were held in which there was a choice of candidates and political parties. The result was a majority for the Communists of only 18.

How was Gomulka allowed to carry out these changes? Molotov had wanted to send in the troops but was prevented by Khrushchev who hoped that Gomulka would eventually realize the precariousness of his position and would get back in line. Indeed, Gomulka did not rock the boat too violently. Russian troops remained on Polish soil, Poland remained within the Warsaw Pact, and even political freedom was circumspect. Gomulka emphasized that the reforms were not going to be used as a springboard to more radical innovations. Once established in power until his fall in 1970 Gomulka proved that he continued to be a Muscovite Communist and remained a faithful ally of the Soviet Union.

Hungary

Hungary had the same causes for complaint as the Poles. The standard of living was very low under communism and frequent food shortages were blamed on the Soviet-style collective farms. Agricultural and industrial goods were sent to the USSR rather than being available to the Hungarian people. There was no freedom of expression and the media was tightly controlled by the government, which also used the State Protection Group (the AVH) and the Hungarian secret police against opponents not only of the Hungarian government but also of communism and the USSR. Soviet control of education enforced a rigid Communist view of history which ignored Hungary's traditions and historical connections with the West. Religion was actively discouraged and Catholics persecuted and imprisoned. The presence of Soviet troops was a constant reminder of Soviet control.

Critics of the Rakosi-Rajk regime in Hungary had been encouraged by the results of the revolt in Poland and were quick to criticize the harsh regime and its economic failings. Khrushchev ordered Matyas Rakosi to resign and replaced him with another Moscow protégé, Ernst Gero. The slight easing of the regime's repression only served to increase criticism from the intellectuals and students and, in the face of demonstrations in Budapest, the government panicked and called on Moscow for help.

On 25 October 1956, 30,000 Soviet troops sealed off Budapest and declared martial law. The situation was further destabilized by the fact that some of the Soviet troops fraternized with the protesters and many units within the Hungarian army seemed less than supportive of the regime. Fighting raged on, with the pulling down of Stalin's statues symbolizing the fall of the former tyrant. Only the security police stayed loyal to the Russians and hundreds of police were lynched by the rebels. One eye-witness recalled seeing two Russian T-34 tanks dragging bodies behind them through the streets as a warning of what happened to freedom fighters. The Russian troops were not strong enough to quash the rebels and, after talks with Imre Nagy, the new Hungarian Prime Minister, the Russian tanks withdrew from Budapest on 28 October, though Khrushchev deployed more divisions on the Hungarian border.

Throughout the country there was an atmosphere of expectation: industrial workers formed revolutionary councils; open elections were held in villages and towns across the country and a coalition government was formed in which some of the older parties such as the Smallholders were represented. It seemed that the Soviets would accept this multi-party government, indeed the Soviet news agency TASS issued a statement that the Soviet Union deeply regretted the bloodshed in Hungary and approved of the removal of Soviet troops.

At this critical phase in the Hungarian revolt, the Suez Canal crisis broke out in Egypt. This distracted Washington's attention from Eastern Europe and offered the Soviets a perfect opportunity to bring Hungary to heel. Khrushchev did nothing at first, hoping that Nagy would bring Hungary back into line without Moscow having to intervene and perhaps being compared to the imperialist powers that were at that very moment invading Egypt.

Insight

The Suez Canal connects the Mediterranean and the Red Sea and allows ships to avoid sailing around Africa. It is a vital connection between the West and the oil-producing states and consequently demanded more attention from the West.

PLEAS TO THE UNITED NATIONS

On 1 November 1956, Nagy demanded the withdrawal of Russian troops from the country and Hungary's withdrawal from the Warsaw Pact. In addition he sent a telegram to Dag Hammarskjold, the Secretary General of the United Nations, asking him to put the question of Hungarian neutrality on the agenda of the UN's General Assembly. He had gone too far. Deng Xiaoping, the official delegate of the Chinese Communist Party, was visiting Moscow at the time and impressed upon Khrushchev the need for a firm hand with Hungary as the revolt was not only against the Soviet Union but also against the whole Communist ideology. How had Nagy hoped to get away with these presumptuous demands? Many Hungarians had been listening to Radio Free Europe (RFE), the CIA-backed station that broadcast into Eastern Europe. This had been broadcasting propaganda since the beginning of the uprising proclaiming the West's backing for Hungary's freedom fighters – perhaps Nagy along with so many of his countrymen believed that the United States would come to Hungary's aid.

Insight

RFE was funded by the United States in order to provide news and information to countries in Eastern Europe.

Staunchly anti-communist, it has been accused of meddling in the 1956 Hungarian revolution, simultaneously providing false hope of US intervention to the Magyars and precipitating a Soviet crackdown because of its inflammatory broadcasts.

On 3 November, 15 Soviet army divisions and more than 4,000 tanks encircled Budapest and at dawn the next day entered the city and used maximum firepower against the inhabitants. Their tactics were extreme: if a sniper was suspected of being in a certain building, that building was destroyed; queues of housewives outside shops were machine gunned; as the last 30 defenders of the Kilian Barracks surrendered they were shot as they emerged.

PLEAS TO THE WEST

Desperate radio appeals were broadcast: 'Civilized people of the world! Our ship is sinking. Light is fading. The shadows grow darker over the soil of Hungary. Extend us your aid.'

No aid came, only sympathy and press condemnation of the Soviet action.

Eisenhower, distracted by the Anglo-French-Israeli action against Egypt and the climax of the American presidential election, did nothing except loudly condemn the action in the final speeches of his campaign and issue a formal protest to the Kremlin. Dulles' promises of liberation and roll back (that the United States would help the peoples of Eastern Europe if they revolted against the control of the Soviets) had been proved a hollow sham. Unable or unwilling to embark on roll back, the United States settled for containment: however deep Eisenhower's hatred of communism, his fear of war was deeper.

The last battle ended on 14 November, by which time between 3,000 and 4,000 Hungarians had been killed and about 200,000 had fled the country, mostly to Austria across the Bridge of

Freedom. Nearly 700 Soviet troops were killed and 1,500 wounded – mostly by Molotov cocktails, the street fighters' only effective weapon against the tanks.

Insight

Molotov cocktail is the generic name for a petrol bomb. An oil-soaked rag is placed in the neck of a petrol-filled glass bottle. The rag is set alight and the whole object is thrown at the opposition. It was named after a Foreign Minister of the USSR, Vyacheslav Molotov.

The rising had been crushed. Nagy had gone into hiding in the Yugoslav Embassy and was replaced by Janos Kadar, but it took several months to restore the kind of hardline control that Moscow wanted. Around 35,000 activists were captured and 300 were executed. Nagy was lured out of hiding with promises of a safe passage, but was betrayed, arrested, imprisoned and later executed. One-party rule had been re-established.

WHY DID THE SOVIET UNION CRUSH THE UPRISING SO DECISIVELY?

The harsh actions taken by the Soviet Union were undoubtedly the main factor why the Hungarian uprising failed; the rebels had little chance against the ruthless use of the Soviet tanks. Khrushchev needed to secure his own position in the USSR and could not afford to show any weakness, especially since China had urged him to deal decisively with the rebels in order to protect the worldwide reputation of communism and to discourage other Eastern European states from taking the same action. Free elections and the withdrawal of Hungary from the Warsaw Pact might mean the end of communism in that country; other satellites might follow suit and that would destroy the Soviet Union's buffer zone against the West. From the perspective of the Soviet Union the events in Hungary had been a major crisis and Khrushchev had proved to be a Stalinist at heart in the way that he dealt with it. Eastern Europe was firmly back under the control of the Soviets.

HUNGARY UNDER JANOS KADAR

Once the Russians had crushed the revolt, Kadar set about restoring order. Martial law was imposed, the secret police were given back their powers, strikes were suppressed and the majority of leading dissidents were imprisoned. Kadar was careful not to antagonize the USSR but also took into account the widespread demand for freedom revealed in 1956. The end of the Russian pillaging of Hungary was of great economic benefit to Kadar's regime as was the aid which poured into Hungary following the USSR's change in policy towards its satellites, with the result that the real income of Hungarians rose by 36 per cent between 1956 and 1963. A new programme to increase productivity and output was introduced in 1965; investment was made on the basis of profitability; salaries and wages depended on productivity. By 1984 over half of Hungary's foreign trade was with the West; the standard of living was higher than in most satellite states; shops were well stocked, streets crowded with privately owned cars, restaurants full – all evidence that the Kadar regime had succeeded in creating a 'people's capitalism'.

Insight

Goulash Communism is another name for economic policies (as detailed above) which wandered from 'pure' Communist economic principles by introducing elements of the free market. Just as a goulash is a stew with a mixture of ingredients, Hungarian communism was a mixed ideology rather than unadulterated communism.

10 THINGS TO REMEMBER

1 *Nikita Khrushchev began de-Stalinization at the Twentieth Party Congress in 1956.*

2 *'Peaceful coexistence', the rejection of violent revolution and 'different roads to socialism' lead to a 'thaw' in relations between East and West.*

3 *Krushchev attended international peace talks at Geneva and Camp David.*

4 *In the Middle East, Africa and Asia, Khrushchev played on fears of American imperialism and extended Soviet influence.*

5 *In Poland, First Secretary Wladyslaw Gomulka introduced reforms, remained committed to Moscow and stayed within the Warsaw Pact.*

6 *Hungary also attempted reforms but Moscow used military might to subdue the Magyars while the West was preoccupied with the Suez Canal crisis.*

7 *Hungary had proposed withdrawal from the Warsaw Pact which could have led to other satellite states following suit thus destroying the USSR's buffer zone with the West.*

8 *The Hungarians had believed Radio Free Europe's propaganda that the West would aid countries trying to gain independence from Russia.*

9 *The new leader of Hungary, Janos Kadar, restored Communist control but also used Soviet aid to improve the country's standard of living.*

10 *His policies have been called Goulash Communism, where traditional Communist ideas were mixed in with elements of a free market economy, improved human rights, and a concern for standards of living.*

7

The arms race

In this chapter you will learn about:
- *the nuclear arms race during the Cold War*
- *technology – Sputnik and Flopnik*
- *Gary Powers and the U-2 incident and the failure of a peace summit*
- *Ostpolitik.*

On 16 July 1945, an eye-witness to the first test firing of the
atom bomb at Alamogordo noted that the whole country was
lit up by a searing light far brighter than that of the midday sun.
Although this person was eight kilometres away from the blast,
only 30 seconds later came a strong blast of air and an awesome
roar which gave the impression that doomsday was at hand. Less
than a month after this event, doomsday came to Hiroshima and
Nagasaki. The horrific aftermath of this action on the people and
the cities illustrated the enormous implications of these types of
weapons. Yet after those two fateful days in August 1945, the
development and proliferation of nuclear weapons continued.
Why did the Great Powers continue to gamble with the future of
the earth by developing these kinds of weapons and did their very
existence really diminish the chances of major wars in the future?

As relations between East and West began to deteriorate in the years
following the Second World War, rivalry increased in the fields of
armaments and space exploration. Soon races developed in these
areas as each side struggled to become superior in the production
of armaments or to become the leader in space exploration.

On 29 August 1949 the USSR exploded its own atomic bomb, code name First Lightning, at Semipalatinsk-21.

Insight

Semipalatinsk-21 is the postcode for the main Soviet nuclear testing facility in north-east Kazakhstan which conducted 456 explosions between 1949 and 1989. It was of intense interest to American U-2 spy planes and, later, spy satellites.

Five days later on 3 September a US Air Force B-29 picked up increased radioactivity as it flew over that area. At first, the United States believed a nuclear reactor had blown up somewhere in Russia but the discovery of certain elements in the radioactivity persuaded the Americans that the Soviets had indeed exploded their own nuclear device similar to the one dropped by the USA on Nagasaki in 1945. How had the Soviets succeeded in developing this device so quickly? They had certainly made use of intelligence obtained by their spies in the West. Klaus Fuchs, a German-born British physicist, and Ted Hall, an American physicist, were found to have been spying for the Soviets and had passed on information which had hastened the development of the Soviet atomic bomb by as much as one year. Yet this information alone did not explain the alacrity with which the Soviet Union followed the United States into the nuclear club. The very nature of the Soviet atomic project was ideally suited to the Communist regime. No expense was spared and the project was given priority over all other concerns. There was no shortage of labour – gulag prisoners were used to build installations and to mine the uranium ore and process it to extract plutonium.

Insight

GULAG was a Soviet governmental agency responsible for more than 476 penal forced labour camps. The dissident Solzhenitsyn described them as places where people were 'exterminated by labour' – he had first-hand experience of life in such a place. An estimated 50 million died in Soviet gulags between 1930 and 1950.

In Igor Kurchatov the Russian scientists had an able team leader who not only inspired his colleagues but was also able to cope with his political masters. Perhaps one should not underestimate the part played by menace in speeding up research: present at the explosion of the bomb was Beria, chief of the Soviet secret police, who commented that it would have been a great misfortune if it hadn't worked.

The Soviet acquisition of the atom bomb forced the United States to reassess its defence capability and led to the development of the hydrogen bomb, a super bomb one thousand times more powerful than the atom bomb. Oppenheimer who had developed the atomic bomb was horrified at the prospect of developing a bomb with such destructive capacity during peacetime and felt that it would be a danger to the whole of humanity. On the other hand, a group of scientists led by Edward Teller and supported by the US military argued that the United States was engaged in a race with the enemy and if this bomb was not developed, the USA would be open to attack by that enemy. President Truman agreed with the latter group, and on 31 January 1950 announced his decision to the world, thus beginning an arms race where both sides hoped they would never have to use the weapons they were developing.

What was the arms race?

The arms race was the struggle for military superiority in the world; just as the Americans developed advanced systems of security and weapons, so too did the Soviets. Both countries developed vast numbers of strategic bombers, intercontinental missiles, submarines and cruisers. Increasingly, nuclear weapons were developed because they were more cost-effective than having to pay for large standing armies. In addition they were more of a deterrent than conventional arms as each side realized if they used nuclear weapons the other side would retaliate in kind, and both sides would suffer horrific consequences. A nuclear arms race developed as, in an attempt to outgun their opponents, each side developed more powerful weapons and tried to build more of each type of weapon than the other side. The idea of having so many nuclear weapons was that they could not all possibly be destroyed should the other side strike first, and the advent of intercontinental ballistic missiles (ICBMs) facilitated retaliation in the event of an attack and led to a type of stalemate situation known as MAD – Mutual Assured Destruction. The race produced so many weapons that there was an 'overkill' capacity (by the 1970s the Soviets had the capacity to destroy every major American city 20 times over, while the United States had the capacity to destroy every major Soviet city 50 times over).

Insight

An ICBM is a land-based ballistic missile that is guided for the first part of its flight but falls freely as it approaches the target. It has the range to carry a nuclear bomb over 5,600 kilometres (3,480 miles).

The arms race was based primarily on fear: the fear that one side would launch a sudden attack on the other; the fear that allies might lack support in times of crisis; the fear that one side would take advantage of its superiority to increase its influence in other parts of the world, and the fear that other countries might turn to the stronger side for help.

The hydrogen bomb

Truman's super bomb took over two years to complete but on 1 November 1952 it was tested on the Pacific atoll of Eniwetok, 320 kilometres (200 miles) west of Bikini Atoll. The bomb weighed 82 tons, took six weeks to assemble and had to be kept in refrigeration prior to its detonation. Observers watching the test from ships at a distance of 48 kilometres (30 miles) saw a 5-kilometre (3-mile) diameter white fireball shoot into the sky accompanied by a wall of heat which was sufficient to heat the wings of a B-36 plane flying 12,000 metres (40,000 feet) high

24 kilometres (15 miles) away to a temperature of 93 degrees. Five minutes later a giant mushroom cloud rose up creating a canopy of 160 kilometres (100 miles) in diameter; from this canopy radioactive mud and rain poured down. The explosion created a crater in the seabed 60 metres (200 feet) deep and 1.6 kilometres (1 mile) in diameter; the coral reef had been vaporized completely.

Nine months later, on 12 August, the Soviets tested their super bomb at Semipalatinsk. Unlike the American hydrogen bomb, the Soviet bomb used lithium and did not need to be refrigerated but could be carried in a conventional bomber. The thermonuclear age had begun with the Soviets marginally in the lead.

National prestige

Prestige played an important part in the arms race as many people on both sides saw it as a straight competition between the relative strengths of capitalism and communism, therefore it was vital that the USA developed a bomb that could use lithium. On 1 March 1954 just such a bomb was exploded in American waters. Its strength had been severely underestimated – the force was three times that which was expected. Situated 132 kilometres (82 miles) away, the Japanese fishing vessel *Lucky Dragon* was affected by the fallout. All 23 members of the crew suffered from radiation sickness and one died. The Japanese government was furious: it seemed that once again the Japanese nation had been unwitting victims of the USA's desire for nuclear advancement. The United States attempted to play down the situation by implying that the *Lucky Dragon* had trespassed or was in fact a Soviet spy ship, accusations which proved to be false.

Insight

The *Lucky Dragon* incident intensified the Japanese anti-nuclear movement, especially since it was discovered that other fishing boats and their catches had been contaminated

(Contd)

by radioactive fallout. From the incident came the Japanese monster movie genre, beginning with *Godzilla* in 1954.

Within the next year both sides had developed bombs which could be easily delivered by air. The nuclear race was gathering pace.

In charge of the United States' Strategic Air Command since 1948 was 'bombs away' Curtis LeMay, a very macho character who freely admitted that if the United States had lost the Second World War, he would have been put on trial as a war criminal for the horrific destruction caused by his bombing raids on Japan. His attitude was bellicose to say the least. He frequently talked about pre-emptive strikes to prevent the USSR gaining any advantage over the USA, and argued that it was in the national interest to begin the next war before the Soviets caught up with the United States. He was eager to expand America's nuclear stockpile and succeeded in doing this with the help of 40 per cent of all US defence spending. In 1950 the United States had 298 atomic bombs; by 1955 these had increased to 2,422 nuclear weapons; by 1962 this had reached 27,100. The number of bombers also increased from 668 in 1951 to 2,500 in 1959. LeMay believed that the United States had to be in a state of military preparedness at all times as the first few hours of any attack would be decisive. He identified 5,000 to 6,000 targets which had to be destroyed in the event of war, including military and air bases and power stations.

Of course, all America's contingency plans depended on their knowledge of Soviet military strength. Unauthorized reconnaissance flights over the Soviet Union had begun in 1950 and, in spite of Truman's express instructions, continued throughout the decade. From 1956 onwards Lockheed U-2 spy planes were used to gather information. These flew at a height of 22,900 metres (75,000 feet) and had a range of 3,200 kilometres (2,000 miles). Aboard were cameras and electronic equipment to monitor radio transmissions and it is said that the photographic detail collected by these cameras was remarkable. Of course, the photographic evidence collected in this way had to be interpreted and sometimes the photographs could be deceptive. The flights themselves were risky as the U-2 incident in 1960 proved.

U-2 incident

On 1 May 1960, Gary Powers, an American pilot, took off from his base in Peshawar, Pakistan, but 20,800 metres (68,000 feet) over the Urals the plane was hit by a Soviet missile. Powers ejected from the plane before it crashed near Sverdlovsk, and parachuted to safety. He did not use the cyanide capsule provided for just such an occurrence and was captured alive by the Soviets. Just before the Paris Summit was about to begin, Khrushchev made an announcement that an American spy plane had been shot down in Soviet air space. The National Aeronautics and Space Administration (NASA) announced that the U-2 was in fact a research plane studying weather conditions at high altitude, denied that spy flights over Russia had taken place and asked for further details.

Khrushchev was able to expose the cover story by producing Gary Powers, numerous cameras, films and tapes and other pieces of espionage equipment – concrete proof that the Americans had not only been spying but also lying. Eisenhower accepted responsibility for the spy flights and publicly announced their termination. No apology was forthcoming and Khrushchev stormed out of the Paris Summit which collapsed in chaos. Gary Powers was put on trial in Moscow and sentenced to ten years' imprisonment; he was released in 1962 in exchange for Rudolf Abel, a Soviet spymaster operating in New York.

Rocket science

During the Second World War, the Nazi government had developed its V1 and V2 rockets as weapons to use against Britain. At the end of the war the United States captured the V1 and V2 bases together with Wernher von Braun, a leading German rocket scientist, and the information thus obtained was put to use in developing the US missile programme.

Russia, too, made use of Nazi technology and expertise by rounding up thousands of German rocket scientists and putting them to work on the Soviet missile programme. Rockets were seen as having the potential to deliver nuclear missiles in double-quick time and with less risk of being shot down than a bomber. The production of these new weapons had not been without problems. A new rocket was being tested by engineers at the secret Baikonur Cosmodrome under the direction of Marshal Nedelin. Nedelin kept a close eye on this work and even sat on a folding chair in front of the rocket urging the technicians to work faster. As a control panel was being fitted, the engine ignited. Technicians were engulfed by flames and fell like burning torches from the top of the rocket. In the end 189 people died. All that was found of Marshal Nedelin was his Marshal's star. In 1957, the Soviets launched their first rocket in Baikonur, Kazakhstan. This was the world's first ICBM, a missile which could carry hydrogen bomb warheads.

The implication of the ICBM was overshadowed by the Sputnik – a 22-inch diameter radio transmitter which weighed 83.6 kg (184 lb). The radio bleeps broadcast by this transmitter shook the world on 5 October 1957 as they were transmitted from outer space. Amateur astronomers and radio operators all over the world eagerly tracked the satellite as it orbited the Earth. The possibilities of military application of the Sputnik were not lost on the USA. On 3 November that year Sputnik II took off carrying the space husky Laika who survived in space for ten days. Laika's breathing, heartbeat and blood pressure were all continually monitored and radioed back to the USSR; however, when it became clear that no arrangements had been made to bring Laika back to earth, there were protests from animal lovers from all over the world!

American public opinion was split between fear of Soviet missiles, and worries about the safety of the dog they called Curly. Prayers were offered up for the dog:

We can only pray in this time of aloneness (sic) and suffering for Curly, that God will be merciful and speed the end. This voiceless cry of mercy, as this satellite spans the Earth, should be long remembered as the symbol of the torture the animal world must go through.

To send Sputniks of such weight into such high orbits required enormous rockets and it soon became clear to the world that the Soviets had solved the problem of the ICBM by developing rockets that could soar across Europe or the Arctic to reach major cities in the West; they could also be used to photograph the territory beneath. Alarm bells started ringing in the USA.

Sputnik was an affront to American national pride; some believed the society had gone soft, that consumerism had overtaken science. This may have caused American scientists to be too hasty in launching a vanguard rocket carrying a 1.8 kg (4 lb) satellite from Cape Canaveral on 6 December 1957. The nation watched with bated breath as the huge rocket rose half a metre in the air, and promptly exploded. The *Daily Herald* in Britain neatly summed up the event with its headline, 'Oh What a Flopnik'. In the United States, a nation mourned.

The missile gap

The 'Gaither Report on Deterrence and Survival' had reported real gaps between US and Soviet science and technology and recommended that the government increase funding for both Strategic Air Command and America's missile force. This report was leaked to the press and promptly began a moral panic; the hysteria that came in the wake of this leak raised the spectre of a missile gap between the USA and the Soviet Union which 'flopnik' seemed to confirm. This missile gap had been caused in turn by a technology gap because of an education gap. The 1958 National Defence Education Act attempted to correct the latter by permitting federal involvement in education when hundreds of millions of dollars were ploughed into education as loans for students of engineering, science and maths. The numbers of Americans attending college in the 1960s doubled as a result.

In the face of this moral panic, Eisenhower remained extremely cool, playing golf following the launch of Sputnik and refusing to be ruffled by claims that the missile gap was widening. Why? Because U-2 spy photos showed that the USSR was in fact making very slow progress in the production of weapons and that the USA not only had more warheads but also led the way in bombers. In spite of Dulles' eagerness to tell the public everything, Eisenhower preferred to keep his own counsel in order that the USSR did not suspect that the United States was aware of the reality of the situation. Instead, he rebuilt bridges with Britain and France following the fracas in Suez the previous year. Britain in return agreed in principle to the USA siting IRBMs (intermediate range ballistic missiles) on British soil. America's European allies in NATO also agreed to site IRBMs; however France refused and the French leader Charles de Gaulle, who was suspicious of the close relationship between the USA and Britain, began to withdraw his country from NATO and to pursue a more independent line.

NASA

1958 was an exciting year for both rocket science and space exploration with three American rockets successfully taking off and with the formation of NASA (National Aeronautics and Space Administration). Although NASA primarily had a scientific goal, science and military aims overlapped. Not only did it consider taking man into space but also developing a spy satellite to replace the U-2.

Public confidence began to recover and many began to believe that they could survive a nuclear attack. Public nuclear air-raid shelters were built and private ones constructed for those who could afford them. Children in schools were taught to 'duck and cover' by a series of cartoon characters and educational films – of little practical use against weapons that could vaporize buildings perhaps, but they increased public confidence and quietened many a nightmare.

As presidential election campaigns got underway the Democrats' candidate, John Fitzgerald Kennedy, made much of the missile gap publicly, although he had been briefed that none existed; the shooting down of a U-2 spy plane by a new Soviet S-75 missile served to increase America's concern and decreased the likelihood of détente at the Paris Summit; it may also have contributed to Kennedy winning the presidential election. As President, Kennedy admitted late in 1960 that a missile gap did exist, but in America's favour; this was done primarily to warn off the Soviets as a crisis heated up in Berlin.

The United States' relief at this news was short-lived, as on 12 April 1961 the Soviets succeeded in launching a man into space. Yuri Gagarin was sent into orbit in a Vostok spacecraft and remained there orbiting the earth for 1 hour 48 minutes. He was given a hero's welcome when he returned to earth but the Soviets, when questioned by the Nobel Prize committee, refused to name the scientist behind this success, claiming in true Communist fashion that the work was a team effort. In the face of this Russian success, President Kennedy pledged that before the end of the decade, the United States would land a man on the moon and return him safely to earth.

Insight

When Armstrong and Aldrin went to the moon, they took with them one of Gagarin's medals as a tribute to the first man in space. *Glasnost* finally made public the name of the lead designer behind Soviet manned flight – Sergey Pavlovich Korolyov, known only by his initials or the soubriquet 'Chief Designer'.

Should the West use nuclear weapons?

The crisis in Berlin in 1961 had seen Kennedy seriously considering the use of nuclear missiles in a limited first strike against the Soviets should they invade West Berlin. Although he had been advised that a limited use of nuclear weapons was possible, Kennedy staunchly refused to consider the use of nuclear missiles against Soviet sites in Cuba, in spite of assurances by the CIA that there were no Soviet nuclear missiles on the island. In fact there were at least 20 medium-range nuclear missiles on Cuba – had Kennedy listened to his hawkish advisers there would certainly have been a nuclear exchange that would have destroyed both the USA and the USSR. Kennedy recognized that in nuclear gamesmanship it was necessary to permit the other side to save face in a crisis.

By 1961 the United States had 12 B-52s constantly in the air 24 hours a day, 365 days of the year, and submarines on the seabed ready to launch SLBMs (submarine launched ballistic missiles). The USSR mirrored the USA with fewer missiles to begin with but, following the Cuban Missile Crisis, they began to stockpile weapons and by the end of the 1960s had overtaken the USA in terms of ICBMs.

China joined the 'nuclear power club' on 16 October 1964 and the danger of nuclear war stepped up a few notches. Unlike the USSR and the United States, Mao had few qualms about using nuclear weapons. He was completely unfazed by the prospect of huge numbers of fatalities should the United States use nuclear weapons against his country, and took the attitude that if 300 million people lost their lives in a nuclear war so be it – after all, war was war. The losses would soon be made up by an increased birth rate, as the 'baby boom' following the Second World War had proved. Mao had been horrified by the Soviet climb-down over Cuba and felt that this was an indication that the USSR was no longer a revolutionary state at the cutting edge of communism. It was time for China to take control of communism. Only three years later, China exploded a three-megaton hydrogen bomb having made the transition from atomic to thermonuclear power in record time.

How safe were nuclear weapons in the hands of the superpowers?

In his book *Has man a future?* (1961) Bertrand Russell, the British philosopher, expressed the opinion that the longer the Cold War went on the more likely was the prospect of 'total destruction'. Several times during the Cold War parts of the world came close to destruction by nuclear weapons, although only a few people were aware how close at the time. The vast majority were blissfully unaware, safe, so they believed, in the knowledge that nuclear devices had a collection of fail-safe devices to prevent them from exploding accidentally. There have been several accidents involving planes carrying nuclear missiles, none of which resulted in nuclear explosions. On 24 January 1961, a B-52 carrying two nuclear bombs disintegrated over North Carolina. One bomb has never been found; the other was recovered but of its six fail-safe devices five were found to have failed. Had the final device also failed North Carolina would have suffered a nuclear blast a thousand times more powerful than Hiroshima.

On 17 January 1966, a B-52 refuelling in mid-air collided with the tanker. Four hydrogen bombs fell to earth near the village of Palomares in Spain. Thankfully their safety devices prevented thermonuclear explosions but explosives in two of the bombs did explode, sending radioactive particles over nearby farmland and further afield, carried by the prevailing wind. A third bomb was recovered intact near the village and a fourth was recovered from the sea by the mini submarine 'Alvin' from a depth of 760 metres (2,500 feet), 8 kilometres (5 miles) offshore. Following a further accident in Thule, Greenland, where a B-52 making an emergency landing crashed, it was decided to end airborne alert operations; the United States would henceforth rely on its early warning systems rather than have a fleet of B-52s constantly armed and airborne. These accidental crashes were worrying but far more dangerous were systems failures. During the Cuban Missile Crisis the atmosphere was so tense that mistakes did occur. In Malmstrom air base several safety precautions were overlooked, any one of which could have led to the inadvertent firing of a nuclear missile. In a Minnesota air base a bear climbed over the perimeter fence triggering a series of synchronized alarms, one of which was the wrong one – a klaxon signifying nuclear war was sounded sending the pilots to their waiting planes. Only the quick thinking of an officer who drove his car into the middle of the runway prevented the planes taking off and delivering their nuclear missiles.

The public was becoming increasingly aware of potential foul-ups that could bring about the end of the world. In 1964 Columbia Pictures released *Dr Strangelove*, a satirical comedy by Stanley Kubrick where a US air base commander loses his mind and orders his squadron to attack the Soviets. In spite of putting into action the emergency procedure to recall the B-52s, because of a series of foul-ups, one continues on its way towards the Soviet Union. The American President informs his Soviet counterpart who sadly informs him that the 'doomsday machine' will in turn launch an automatic retaliation against the USA. The end of the film shows the beginning of the resulting nuclear holocaust. Although the Pentagon denied such a situation could occur, an incident in Moorestown, New Jersey, showed that mistakes could be made when a satellite appeared on the radar screen and was mistaken for a missile launched at Tampa from Cuba. Luckily the mistake was noticed in time.

Détente and the arms race

Events in Eastern Europe during the 1960s had indicated that dangerous pressures were developing which could destabilize the Eastern bloc. The Brezhnev Doctrine attempted to prevent these from developing further by emphasizing that military intervention on the part of the Warsaw Pact troops would be forthcoming in the event of divergent policies being followed by the satellite states.

To Leonid Brezhnev, the Soviet leader, détente offered the possibility of stabilizing the situation in Eastern Europe while pushing ahead in other promising areas such as the Third World or developing countries. In the United States there had been massive spending on the war in Vietnam and the economic benefits of détente made it very appealing to Washington. The prospect of détente with China offered the possibility of driving a wedge between the USSR and China, thus lessening the threat posed by the combined power of the two Communist giants.

To the Great Powers, détente was not merely about peaceful coexistence and it could be argued that by 1979 détente had actually done more to intensify the Cold War than it had to lessen its effects. There were certain developments during the period of détente which encouraged optimism at the time, particularly negotiations concerning arms control. It should be noted that arms control or arms limitation did not imply disarmament. The aim was to freeze or at least slow down the arms race in order to cut spending and achieve a balance of power rather than end it altogether.

In 1970, the SALT (Strategic Arms Limitation Talks) began, leading to the first ABM (Anti-Ballistic Missile) Treaty of 1972. This established a balance of nuclear warheads between the USSR and the United States. The SALT discussions continued to try to find a basis for agreed arms reductions until the SALT 2 Treaty was signed in 1979, although it was overtaken by events and not ratified by the American Congress. In 1975 the Helsinki Accords recognized the existing borders of Europe and brought up the issue of human rights when the signatories agreed to respect freedom of belief and expression.

Détente did have its limits. The arms race was almost impossible to slow down in spite of its threat to the very existence of the world. While there was a substantial and ever growing anti-nuclear protest movement, especially in Britain and West Germany, there were many who believed the arms race guaranteed world safety as long as both sides cancelled each other out in the 'balance of terror' – the aptly named MAD scenario. One should not forget the powerful vested interests that existed on both sides of the iron curtain and put pressure on their respective governments; military and industrial vested interests wanted to keep arms spending for both ideological and business reasons. Critics of détente were frustrated by the USSR's failure to improve human rights and suspected that the Soviets were failing to keep to the terms of the SALT 1 agreement. In fact both sides were positioning more missiles against each other and technological developments quickly made SALT 1 irrelevant. The Soviet invasion of Afghanistan brought détente to an end and began the second Cold War.

Ronald Reagan and the second Cold War

In 1980 Ronald Reagan replaced Carter as President of the United States. He firmly believed that détente had caused the USA to lose ground to the USSR and returned unequivocally to an anti-Soviet policy. Included within this policy were initiatives such as expanding the United States' armed forces, developing a new type of nuclear bomb (the neutron bomb) and new types of missiles (including the MX, Cruise and Pershing missiles), and developing a new form of defence against nuclear attack – the Strategic Defence Initiative (SDI) or Star Wars as it became known. Anti-Soviet rhetoric returned to international affairs and Reagan frequently referred to the USSR as the 'Evil Empire'.

Insight

In August 1984, while recording a sound check which was unfortunately already being broadcast, Ronald Reagan quipped: 'My fellow Americans... I've just signed legislation outlawing Russia for ever. We begin bombing in five minutes.'

During this period the United States developed a new type of bomb – the neutron bomb which could kill many people without destroying so much property. A nuclear explosion causes heat, blast and radioactive fallout, but a neutron bomb makes use of this energy and converts it instantly into high energy radiation. A small neutron warhead might cause a blast and fireball which would affect only 230 metres (750 feet), but the radiation it released would prove lethal to living organisms over a radius of 2.5 kilometres (1.5 miles). The radiation would not be longlasting, and the area could be reoccupied within a matter of days. It opened the possibility of being able to fight a limited nuclear war largely confined to military forces and not affecting civilians as a conventional nuclear war would.

The United States developed the MX missile which was also known rather ironically as the 'Peacekeeper' missile. These missiles had been under development since 1971 and were ICBMs with a range of approximately 11,250 kilometres (7,000 miles), which carried 10 or 12 independently targetable thermonuclear warheads. The MX's accurate guidance system gave its 300 kiloton warheads greater potential to destroy reinforced missile silos and command bunkers situated in the USSR.

In November 1983 the first of 160 nuclear missiles reached Greenham Common in Berkshire, UK as part of NATO's plan to strengthen Western Europe's nuclear defences. This Cruise missile was a new type of missile which could be launched from land, ship or plane, but the ones deployed in Europe were to be ground-launched. The missile could fly at 900 kilometres (600 miles) an hour at approximately 20 metres (65 feet) above the ground, enabling it to slip under radar screens to deliver its 200 kiloton nuclear warheads with deadly accuracy. According to one RAF expert it could hit not just a given house to within 10 metres (32 feet) of its target over 3,000 kilometres (1,800 miles) but even a given room in that house. Pershing 2 missiles were to be stationed in West Germany in direct response to the deployment of mobile SS-20 missiles by the USSR in Eastern Europe.

Reagan launched the Strategic Defence Initiative (SDI) or Star Wars, an expensive programme to develop anti-missile weapons using laser beams. It aimed to exploit the huge gap that existed between American and Soviet technology and aimed to make it impossible for Soviet missiles to reach American targets by creating a huge laser shield in space. Such a system was in direct contravention of the Anti-Ballistic Missile treaty of 1972 which had stabilized the nuclear balance and had ensured that if either side launched an attack, their own destruction would be guaranteed (MAD). If successful it would mean the United States would not be the victim of a 'first strike' and might feel able to initiate a nuclear strike, fully confident of its own safety. The Soviets had received news of the SDI before its official announcement on 23 March 1983 and were afraid they would not be able to match the American programme for purely financial reasons. Star Wars may have been meant as a purely defensive system but the Soviets regarded it as provocative.

Insight

The SDI was soon derided by physicists as being impossible given the existing technology and became known increasingly as the Star Wars Initiative (after the cult film by George Lucas, a fictional account of a young Jedi Knight battling against an evil empire). Reagan's career in Hollywood had left its mark.

Two further incidents in 1983 pushed Soviet nerves nearly to breaking point. On 25 October the United States invaded Grenada fearing a Marxist takeover of the Caribbean island; Britain protested at American involvement in a Commonwealth country and for a time there was a flurry of Anglo–American communication. Soviet agents may have feared the worst especially as, just days after the invasion, NATO began its 'Able Archer' war games designed to test NATO's nuclear-release procedures. The exercise involved temporary radio silence and changes in NATO codes and frequencies. The Soviets believed that 'Able Archer' was a cover for an imminent NATO attack and several nuclear-capable planes were placed on alert in East Germany. The United States failed to realize how dangerous the situation had become until the Director of the CIA met with the British double-agent Gordievsky. This proved to be a turning point which paved the way for talks in Reykjavik, caused the Americans to tone down their military exercises and persuaded Reagan that it was necessary to begin discussions with the USSR.

These were facilitated by the appointment of a new General Secretary in the USSR. Mikhail Gorbachev, age 54, was elected unanimously by the Politburo on 10 March 1985. Three months earlier he had nailed his reformist colours to the mast when he had spoken of *perestroika* and *glasnost* to a party conference. He realized the need for reform within the Soviet Union and saw that one way to fund this was by reducing spending on defence. Prime Minister Margaret Thatcher had already proclaimed him a man she 'could do business with' when he and his wife had visited Britain in 1984. Would Reagan be able to work with Gorbachev?

Reagan and Gorbachev

Arms reduction talks, broken off after the shooting down of Korean Airlines flight KAL 007, were resumed and a meeting in Geneva between Gorbachev and Reagan was planned for November 1985. It was not a success. Both men adopted adversarial stances, each accusing the other of dividing the world and of accelerating the arms race. There seemed no hope of agreement. Following a short walk together the two leaders sat down beside an open fire to continue their discussions and to the surprise of all concerned they appeared to enjoy each other's company. The second day followed a similar pattern, disagreements in the morning and the development of personal rapport in the afternoon. When a final joint communiqué was signed the leaders agreed that a nuclear war should never be fought and that the two sides should not attempt to achieve military superiority. Although nothing concrete had been agreed, a dialogue had been opened.

Unfortunately, following the apparent success in Geneva, the United States resumed an anti-Soviet, belligerent stance: two American warships deliberately entered Soviet territorial waters gathering intelligence; American raids on Libya in reprisal for terrorist acts killed over 100 Libyans; the United States exploded another nuclear device and continued to finance the Mujahideen to the tune of $630 million.

In October 1986 a mini-summit was agreed between the two powers at Reykjavik, but nothing came of the meeting as Reagan clung obstinately to his dream of SDI.

Later in 1986 Reagan became embroiled in mysterious deals involving the sale of arms secretly to Iran and the diversion of profits made thus to help the Contras in Nicaragua. As Congress had refused to vote the President the funds he wanted for the Contras, this secret dealing led to public outrage and the affair was christened 'Irangate' by the media. Around the world his credibility plummeted, and his popularity with the American public fell, but remained high with Margaret Thatcher (the British Prime Minister).

Insight

The Contras were rebel groups fighting against the left-wing Sandinista government in Nicaragua and supported financially and militarily by the USA. President Reagan believed them to be 'the moral equivalent of our Founding Fathers'. The Reagan administration was found to have been selling arms to the Iranian government in an attempt to obtain the release of US hostages being held in Lebanon. Profits from this deal were diverted to supply the Contra guerrillas in Nicaragua.

In February 1987 Gorbachev agreed to the elimination of all Soviet and American intermediate-range nuclear missiles in Europe. The Intermediate-range Nuclear Forces (INF) Treaty had no strings attached and made no mention of abandoning SDI. The signing took place in the East Room of the White House and was televized live in both the United States and the USSR. The treaty eliminated an entire class of Soviet and American nuclear arms from Europe – all the SS-20s, the Cruise and Pershing missiles that had caused so much protest were to be dismantled. The process of verification was open and extensive, with officials on both sides having the right to inspect missile sites and factories.

While walking in Red Square during the Moscow Summit in 1988, a journalist asked President Reagan whether he still believed the USSR was an 'evil empire'. Reagan replied he did not. The journalist pressed him further and asked why his opinion had changed. Reagan replied, 'I was talking about another time and another era.' The Moscow Summit was pure theatre, merely the reaffirmation of friendship. As ever the stumbling block was SDI.

Gorbachev's bombshell

On 7 December 1988 Gorbachev addressed the United Nations General Assembly and made one of the most astounding speeches ever delivered to the UN. He announced unilaterally a cut of 500,000 men in the Soviet armed forces, the removal of 10,000 tanks, 8,500 artillery pieces and 800 combat aircraft from Europe, large withdrawals from Manchuria and from the border with China. Reagan remained convinced that American strength and determination had forced the Soviets to give in; what he failed to realize was that Gorbachev was not an old-style Soviet leader: he was committed to arms reduction and was unwilling to play games with the future of the Soviet people at stake. To him, compromise, mutual trust and co-operation were the way forward.

Public reaction to the arms race

In 1958 public concern regarding the dangers of nuclear missiles led to the formation of CND, the Campaign for Nuclear Disarmament. In Britain CND's annual Easter march from London to Aldermaston called for unilateral nuclear disarmament of Britain's nuclear arsenal and for the removal of American bases from British soil. In the 1960s a number of marches, sit-down protests and civil disobedience shocked the British establishment and the protesters were portrayed as unwashed beatniks by the British media. The arrest of 89-year-old philosopher Bertrand Russell and his subsequent imprisonment, however, led to international outrage and protests to the British government.

During the 1964 general election campaign, the Labour Party, following pressure placed upon it by the CND movement, campaigned on a promise to cancel government plans to buy American Polaris nuclear missile submarines. Labour was duly elected but Harold Wilson, the Labour Prime Minister, went ahead with the purchase and reneged on his campaign promises. This undermined CND's power and credibility and left it severely weakened for over a decade.

In Europe similar anti-nuclear groups campaigned for disarmament. In Holland, religious organizations took the lead forming the Dutch Inter-church Peace Council. In both East and West Germany there was strong support for peace and disarmament organizations. Recently opened files of the Stasi, the East German secret police, reveal that they were active within the East German peace groups and in 1982 the Director of the CIA claimed that the USSR had channelled approximately $100 million each year into the Western disarmament movements. In Eastern Europe the people, raised on a diet of government propaganda and censorship, were less concerned. Few had any inkling of the Cuban Crisis until the whole thing was nearly over. The war in Afghanistan and the coming of *glasnost* saw the anti-nuclear movement extend to the Soviet Union and its satellites.

During the 1970s the anti-nuclear movement underwent a renaissance with the decision to site Pershing II and Cruise missiles in Europe. At the Greenham Common airbase in Berkshire, a women's peace camp was set up outside the perimeter fence to protest at plans to deploy Cruise missiles there. Relations between the Greenham Common women and the soldiers at the base were naturally strained. One of the women, Judith Day, recalled how, during an all-night vigil at the gates to the base, American soldiers returning from a night out in the local hostelries took great delight in urinating on the women sitting outside the gates.

Not all encounters with the American forces were so negative. During one altercation at the gates an American woman living on the base came out to talk to the Greenham women protesters and to find out more about their beliefs. Before long an American soldier approached her and politely asked her to return to the base.

The woman smiled and explained that Judith was her cousin and that they were just 'catching up' on family matters; the soldier retreated respectfully. Some minutes later the same soldier returned and insisted, very respectfully, that the American woman return to the base immediately. Judith Day later discovered that her 'cousin' was actually the wife of the commander of the base. The peace camp remained in place for 19 years in a permanent vigil. In December 1982 an estimated 30,000 people linked hands around the base in protest, on 1 April 1983 70,000 linked arms forming a human chain from Greenham to Aldermaston. Newbury District Council tried twice to evict the women from the site; each time the peace camp was re-established and it was not until 2000 that the peace camp finally came to an end.

Public protest to both Soviet and American governments helped to play a role in the signing of the INF Treaty in 1987. With the collapse of the USSR, the anti-nuclear movement has since shifted its attention towards Asia and China's nuclear testing and also towards the new nuclear arms race between India and Pakistan.

The arms race was not without its moments of black comedy. During the Cold War, Britain secretly planned to build a nuclear landmine. Code-named 'Blue Peacock', the device was to be 'run' by live chickens. The seven-ton mine was the size of small truck and was designed to be buried or submerged by a British Army retreating from Soviet forces. It was intended that at its core would be plutonium surrounded by high explosives. The intention was to detonate the landmine by remote control or timer to cause mass destruction and to contaminate a wide area, thus preventing subsequent enemy occupation of the area. The scientists working on the project realized that in winter vital components could become too cold to activate and the mine might fail to explode. Various solutions to this problem were explored including filling the casing of the bomb with live chickens, which would give off sufficient heat, prior to suffocating or starving to death, to keep the delicate explosive mechanism from freezing!

10 THINGS TO REMEMBER

1 *The first American atom bomb exploded on 16 July 1945. On 29 August 1949 Russia used its first atom bomb, and China joined the nuclear club on 16 October 1964.*

2 *A superpower arms race led to a stalemate known as MAD (mutually assured destruction).*

3 *SALT talks during the 1970s slowed the nuclear arms race but many believed that MAD guaranteed world safety so spending on nuclear weapons continued.*

4 *Each side used spies and spy planes to discover the military strength of its enemy – not always with success as the U-2 incident proved in 1960.*

5 *The Russian's Sputnik satellite raised fears that a missile gap had developed between the USSR and the USA – this was unfounded.*

6 *NASA became increasingly important in the 1960s when, following the Russian cosmonaut Yuri Gagarin's journey into space, Kennedy pledged that the USA would land on the moon first.*

7 *Under Reagan, the USA developed new nuclear weapons and missiles, expanded its missile bases into Europe and launched the Strategic Defence Initiative to develop anti-missile weapons using a laser beam shield situated in space.*

8 *Mikhail Gorbachev introduced* perestroika *and* glasnost, *opened a dialogue between the USA and the USSR and facilitated the elimination of all Soviet and American intermediate-range nuclear missiles in Europe.*

9   *On 7 December 1988, Gorbachev announced in the UN that he was unilaterally and substantially reducing the Soviet armed forces.*

10 *In Britain the Campaign for Nuclear Disarmament (CND) and the women protesting around Greenham Common pressurized the government not to station American nuclear weapons on British soil.*

8

Kennedy and Khrushchev

In this chapter you will learn about:
- *the Cuban Missile Crisis*
- *the U-2 sighting of missile sites on Cuba*
- *the ExComm two-week debate*
- *a win–win outcome.*

The United States had always regarded the Caribbean as its backyard, a source of trade, wealth and leisure and an area which formed part of the US security zone. During the nineteenth century, President James Monroe had emphasized the importance of this area by issuing the Monroe Doctrine – a statement which declared the area of the Americas to be a sphere of US influence. The United States had demonstrated its unwillingness to accept Communist influence in the Latin America/Caribbean area when it had intervened in Guatemala in 1954 to rid the country of a left-wing government which was too extreme for the United States' liking, particularly when the Guatemalan government began to interfere in the affairs of the United Fruit Company – a company with direct connections to Washington and John Foster Dulles.

Although the USA was a signatory to the charter of the Organization of American States, which declared that no state might interfere in the affairs of another, Washington gave permission for the CIA to train and prepare a group of anti-communist Guatemalan exiles to conduct a guerrilla war against the Guatemalan government. Led by General Carlos Castillo Armas and supplied by the CIA, these troops eventually persuaded the Guatemalan officer corps to desert from the Guatemalan army causing President Arbenez to flee into exile. The CIA was thrilled with this coup and was convinced that the Caribbean and Latin American area would remain within the United States' control without further challenge.

Approximately 150 kilometres (90 miles) off Key West on the coast of Florida lies the Caribbean island of Cuba. The United States had liberated Cuba from Spanish rule following a ten-week war in 1898, had built a huge naval base at Guantanamo Bay, and American companies had invested in the mining and agriculture of the country.

Since early 1933, Cuba had been ruled by a pro-American dictator, Fulgencio Batista y Zaldivar. The United States not only helped keep him in power but also dominated Cuba's trade and bought most of the main crop, sugar cane. The United States owned most of the land and the larger industries and Cuba became well known as a holiday destination for rich Americans. Tourism in this Caribbean playground was dominated by the Mafia and the island gave many Americans a weekend taste of the tropics and access to prostitution, drugs and gambling. The gulf between the rich and poor in the country was tremendous; living conditions in the rural areas were almost medieval. Batista's government was harsh and corrupt and very unpopular with many of the Cuban people.

The first to raise the flag of protest, on 26 July 1953, was Fidel Castro, a young lawyer who offered Cubans the chance to change their lives, to restore their dignity and to break free of US control. The uprising failed: he was imprisoned and later sent into exile in Mexico and the USA. On his release he returned to Cuba and began plotting the overthrow of the Batista regime from his base in the Sierra Maestra Mountains in the Oriente province of Cuba. Here he launched guerrilla attacks on Batista's forces, aided and abetted by Ernesto Guevara, a doctor from Argentina better known to the world as Che Guevara. This doctor's first love was revolution, especially against the USA.

Castro's revolution

Batista's use of terror lost him a great deal of support from the Cuban people and on 1 January 1959 he fled the country. Castro marched into Havana a week later, formed a coalition government and began a series of reforms designed to end corruption and terror in Cuban politics and to improve Cuban prosperity, particularly that of the peasants who worked on the land and in American-owned sugar mills. He claimed he was fighting for a democratic Cuba and an end to dictatorship, but at first Castro had no programme to nationalize American interests or the sugar mills, nor had he declared his allegiance to Marxism-Leninism. Rather, his government was more Cuban nationalist than Socialist. He visited New York claiming to 'come for good relations' but did not meet President Eisenhower. He was later to complain that 'the US President did not even offer me a cup of coffee'. To Castro's disappointment he met Vice President Nixon who, having listened to all that Castro had to say, decided that Cuba was now run by a Communist who could not be trusted.

Castro commenced his policy of land reform, distributing land he had confiscated to the landless peasants previously exploited by both Batista and American companies. When American oil companies refused to refine oil bought cheaper elsewhere, Castro nationalized the refineries. Compensation was offered, but the United States refused his terms. Following a visit from Anastas Mikoyan in February 1960, Castro signed a trade agreement with the Soviet Union and nationalized American interests in Cuba worth over a billion dollars. The United States tried and failed to moderate Castro's policies by setting up an economic blockade and refusing to buy Cuban sugar, the country's main export. The Soviet Union quickly stepped in to buy the crop and also to ship petroleum to Cuba following Eisenhower's refusal to sell petroleum products to the Cubans. It was natural for Cuba to move ever closer towards the Soviet Union as the United States cut all ties with her Caribbean neighbour. As Kornienko, a close associate of Khrushchev, observed, Castro and his associates were not Communists, they were pushed in that direction by the United States.

The direct involvement of the Soviet Union in a Caribbean state interfered in the unspoken 'spheres of influence' governing the Cold War.

American attempts to destabilize Cuba

Confident that the CIA could repeat its success in Guatemala, Eisenhower approved a number of CIA-led covert operations with the intention of destabilizing Cuba. A series of sabotage raids were conducted; bombs were exploded in warehouses and on ships bringing imports to the island; domestic cats were used to set fire to the sugar cane crop – as one saboteur noted, if you set fire to a piece of petroleum-soaked material attached to the cat's tail, the cat would run two to three kilometres in an effort to extinguish the fire, all the time setting alight the sugar cane crop as it ran. Walt Elder, assistant to the Director of the CIA, recalled how the agency acquired a stock of poisoned capsules with a view to using them on Castro, and how they even recruited the Mafia to their cause. At one point they succeeded in recruiting Marta Lorenz, Castro's secretary and one-time lover. She was trained to kill by the CIA and succeeded in returning to Cuba and gaining admittance to Castro's bedroom. He was well aware of her intentions and asked her point-blank whether she had come to kill him. She replied that she had, at which point he took out his revolver and gave it to her saying, 'Nobody can kill me' and urging her to 'Do it!' She refused and returned to the United States.

Countless ridiculous exploits were planned by the CIA, many concerning the use of one of Cuba's main luxury items and a weakness of Castro's – the cigar. Plans were laid for Castro to receive exploding cigars, cigars containing a chemical which would cause his beard to fall out thus exposing him to ridicule, cigars laced with LSD to be given to him before he appeared on television thus causing him to act like an idiot. As a former operative with the CIA remarked, they were desperate!

Insight

Kennedy, too, enjoyed a Havana cigar. He ordered 1,200 H. Upmanns brand *petit coronas* and upon receipt signed an executive order which imposed a trade embargo on Cuba. It was illegal for US residents to purchase or import Cuban cigars wherever they were in the world.

The CIA also trained a force of Cuban exiles in Guatemala. The intention was that this exile brigade would land in Cuba, and lead an uprising against Castro and his government.

The Bay of Pigs invasion

On 20 January 1960 a new President of the United States of America had been inaugurated – John Fitzgerald Kennedy. Prior to his inauguration he had been briefed by Eisenhower on the US plan to help the anti-Castro guerrillas. Although he was surprised at the small numbers involved in this potential operation, Kennedy made no objection. After all, on the campaign trail to the presidency, the Democrats had frequently been accused by the Republicans of being soft on Cuba. Consequently Kennedy had promised action if elected. However, Kennedy, fearful of world opinion, was unwilling to 'go public' about these plans, indeed he stipulated that American involvement had to be concealed and refused to countenance any US military involvement. In a press conference three days before the scheduled invasion Kennedy publicly emphasized that under no circumstances would there be an intervention in Cuba by United States armed forces.

The invasion of the Bay of Pigs was a disaster. A group of approximately 1,400 lightly armed Cuban exiles landed on Cuba to face 20,000 Cuban troops. The exile brigade had been supported by six US bombers, painted in Cuban colours and flown by rebel Cubans, which had failed to ground the Cuban air force but had dropped napalm bombs on Cuban civilians and troops causing horrific injuries and deaths. In spite of pleas to the USA for more aerial support, Kennedy realized the hopelessness of the situation and refused. There was no popular uprising to support the rebels and many Cubans who had never considered themselves as revolutionaries took up arms for the first time to defend their country from the invaders. At the end of three days of fighting, their supply ships sunk by the Cuban air force, the survivors of the invading exile brigade surrendered. One hundred men had been killed and only 14 were rescued by the US navy. Around 1,200 were taken prisoner and were later sent back to the United States in return for $50 million ransom paid in food and medical supplies.

It was clear that the United States had made a mistake: Kennedy, by being so determined to minimize the political risk to himself, had weakened the prospect of the invasion's success; the CIA had not only overestimated the Cuban support for the invasion but had also wrongly assumed that Kennedy would support a failing mission by direct action. It was a steep learning curve for the new American President. He had realized that he could not accept advice from his advisers unquestioningly but he also became convinced of the potential threat Cuba posed to the security of the United States. When Kennedy met Khrushchev in June, the Soviet leader radiated confidence and rubbed salt in the wound by insisting that the United States was on the wrong side of history and that increasingly communism would win the day. Khrushchev's translator Sukhodrev remembered that Kennedy, not renowned as a smoker, had chain-smoked that day, and how he had even smoked Sukhodrev's cigarettes in his nervousness. Kennedy may well have begun to wonder whether the West was losing the Cold War.

Cuba grows closer to the USSR

In Cuba the failed invasion rallied the people behind Castro's government and persuaded him to hitch his wagon to the Socialist revolution. Henceforth Cuba would follow communism, the only sensible response to American imperialism.

In October 1961 Operation Mongoose, a covert operation programme to overthrow Castro, was initiated by the CIA with full presidential knowledge and support. Between January and July 1962, 60,000 acts of sabotage including arson, explosions and even murders were carried out. In the spring a series of large-scale military exercises, including amphibious landings, were carried out on nearby Caribbean islands, the purpose being to increase the pressure on Castro and to show off American military capabilities. It seemed to many international observers that the United States was about to invade. Both Russia and Cuba became convinced that this was the United States' intention.

Khrushchev's bright idea

Visitors to Khrushchev's dacha on the Black Sea were often given a pair of binoculars and bidden to look through the window. Invariably they would say that they could see nothing, whereupon Khrushchev would seize the binoculars, look intently through them for a few moments and declare that he could see the American

Jupiter missiles positioned in Turkey directly pointing at his summer house! It was his little joke, but these missiles were no joke. They were a direct threat to the Soviet Union and could launch a nuclear attack on the country in a matter of minutes. The existence of these missiles, together with the threat posed to Cuba, Russia's shop window of socialism in Latin America, gave Khrushchev an audacious idea of 'throwing a hedgehog at Uncle Sam's pants'. Russia would station nuclear missiles on Cuba thus protecting the island from an American invasion and giving the United States a taste of its own medicine by directly threatening the major cities on mainland America. Although shocked by this plan, only Mikoyan disagreed with Khrushchev, arguing that Castro would refuse to station the missiles on Cuba and that the Cuban landscape was unsuitable for such a plan. Without trees, how could the missiles remain hidden?

Although initially worried about the effect the presence of missiles might have on the image of the Cuban revolution, Castro was interested. He felt that missiles might provide a shield against American imperialism and improve the balance of power in the Caribbean. Furthermore it was Cuba's duty. In July 1962, 65 Soviet ships, ten of them carrying military equipment, set sail for Cuba. By September, construction of the missile sites in San Cristobal, Western Cuba, was underway. From here nuclear missiles could be launched at the United States.

The CIA received over 500 reports from agents in Cuba that the Soviets had placed nuclear missiles on Cuba, but these reports were dismissed. After all, why would Khrushchev take such a risk? Several weeks later, on 14 October 1962, these sites were photographed by a U-2 spy plane. The photographs were analyzed by the photo intelligence branch of the CIA and the President was informed of their existence on 16 October. Kennedy was horrified and exclaimed that it was exactly as if the United States had suddenly begun to put missiles in Turkey. An adviser had to remind him that the United States had done precisely that.

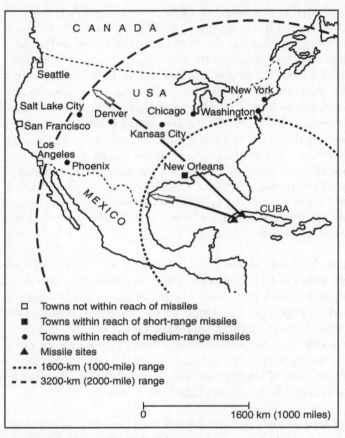

Figure 8.1 American towns within range of missiles from Cuba.

ExComm hawks and doves

Kennedy put together a group of senior advisers to discuss the crisis. This Executive Committee of the National Security Council, or ExComm as it became known, was to meet almost continuously for the next two weeks. It agreed unanimously that nuclear weapons in America's backyard were unacceptable and that they must be removed. It was calculated that the missiles would become operational within two weeks; therefore a two-week time limit was imposed within which to remove the missiles.

> ## Insight
>
> All discussions conducted by ExComm were recorded secretly by President Kennedy who installed a tape recorder in the White House basement with wires to concealed microphones in the Oval Office.

ExComm divided into two groups – the hawks and the doves. The hawks, mainly military men, wanted to invade Cuba and eliminate communism; the doves wanted to avoid anything which might lead to escalation and retaliation – they preferred a diplomatic approach which included discussions with Castro and Khrushchev.

The Joint Chiefs of Staff wanted a decisive military solution, and put out a secret all forces alert to be ready for an air strike and possible invasion. The preparations were hush-hush and, to ensure they remained secret, the doors of the barracks were chained shut, and the men were only allowed access to telephones in strictly controlled areas.

ExComm debated the best way to neutralize the missiles: should they launch a pre-emptive air strike to bomb the missile sites or force the Soviets to remove them by some other means? If they were to bomb the sites, would the air force be able to take out all the missile sites, the SAM anti-aircraft missile defences and the back-up facilities decisively? It was estimated that there could be no guarantee of eliminating all the missiles – the best that could be hoped for was that 90 per cent would be destroyed.

At first Kennedy was in favour of a pre-emptive strike, but not all of ExComm was convinced. The Pentagon tried to persuade the President that a neat surgical attack was impractical and the air force General Curtis LeMay called for an all-out air offensive with hundreds of bombing sorties. Those opposed to this warned

Kennedy that there would be major casualties, both American and Cuban, which could jeopardize world opinion. They believed an air strike could too easily lead to an escalation of the crisis. Gradually Dean Rusk, the Secretary of State, and Robert MacNamara, the Secretary of Defence, persuaded ExComm against the air strike option.

On Thursday 18 October 1962, ExComm was informed that the installation of the Soviet SS-4 medium-range missiles was nearly complete but that the longer-range SS-5 missiles would probably not be functional until the end of the year.

Cuba in quarantine

ExComm now considered an alternative to an air strike – a naval blockade. All ships bound for Cuba were to be stopped and searched. This would prevent further missiles being landed and would buy time for the United States to consider its options. Kennedy decided to back the blockade option and on 22 October informed America's allies of his intentions. Until this point they had been unaware of the crisis, but both Britain and France pledged their support. Kennedy was concerned that the blockade might lead to a Soviet reaction in Berlin and so the B-52 nuclear bomber force was placed on alert and armed with nuclear warheads. It was decided to inform the world of the situation via a television broadcast during prime time viewing that evening. Prior to this broadcast the Soviet Ambassador Dobrynin was given a copy of Kennedy's speech and a copy of a personal message to Khrushchev. The Ambassador knew nothing of the deployment of Soviet missiles in Cuba and, according to Dean Rusk, aged ten years as he read the documents. The Ambassador took a short time to compose himself, then relayed the message to Moscow. There, the leadership was convinced that the stage was set for an American invasion of Cuba, and sent instructions to the Soviet commander in Cuba authorizing him to use tactical nuclear weapons should the Americans land.

Kennedy addressed the nation from the White House setting out the evidence of the site of Soviet missiles and outlining the US policy of quarantine – the word blockade had been dropped as it was considered too aggressive. While he was speaking, all US military forces worldwide went on DEFCON 3 – a heightened state of nuclear alert.

Insight

The DEFCON range indicates the readiness of US defence capabilities on a scale of one to five, five being the lowest state of alert in peacetime and one the highest or imminent possibility of war. During the Cold War this would have inevitably meant all-out nuclear war.

In the Caribbean, 180 US naval ships were deployed to blockade Cuba. Khrushchev now entered a period of improvisation as he had no contingency plan should the missile sites be discovered. The Warsaw Pact forces were put on alert. TASS, the Soviet news agency, charged Kennedy with a violation of international law and with threatening world peace, and Khrushchev accused Kennedy of trying to provoke a military conflict. Following Kennedy's speech to the nation, Cuba too believed that the blockade was the first step on the road to invasion and quickly moved to mobilize the Cuban people to fight to the last man to support the Soviet troops in Cuba.

On Wednesday 24 October, the Secretary General of the United Nations, U Thant, sent identical letters to both Kennedy and Khrushchev pleading with both governments to suspend the blockade and the shipments for a couple of weeks in order to reduce the risk of war. Later that day one Soviet ship containing 24 nuclear warheads beat the blockade and docked in the Cuban port of La Isabela. Khrushchev issued a caution to Kennedy not to stop Soviet ships at sea, otherwise Soviet submarines would sink the American vessels. He warned, 'If America insists on war, we'll meet together in hell.' At 10.25 a.m. reports came through to ExComm that some of the Soviet ships had stopped dead in the water. In Dean Rusk's immortal words, 'We're eyeball to eyeball, and I think the other fellow just blinked.'

Unbeknown to him, five Soviet ships carrying nuclear missiles had been ordered back to the Soviet Union the day before in spite of the fact that Ambassador Dobrynin had told Robert Kennedy (the president's brother) that the Soviet captains had orders to continue on their course to Cuba.

ExComm was well aware of the escalating nature of the crisis and the need to avoid actions that might humiliate the Soviets or be misconstrued, thus leading to a knee-jerk nuclear reaction on the part of the Soviets. The Joint Chiefs of Staff, for the first and only time in the Cold War, raised the level of military alert to DEFCON 2 – the highest level of alert short of war. Meanwhile, in the quarantine zone of the Caribbean, the Soviet tanker *Bucharest* was stopped and searched by the USS *Gearing*; as it contained only oil, it was allowed to continue to Havana. Later that day in the United Nations Security Council in New York, a heated exchange took place between the US Ambassador Adlai Stevenson and the Soviet Ambassador Valerian Zorin. This exchange, a moment of tense drama, was captured on film for posterity and has gone down in history as one of the most famous exchanges in the history of the UN.

Questioned by Stevenson as to whether the USSR had placed missile sites on Cuba, Zorin stonewalled, refusing to answer because of Stevenson's inquisitorial attitude. He told Stevenson he would have his answer in due course; Stevenson replied, 'I am prepared to wait for my answer until hell freezes over.'

By 26 October, President Kennedy was under increasing political pressure, as the November congressional elections approached, to crack down hard on Castro. ExComm discussed plans for an invasion and 25,000 US marines were assembled in the Caribbean to join the 100,000 soldiers already assembled in Florida; two US aircraft carriers headed towards Cuba and the air force presented plans for an air strike beginning with 2,000 sorties. It was estimated that American casualties would be approximately 18,500 in the first few days of fighting.

Unbeknown to Washington, nuclear war was hanging by a thread under the seas surrounding Cuba. The USS *Beale* had been tracking a Soviet submarine and had begun dropping depth charges to warn the submarine of its proximity to the restricted area. According to the Soviet signals intelligence officer the depth charges felt like 'sledgehammers on a metal barrel'. USS *Beale* was unaware that the submarine was carrying a nuclear torpedo and had instructions to use this should the hull be pierced by depth charges or fire from the surface. The submarine was running out of air and needed to surface and there followed an argument about what action to take between the captain, a political officer and the chief of staff of the submarine flotilla. Things escalated to the extent that the captain ordered the nuclear torpedo to be made ready for combat. It is unclear what happened next but sense prevailed and the submarine rose to the surface rather than using its torpedo to break free of the encircling American warships. The vital importance of this incident was only recognized in 2002 at the Cuban Missile Crisis Havana Conference following the declassification of government documents and navy deck logs.

In the Kremlin, Khrushchev became increasingly concerned that Kennedy was losing control of events and sent a very long and emotional personal letter to the President which urged, 'We and you ought not to pull on the end of the rope in which we have tied the knot of war, because the more we pull the tighter the knot will be tied.'

The letter offered a political solution: the Soviets might withdraw the missiles if the USA agreed neither to invade Cuba in the future nor to support other forces who might invade. Robert Kennedy had maintained a private channel of communication with the Kremlin throughout the crisis with the help of Anatoly Dobrynin, the Soviet Ambassador. In the early hours of 27 October they met again. Dobrynin raised the presence of American missiles in Turkey and the threat they posed to the security of the Soviet Union. Following a short phone call, Robert Kennedy, acting as a go-between, responded that the President was willing to examine the question of Turkey favourably. This news was immediately passed to Moscow – it seemed that the crisis might yet be solved peacefully. This spark of hope was all but extinguished by events later that day.

In ExComm on Saturday 27 October the news came that the six missile launchers on Cuba appeared to be operational and that the next 48 hours would be critical. Then the shocking news came that the Soviets had launched MiG fighters to intercept a U-2 plane which had entered Soviet air space over Siberia. MacNamara was convinced it meant war; Kennedy was more relaxed, as he said, 'There's always some son of a bitch who doesn't get the word.' The U-2 plane escaped without harm.

The next blow came with a letter from Khrushchev which had been broadcast on Radio Moscow. It should be remembered that at this time no direct link existed between the Kremlin and the White House, and a radio broadcast from Moscow was one way of reaching the White House quickly and efficiently. This letter was far more formal than the one received the day before. It stated that the Soviet missiles on Cuba would be removed in return for the removal of US missiles in Turkey. The hawks on ExComm were outraged as there had been no mention of Turkey in the previous letter. They speculated that Khrushchev had been dismissed or at the very least overruled by the hardliners in the Kremlin. Only the President and his brother knew that Khrushchev was responding to their proposals of the previous meeting between Robert Kennedy and Dobrynin. Discussions in ExComm were heated. Kennedy pointed out that world opinion would think the deal over Turkey was an acceptable one to avoid nuclear war. The Chiefs of Staff argued that such a move would severely weaken NATO. As the day progressed, Kennedy became aware that he could not progress without possibly sparking a nuclear conflagration; neither could he retreat without it looking like surrender.

Cuba's view of the situation

The evening prior to Kennedy and Dobrynin's discussions, Castro had visited the Soviet Embassy in Havana where he sent a telegram to Khrushchev. In it he warned Khrushchev that an American invasion was imminent and he assured Khrushchev that the Cuban people would be willing to fight to the last man. He strongly suggested that the Soviets prepare a nuclear strike in retaliation for the expected invasion and informed them that he had ordered his own units to fire on any US aircraft flying over Cuba. Castro had upped the ante.

The morning of 27 October began badly in Cuba as a tropical storm lashed the island. This torrential rain caused Soviet technicians who were preparing their missiles to fear the rain would short-circuit their electronics. The continuing violation of Cuban air space by low-flying U-2s put everyone's nerves on edge. News that American U-2s had been spotted over the island sent Soviet anti-aircraft guns into action and the deputy Soviet commander authorized the firing of a SAM missile. The missile exploded alongside the U-2 plane causing it to crash, killing the pilot. This incident may have raised the morale of the Soviet soldiers in Cuba but Khrushchev was furious. The six short-range nuclear missiles which the Soviet generals in Cuba had authority to use without consultation with the Kremlin would be enough to start a nuclear war.

In Washington, US military contingency plans called for a reprisal, but Kennedy refused to give permission – a decision which probably avoided nuclear war. Instead he decided to gamble: he would ignore Khrushchev's letter broadcast on Moscow radio and respond instead to his first letter. Consequently at 8.00 p.m. President Kennedy signed a letter which guaranteed an end to the blockade and no invasion if Russia withdrew its missiles. The world held its breath.

Reaction of the people

Since the President's broadcast, the American people had been stocking up on supplies, many of them spending money they didn't have, so convinced were they that they would not have to pay it back; there was a run on the banks and the stock exchange on Wall Street fell. Children in schools were taught wildly inappropriate methods to defend themselves in case of nuclear attack and were urged by a cartoon character, Bert the Turtle, to 'Duck and Cover'. The Soviet people were not so well informed: some journalists with connections to the Kremlin sent their families out of Moscow believing the American bombers were on their way. Parents in America kept their children at home, or waved them off to school wondering if it would be the last time they would see them. Even MacNamara wondered at the beauty of the autumnal evening as he left the White House that Saturday evening and speculated whether it was the last he would see.

At the end of the ExComm meeting on Saturday evening, a few of the members decided that Robert Kennedy should meet once more with Dobrynin to inform him of the President's letter and to discuss a deal over the weapons in Turkey. It was important that this should remain a secret for fear that it would look like an American climb-down and might lead to an escalation of the crisis. To this end Dean Rusk dictated a letter to an American official at the UN which was to be issued by U Thant the following day, should Washington deem it necessary. U Thant was to call for the removal of both the Soviet missiles from Cuba and the American missiles from Turkey. Thus, should the secret deal become public, Kennedy could pass it off as a suggestion from the UN.

Robert Kennedy met once more with Ambassador Dobrynin. He emphasized that the crisis was escalating as the hawks within the military were anxious to bomb the missile sites if the missiles were not withdrawn. If the missiles were dismantled, the blockade would be withdrawn and there would be a guarantee that no invasion of Cuba would occur. The issue of missiles in Turkey was raised and Kennedy emphasized the necessity for secrecy regarding this aspect, but assured Dobrynin that within four to five months the Turkish missiles would be withdrawn.

Dobrynin reported this meeting to the Soviet Praesidium meeting in Khrushchev's dacha outside Moscow.

Khrushchev was aware of the intense pressure on President Kennedy and urged his colleagues to take a dignified stance on the crisis. All too aware that time was running out, the Soviets had been given 24 hours to reply to Kennedy's letter, and afraid that attacks on the missile sites were imminent, it was agreed to accept Kennedy's proposal. The acceptance was broadcast on Moscow radio at 9.00 a.m. on Sunday 28 October. Within hours Kennedy had broadcast a statement of acknowledgement and the world breathed a collective sigh of relief.

Win–win

In the United States the result was hailed as an American victory. Only the hawks were displeased and believed that they had been denied a fight. Comments such as, 'We've been had,' 'The greatest defeat in history' and 'We should invade today' reverberated around the Pentagon.

In Moscow, Khrushchev too claimed a victory and hailed the conclusion as a triumph for common sense. He emphasized that the Soviet Union had safeguarded the Socialist Revolution in Cuba for posterity by gaining a promise from the United States that it would never invade the island. It was a great result for diplomacy and not a shot had been fired. Privately the result was seen as a humiliation and Khrushchev was deposed the next year.

Only Castro was less than pleased. He had not been consulted by Moscow about the withdrawal of the missiles and cursed

Khrushchev and refused to see the Soviet Ambassador. He felt completely let down by the Soviets and regarded the outcome as a moral defeat. Within two months no trace was left of the missiles on Cuba.

In Turkey the agreement was hailed as a victory. The government in Ankara was delighted that no mention had been made about the American missiles which they wanted to remain on Turkish territory for defensive purposes. Little did they know that a deal had been done.

Kennedy emerged as the young hero who had kept his cool and taught the Soviets a lesson. His failure in the Bay of Pigs forgotten, Kennedy was now a world statesman and peacemaker. The Democratic Party won their biggest majority in the Senate in 20 years, a mere ten days after the crisis.

Result of the crisis

The United States and Russia had realized that along with their great power came responsibility to the rest of the world. The policy of brinkmanship, of pushing each other to the very brink of war, was too deadly a game to be played and with the existence of nuclear weapons it could result in worldwide catastrophe. The difficulties facing the two leaders as they attempted to communicate directly became apparent during the crisis, and it was decided to set up a 'hot-line' teleprinter link between Moscow and Washington. The dangers of nuclear weapons had never been more apparent and a series of nuclear arms control talks began, culminating in 1963 with a nuclear test ban treaty signed between the United States, Britain and Russia.

In 1963 Kennedy was assassinated in Dallas, apparently by Lee Harvey Oswald, a loner who had links with both Cuba and Russia. Conspiracy theories still abound as to the assassin and his motives. In 1964 Khrushchev was deposed as the Soviet leader.

He died of natural causes, not state-induced causes as was the norm under Stalin. Only Castro still remains, 40 years after the Cuban Missile Crisis.

The election of President Obama on 4 November 2008 was broadly celebrated in Cuba and brought the prospect of reconciliation or at least coexistence with Cuba. US Secretary of State Hillary Clinton spoke of the failure of previous US policy towards the island and welcomed an offer for talks from the President of Cuba Raul Castro. President Obama spoke of a new beginning with Cuba and eased restrictions on Cuban Americans wishing to visit relatives on the island and send money home. However at the time of writing the American President is once again being portrayed as an imperialistic warmonger; talks begun at the beginning of the new administration have stalled and Cubans have been enraged by what they regard as the US carrot and stick approach – relaxation of certain policies but a continuation of denunciations of the Castro government's record on human rights. In November 2009 President Raul Castro led the country's largest military exercise in recent years and called on Cuban forces to be ready for an American invasion – it seems things are back to normal.

10 THINGS TO REMEMBER

1 *In January 1959, Fidel Castro established a new government in Havana which turned towards the USSR for trade and aid.*

2 *The CIA aided several covert operations to destabilize Cuba, including the Bay of Pigs invasion in 1960.*

3 *The failed invasion caused Castro to declare that Cuba would follow communism.*

4 *Khrushchev, annoyed by US missiles in Turkey aimed at the USSR, suggested stationing nuclear weapons on Cuba to 'protect' the island.*

5 *The Soviet missile sites on Cuba were detected by a U-2 spy plane and led to Kennedy forming ExComm, a group of senior advisers to discuss the crisis and possible action.*

6 *A pre-emptive air strike was considered but dismissed for fear of escalating the crisis and alienating world opinion.*

7 *A naval blockade was established to stop and search ships bound for Cuba in order to prevent further missiles being landed. This was interpreted by Cuba as the first stage of an American invasion.*

8 *After sabre-rattling on both sides, and secret negotiations between Dobrynin the Soviet Ambassador and Robert Kennedy, President Kennedy signed a letter to Khrushchev which guaranteed an end to the blockade and no invasion of Cuba if Russia withdrew its missiles – Khrushchev accepted.*

9 *Brinkmanship had proved to be too dangerous. A 'hot line' improved communications between Moscow and Washington and a series of nuclear arms control talks began.*

10 *Khrushchev's diplomacy was publically praised but privately censured. Castro felt let down while Kennedy emerged as a world statesman and American hero.*

9

A new domino

In this chapter you will learn about:
- *the tension brewing in the Far East leading to the Sino–Soviet Split*
- *the 'Vietnamese grasshopper' ridding itself of the 'French elephant'*
- *American and Vietcong tactics*
- *the Tet offensive*
- *the television war and anti-Vietnam protests*
- *Vietnamization.*

A young child barefoot and dressed in shorts and an open-necked white shirt runs screaming in terror down a road. A young girl runs behind him. She is naked; her clothes have been burned off in an American napalm attack. Behind them are American GIs, some cameramen filming and small groups of Vietnamese people fleeing the fighting; further back one can see the village of Trang Bang, now a mass of grey smoke. Once seen, this photograph taken by Nick Ut is unforgettable. What had brought about this tragedy? Why were innocent citizens affected in such horrific ways? The answer lies in the history of the Cold War in South-East Asia.

Russia and China

One of the results of the Korean War was that the Cold War became a worldwide conflict rather than one based predominantly in Europe. East and West distrusted each other more than ever before and in the Far East this distrust was compounded by the fact that the United States faced the combined strength of two Communist superpowers, Russia and China. Their friendship dated from the Treaty of Friendship signed before the Korean War, which resulted in Russian aid flooding into China and Russian expertise being used to build such projects as a bridge over the Yangtze River. It seemed that the two Communist powers were symbiotic – thinking and acting as one: Russian experts worked in China; 10,000 Chinese were trained in Russia; China traded with Russia; and Russia lent China millions of dollars to help fight the Korean War. It seemed the two would be invincible against the West, particularly when, in 1957, Russia promised to supply China with nuclear weapons. It also appeared that Mao was right when he predicted that communism would eventually spread across the whole world.

In an attempt to stand up to the increasing Communist threat, the United States hastened to create an alliance of non-communist countries in the Far East in the hope that this alliance would be able to withstand the spread of communism. This alliance was known as SEATO – the South East Asia Treaty Organization – and the United States confirmed its support by signing a Peace Treaty with Japan in 1951 and a defence treaty with nationalist China in February 1955. The latter kept Chiang Kai-shek in power with huge amounts of American aid and an American fleet to protect Formosa.

The United States misjudged the situation in South-East Asia. Washington believed that China was a mere Russian puppet under Moscow's control. China did indeed turn to Russia, but this was because of the United States' attempts to isolate the country through trade, diplomacy and in the United Nations. In fact, Mao's communism was very different to Russian communism but China did want to spread communism throughout South-East Asia using violent revolution or, as Mao wrote in his book *The Thoughts of Chairman Mao* (second edition, 1966), via 'the barrel of a gun' if need be. The United States feared China might initiate the domino theory feared by Washington – if one 'domino' in South-East Asia fell to communism, others would follow suit in a 'knock-on effect'. Eisenhower felt that this could easily lead to the loss not only of Asia, but also India and Japan, and finally the whole of Europe would be in danger. The Korean War seemed to validate this theory and when China tried to gain some offshore islands in 1955, the Americans, following their policy of brinkmanship, threatened to use tactical nuclear missiles thus forcing China to back down.

Insight

This incident is also known as the Taiwan Strait Crisis. China seized the Yijiangshan Islands, forced Chiang Kai-shek to evacuate the Tachen Islands and shelled Quemoy and Matsu.

The domino theory increased American determination to support South-East Asia should 'dominos' be threatened; as in Korea, only strong American action would resist the 'yellow peril'.

Sino–Soviet split

The alliance between Russian and Chinese communism had never been a very stable one. Before Mao came to power in 1949, there had been disagreements over the very nature of Chinese communism which, unlike in Russia, depended on the support of the peasants rather than the industrial workers. Resentment had been brewing between Stalin and Mao, especially since the former had been lukewarm in his support for Chinese communism against Chiang Kai-shek during the Chinese Civil War.

There were disagreements too in the field of agriculture: where Stalin pushed for the mechanization of farming, as had happened in Russia, Mao wanted to provide more work for the Chinese peasants, not less. Stalin tended to view China in much the same way as he viewed Hungary and Czechoslovakia, as a satellite state to be used for Russia's benefit. Mao was determined to pursue an independent line but, at the same time, was aware that China needed an ally and one that would provide aid, advice and support. When Khrushchev came to power, relations between the two countries seemed to plunge into crisis following his speech denouncing Stalin. Mao may not have agreed with Stalin on every point, but he did think that Stalin had been an effective leader of the Communist world and perhaps wondered whether Khrushchev's denunciation of him was obliquely referring to the situation in China.

Nor did Mao agree with Khrushchev's idea that communism could be achieved without revolution; to Mao, revolution and war went hand in hand if the expansion of communism was to be successful. As a close follower of Marxist-Leninist ideas, Mao failed to understand how Khrushchev could entertain the thought of peaceful coexistence with the West, especially with that arch-capitalist exploiter, the United States. He believed that communism should take a hard line against the West since the Korean War had demonstrated that the United States, in theory strong, was in reality weak. Increasingly, Mao formed the opinion that the Soviets were only interested in spreading communism where it would further the interests of the Soviet Union.

From 1955 onwards relations between the two countries became increasingly strained. Mao objected to Russia's offers of aid to Third World countries such as India and Burma. Russia on the other hand refused assistance when China attempted to take over offshore islands occupied by Chiang Kai-shek. In 1958, Mao began his second five-year plan known as the 'Great Leap Forward', which once again put the emphasis on agricultural production which would fund industrial development. However, the industries established were labour-intensive, and central planning was abandoned in favour of local organization.

Insight

The Great Leap Forward planned to develop agriculture and industry as Mao believed that both were absolutely vital. Industry could only prosper if the workforce was well fed, while the agricultural workers needed industry to produce the modern tools needed for modernization.

Russia criticized this plan as a dangerous experiment which ignored the experience of other Socialist countries (namely Russia). In 1960 Russia withdrew not only its aid but also its technical experts from China, leaving half-built factories to fall into ruin and other projects incomplete. In the military sphere, Khrushchev tore up the agreement to share nuclear secrets with China and military aid to China came to an end. Speculation about a Sino–Soviet split was rife in the West. Western journalists based in the Far East commented that the Chinese leadership believed that Khrushchev was too soft on the West; that the United States was a mere 'paper tiger' on its last legs and the victory of communism was imminent; that as Russia clearly was no longer up to the job, the Soviets should step aside and let the Chinese take over the leadership of world communism.

In 1963, Mao made the split public and a torrent of propaganda followed from both sides. The Sino–Soviet split divided the whole Communist world, the vast majority of which supported Russia and caused the Chinese to become more introspective, relying increasingly on their own efforts and resources. The mistrust increased and developed into fear when, in 1969, there was an incident on the 7,250-kilometre (4,500-mile) border between the two countries where 31 Russian guards were killed by Chinese troops. Now, the fear of Russian nuclear weapons galvanized the Chinese to build nuclear shelters while the Russians feared the vast army and aggressive attitude of the Chinese leaders. Instead of the division of alliances being simply East versus West, or Communist states versus non-communist states, there now existed a triangle of power.

A new domino

Before the Second World War, Indo-China was part of the French colonial empire. This area had been conquered by the

Japanese during the war and the Communists, led by Ho Chi Minh, organized guerrilla resistance to the occupying power by forming the League for the Independence of Vietnam, or the Vietminh. The United States had supported these resistance groups during the war, but once the war ended France took up the reins of power once more in an attempt perhaps to blot out the humiliation of the fall of France in 1940. Ho Chi Minh and his supporters had hoped to create a country free of external influence, but France despatched troops to re-establish control of the area.

A bitter war ensued between the 'elephant (France) and grasshopper (Vietnam)'. At first, the United States was critical of French actions in Indo-China, but as it became clear that the Vietminh were receiving help from the Soviets and, after 1949, Mao's government in China, their attitude changed and they supported France. In spite of this the war went badly for France and 8,000 troops were killed in Dien Bien Phu in 1954. This 'Dirty War' was not what the French had expected and they surrendered; 90,000 French troops had been killed, wounded or were missing. Later that year the Great Powers met in Geneva to discuss the situation. The Geneva Accords that resulted from this meeting insisted that Indo-China be divided into the independent states of Cambodia, Laos and Vietnam; they divided the latter country in two at the 17th parallel and decreed that all foreign troops were to leave the country. Free elections were to be held in 1956 with a view to reuniting Vietnam and creating a multi-party system of government. Cambodia and Laos were to be independent countries with multi-party systems of government. These agreements brought only a brief respite to the area.

In the North of Vietnam, Ho Chi Minh created a Communist government while in the South, Ngo Dinh Diem created the Republic of Vietnam, a nationalist, Catholic, anti-communist government ruled by himself and aided by various members of his family and friends. Diem was supported by the United States as they saw no better alternative, but his government was less than satisfactory.

Figure 9.1 Main areas of conflict in Vietnam.

In Washington, incoming President Kennedy was warned by Eisenhower of the dangers inherent in South-East Asia becoming a Communist area; Vietnam had the potential to be another 'domino' which could lead to the fall of all the other countries in the area and possibly India, thus threatening Europe.

In the meantime, Ho Chi Minh's authoritarian state was reforming the land-owning structure in the North in an attempt to build up support for the Communist government in the forthcoming free elections. Landlords were pilloried, imprisoned and executed, and their land distributed to the peasantry. A million refugees fled to the South. In addition, from 1960 onwards guerrilla troops (the National Liberation Front) were trained in the North contrary to the Geneva agreements. These guerrillas, known as the Vietcong, terrorized villages and country districts in the South forcing them to support them with food, shelter, information and recruits. They were supplied by the North via a series of routes through the jungle and over the highlands of neighbouring Laos, known as the Ho Chi Minh Trail.

The United States saw these Communist activities as a direct threat to the free world, yet the regime was undecided and divided as to how best to cope with the rise of communism in the area. Kennedy refused to send US combat forces to South-East Asia, preferring instead to send military advisers to train South Vietnam in counter-insurgency. By the end of 1961 there were 3,000 US military personnel engaged in covert activities in Vietnam. During 1962 the situation worsened and by the end of that year the numbers of US military personnel had increased to 11,500. However, Kennedy denied any military presence in spite of the rumours that US pilots were flying combat missions, creating a situation which was tantamount to an undeclared war.

Diem's government became increasingly intolerant of other religions in the South. The Buddhists were singled out for particular attention, their pagodas raided, shrines destroyed and monks arrested. This persecution became so bad that several Buddhist monks doused themselves in petrol and set themselves alight – their self-immolation a public protest against Diem's policies.

News of a further clampdown on Buddhists reached Washington in late August when the upper echelons of the administration were on vacation. An Assistant Secretary of State for the Far East drafted a telegram to the US Ambassador in Saigon suggesting that the search begin for a successor to Diem and was hastily approved by the President and his advisers. Ambassador Lodge in

Saigon interpreted the telegram as a command to organize a coup against Diem and issued orders accordingly to the CIA station in Saigon. Washington the following week saw heated disagreements regarding the wisdom of this course of action. This conflict among his advisers caused Kennedy to cable the Ambassador warning him that he might decide to stop the coup at any moment and that the Ambassador should be prepared to call a halt at the very last minute should Kennedy decide to reverse his previous decision. Diem was blithely unaware of this plotting and, when visited by Robert MacNamara, the Secretary of Defence, and General Taylor, rejected any suggestion that his regime was repressing the Vietnamese people and emphasized instead the wisdom of his policies. Washington was persuaded of the need to begin to disengage itself and announced its intention to pull out 1,000 military personnel by the end of 1963.

On 1 November 1963 a coup led by South Vietnamese rebel generals surrounded the presidential palace and seized key facilities in Saigon. The next day Diem agreed to stand down, fled from the palace with his brother and sought refuge in a church. From here they were persuaded to enter an armoured personnel carrier which drove them to the rebel headquarters. When the doors of the vehicle were opened, the bodies of Diem and his brother with their hands tied behind their backs were found – they had been shot. A visibly shaken President Kennedy left his meeting on being told of the murders. Within three weeks he too was assassinated – killed by a sniper while driving through the streets of Dallas.

The likelihood of war increases

Lyndon B. Johnson announced his decision not to be the President that allowed South-East Asia to 'go Communist'; the United States would stand by its friends and as South Vietnam was an ally under the South East Asia Treaty (SEATO) he proceeded to escalate American military presence in Vietnam. One difficulty about helping South Vietnam was its governmental instability. After 1963, there was coup after coup and frequently Chief Ministers lasted less than six weeks. Although there was little support for communism in the elections, the results showed that the people were divided in their support for various political and religious groups; in fact, there were over 20 different political parties. The Vietcong's campaign of murder, intimidation and kidnapping against government employees hindered the functioning of any South Vietnamese government.

Gulf of Tonkin

In August 1964, US naval vessels conducting surveillance in international waters in the Gulf of Tonkin were fired upon by North Vietnamese patrol boats. The USA had been trying to acquire information about the operation of Soviet-built anti-aircraft missile bases and radar stations along the Gulf of Tonkin. An attack on these stations by South Vietnamese patrol boats had been carefully monitored by the USS *Maddox* in order to ascertain the effect that this attack would have on these bases. On 2 August the *Maddox* had been chased by North Vietnamese torpedo vessels and these had fired torpedoes as it sailed away. A slight skirmish resulted during which one of the torpedo boats was sunk and the other two damaged. Two days later further attacks were reported and the US government reacted with outrage at this unprovoked aggression.

In reality, the second encounter never took place. The *Maddox* had been buffeted by a tropical storm and had intercepted messages which gave the impression that it was about to be attacked by North Vietnamese torpedo boats. The tropical storm had affected the destroyer's equipment and the crew believed that torpedoes had been loosed off against them. In fact, air support from a nearby carrier could find no evidence of a North Vietnamese naval attack, but Johnson, anxious to revitalize the presidential election campaign, immediately ordered the first bombing of North Vietnamese bases in retaliation. He also approached Congress to seek a resolution which would give him the power to take all necessary measures to defend US forces and to prevent further aggression. The proposed resolution went further and suggested that the President be given sole responsibility for determining when peace and security had been established in the area. Public opinion was 85 per cent behind the administration and, on 7 August, after minimal debate the Gulf of Tonkin resolution was passed with only two dissenting voices in the Senate and none in the House of Representatives. This resolution gave Johnson the authority to conduct the conflict in any way he saw fit – it was like 'Grandma's nightshirt' – it covered everything.

Johnson's success in the presidential election gave him public support for his plan to take a firm stance against communism in South-East Asia. By the end of 1964 there were 23,000 US military personnel in Vietnam.

Events in Russia and China had an indirect effect on Vietnam. The Sino–Soviet split led to a situation where the two powers vied to supply the North Vietnamese in their struggle to take the South. The Chinese relished the idea of backing North Vietnam against the United States but the Soviet Union was by now pursuing a policy of peaceful coexistence with the USA and had to be more discreet in their support and aid. Russian military aid was promised on condition that Hanoi would conform to Moscow's view of the Communist world rather than Beijing's. The North Vietnamese were not easy to deal with and one Soviet diplomat commented that they were 'a bunch of stubborn bastards', so frustrated was he that Hanoi would not consider opening negotiations with Washington.

Operation Rolling Thunder

Secure in their military support from both the Soviets and the Chinese, the Vietcong were able to intensify their raids on the South. It is estimated that they had approximately 170,000 individuals ensconced in the South who could attack at will. A series of attacks on American targets from November 1964 to February 1965 finally persuaded President Johnson to retaliate. Operation Rolling Thunder was the code name of this sustained retaliation, a heavy bombing offensive on military positions in North Vietnam which attempted to end Hanoi's support for the Vietcong by destroying supply lines, ports and bases. It was hoped this campaign would remove the need to commit American troops to the war on the ground and would encourage the North Vietnamese to come to the negotiating table.

By 1970 the Americans had dropped more bombs on Vietnam than they had on any other previous target; someone estimated that they dropped more explosives than were dropped by all nations during the Second World War. In spite of the high explosives, cluster bombs and napalm which poured down from the American bombers, it was obvious early on that this was not a tactic to use against a militarily undeveloped nation. Most supplies were still transported by bicycle or carried on the backs of porters, therefore bombing of roads and means of communication had little effect on the supply chain, yet Washington was reluctant to cease bombing for fear the United States would look weak.

Bombing was also used against the Vietcong in the South, and in an attempt to deprive them of their forest cover the Americans employed chemical herbicides to defoliate the trees and destroy the rice crops on which the Vietcong depended for food. The most notorious of these defoliants was 'Agent Orange', a substance which contained dioxin, a carcinogen which poisoned not only the rivers and streams and the Vietnamese people but also the American personnel who loaded the chemical barrels onto the planes. The long-term effect of Agent Orange was to pollute the rivers and streams, the fragile eco-system and also the Vietnamese people.

Insight

Today, scientists believe the effects of Agent Orange (a defoliant laced with dioxin) remain in the soil and are responsible for high instances of genetic defects in areas where the chemicals were used.

The United States commits to ground involvement

On 8 March 1965, the first American troops came ashore at
Da Nang to defend American installations, but over the next few
months their numbers increased and so too did their military
brief; the troops were now permitted to patrol the countryside
and seek out and destroy the Vietcong. This escalation was not
made public to the American people, although news reports clearly
indicated that the USA was becoming more and more embroiled
in the conflict. In the United States innumerable pleas were made
by officials to limit America's commitments in Vietnam as it was
clearly becoming a long, drawn-out conflict with no realistic
hope of victory. In Johnson's opinion it was equally unrealistic
to withdraw as this would be hailed by the Communist world as
a humiliating defeat for the United States. In July the President
announced that the United States would stand firm in Vietnam.

South Vietnam was transformed with the arrival of the American
troops as enormous resources were poured into the country. Major
construction projects were completed in record time – hospitals,
airfields, ports, roads, bridges and supply bases. A huge amount of
technical equipment and consumer goods could be found wherever
there were Americans, and much of this found its way onto the
black market. It was not unusual to find American rifles, flak
jackets, office equipment, whiskey, cosmetics and cigarettes on
sale in Saigon street markets.

America's technological superiority was obvious in their weapons
but increasingly North Vietnam kept up using heavy artillery
and rockets, MiG fighter planes and Soviet PT-76 tanks. This
said, it was the low-tech weapons and fighting methods that were
important, something which the Americans failed to appreciate.

The first major confrontation took place between the US and
Communist forces in the Central Highlands in November 1965.
Both sides claimed victory, the North Vietnamese because they
had retained their positions and the USA because they had lost

fewer troops than the Communists. What Washington failed to comprehend was that North Vietnam was willing to pay a high price in casualties whereas the American people were not.

General Westmoreland, the commanding general in Vietnam, had three main objectives: to defend American bases and installations; to initiate search and destroy missions on the Vietcong; and to conduct 'mopping up' operations against the remaining Communists. These objectives were pursued against a background of continued bombing and an attempt to 'win the hearts and minds' of the Vietnamese population; aid was supplied in an attempt to settle the countryside by making the peasants prosperous and therefore loyal to the non-communist regime. Schools were built, wells were dug, and tools, seed, cattle, chickens and pigs were provided to enable farmers to begin again.

Although partially successful, the pacification programme was devised in haste and was not given enough time to develop – often the 'pacification' was actually bullying of village communities. In addition, the Vietcong's influence could return at any time, especially if American actions were extreme and alienated the people. The search and destroy missions involved the use of helicopter gunships to ferry troops to remote areas thus avoiding booby traps and surprise attacks by the Vietcong on the ground. These helicopters had great difficulty in distinguishing between civilians and Vietcong and it became all too easy for American GIs to shoot first and ask questions later. With the average age of GIs being 19, inexperience and nervousness led to mistakes. The use of drugs as an escape from the horrors of war was commonplace. Heroin from Laos was easily available and smoking marijuana or dope was commonplace. Atrocities took place which turned the Vietnamese people against the Americans and the American public against the war. One of these was the massacre at My Lai in March 1968 where 300 villagers, mainly women and children, were shot down in cold blood because they were believed to be sheltering Vietcong guerrillas – actions that were unlikely to win the 'hearts and minds of the Vietnamese people'. Lieutenant William Calley was charged with the crime, but served only three years in prison.

Peace initiatives

It was apparent that no clear battle lines existed in the war in Vietnam and it continued to escalate in spite of a series of peace initiatives; in 1967 there were six attempts by intermediaries to initiate peace negotiations – all failed, perhaps because the diplomatic initiatives were undermined by military events at a critical moment. In the United States there was increasing dissatisfaction with the way the government was pursuing the war. The cost had escalated to $20 billion a year and had put a stop to Johnson's attempts at welfare reform at home; the numbers of American troops in Vietnam reached 485,000 by the end of 1967, and by 1968, 300 of these were dying each week.

Insight

Johnson had initiated a series of social reforms which aimed to eliminate poverty and racial intolerance. The spending on education, medical care, transportation and inner-city problems was curtailed by spending on the war.

The Tet offensive

During the Tet religious festival of January 1968, the Vietcong made a series of surprise attacks in more than 100 major South Vietnamese cities and American bases. These simultaneous attacks showed that the Vietcong could strike in the heart of American-held territory. In Saigon a unit had even penetrated the US Embassy compound, a feat that stunned the American public and suggested that the war could not be won.

Insight

Tet is a festival to celebrate the end of the lunar calendar and the beginning of spring. Following lavish meals, the Vietnamese join parades and let off firecrackers to ward off

(Contd)

evil spirits. Both North and South Vietnam had broadcast
that there would be a two-day ceasefire during the festival.

In fact, the Tet offensive was not the success for the Communists
that it appeared to be: it had been designed to ignite a popular
rising throughout South Vietnam but this failed; huge numbers
of the Vietcong's best troops had been lost and it was severely
weakened in terms of resources and ability to strike in future. In
propaganda terms, the Tet offensive had been a resounding success.
Public opinion in the United States had turned decisively against
the war as the chant 'Hey, hey LBJ; how many kids did you kill
today?' could be heard, and on 31 March Johnson broadcast on
television that the United States would stop all bombing above the
20th parallel in the hope of encouraging peace talks to take place.
He also announced his decision not to run in the forthcoming
presidential elections – Hubert Humphrey was the Democrats'
choice as presidential candidate, while Richard Nixon was
nominated as the Republicans' candidate.

Preliminary peace talks began in Paris in May 1968 but soon ran
aground on the issue of who was to sit at the negotiating table.
President Thieu of South Vietnam refused to negotiate if the
Vietcong were present and was encouraged to do so by Nixon who
promised him a better deal under the Republicans. On 31 October
Johnson called off all American bombing, but still Thieu refused to
negotiate. On 5 November Nixon was narrowly elected President
but his 'new team' with 'fresh ideas' did not end the fighting in
Vietnam for another five years.

Vietnamization

In 1969 the new American President decided on a process of
Vietnamization, the transferral of responsibility for conducting
the war to the government in Saigon. Henceforth the South
Vietnamese must take over their own defence. The first troops were
withdrawn in June 1969 and in 1970 the USA pulled completely
out of the ground fighting while continuing its air support to the

South. In August 1972 the Politburo in Hanoi voted to authorize a negotiated settlement. Hanoi was well aware of the approaching American presidential election and calculated that they could extract better terms by casting Nixon in the role of peacemaker thus boosting his image in the eyes of the American public. In spite of President Thieu's opposition to Kissinger's deal with Hanoi, the latter announced at a press conference that peace was imminent. Nixon won the election with a landslide result. A month later peace negotiations broke down and Nixon attempted to force Hanoi into an agreement by a B-52 bombing campaign for 12 days over Christmas; Hanoi returned to the negotiating table.

Insight

Kissinger was National Security Adviser, Secretary of State and a leading player in American foreign policy from 1969 to 1977. He initiated détente with the USSR and China and was awarded the Nobel Prize for his negotiations in the Paris Peace Accords. His role in other aspects of American policy abroad was more controversial.

Within a month a ceasefire agreement was signed. These Paris Accords led to the withdrawal of US troops and the return of prisoners. Vietcong troops were allowed to remain in the South against Thieu's wishes, and the South was to continue to receive US economic aid and military assistance should Hanoi resume military action. The most important issue of who would govern South Vietnam was left unresolved. On 29 March 1973 the last group of American soldiers left Vietnam.

Peace with honour?

The Vietnamese people still had to endure fighting for another two years. The aid promised in Paris to the South began to falter as Nixon and his regime became preoccupied with the unfolding Watergate scandal. Vietnam suffered massive inflation, huge unemployment and terrible corruption. In 1975, the North launched yet another attack capturing the Central Highlands and advancing inexorably towards Saigon. The last helicopters took off from the rooftop of the US Embassy in Saigon on 29 April 1975. The terrible sight of South Vietnamese refugees trying to cling on to the overloaded helicopters, some falling to their deaths, was watched on television around the world. On 30 April a North Vietnamese tank crashed through the gates of South Vietnam's Presidential Palace and Vietnam was reunited under Communist rule; a humiliating end to the United States' longest war.

1975 also saw the triumph of communist armies in Laos and Cambodia. It seemed that the domino effect so feared by Eisenhower had indeed come to pass.

Implications of the war

For Vietnam the consequences of the war were tremendous. There had been huge casualties, approximately 2–3 million Vietnamese, Cambodians and Laotians had lost their lives; America's chemical weapons had poisoned the area; drugs and prostitution polluted the cities; refugees fled from the country in their hundreds of thousands, many fleeing by sea as 'boat people'.

Vietnam joined COMECON in 1978 and received aid from the Soviet Union, but the price of that aid was high as it earned Vietnam the enmity of both China and the USA. Vietnam joined the United Nations in 1979 despite some opposition from the United States, but when Cambodia (Kampuchea) was invaded in 1978, China retaliated by declaring war on Vietnam in 1979. By 1983 the Soviets were spending the equivalent of 3 million US dollars a day to support Vietnam, and further support was provided to Laos.

Insight

The Council for Mutual Economic Co-operation (COMECON) was Moscow's answer to the Marshall Plan, arranging trade between Communist countries in a manner which primarily benefited the USSR.

In the United States the reverberations of the Vietnam War still continue. The level of casualties had been high and most Americans had a relative or friend who had died in 'Nam. The huge economic cost of the war had meant cutbacks in spending on social reforms, and Johnson's plans for a 'Great Society' based on welfare reform had to be put on hold. An anti-war movement developed in the United States among the young: thousands of young men burned their 'draft' cards and refused to fight; sit-ins and demonstrations in universities caught the attention of students all over the world, and they followed suit. A peaceful student demonstration at Kent State University in Ohio 1970 saw the National Guard opening fire and killing four students, some of whom had not even been part of the anti-war demonstration. It seemed that the government was ignoring the very American constitution which they claimed was the blueprint for democracy.

Insight

Students in Kent State University had been protesting against the invasion of Cambodia when they were fired upon by the Ohio National Guard. Four students were killed and nine others wounded. John Filo's photograph of the event became a lasting image of the anti-war movement.

The televizing of the war and its atrocities led to the American people questioning their whole ethos. How could a GI set fire to the homes of helpless peasants with such a cavalier attitude as seen in a CBS news report televized on 5 August 1965? The nightly reports of the carnage and destruction may have desensitized the American people but it also led them to question the rightness of their cause. The Americans were told they were fighting for the hearts and minds of the Vietnamese people, but how could they hope to achieve this with the kind of tactics they employed against many thousands of innocent Vietnamese? The destruction of the land and agriculture would hardly endear them to the local populace.

The war had social effects back home too: the sale of drugs in Vietnam fed back into the United States and exacerbated an existing problem; marriages fell apart because of post-traumatic stress disorder.

> **Insight**
>
> Post-traumatic stress disorder is an emotional illness which develops usually as a result of a life-threatening experience. Called Post-Vietnam syndrome during the 1970s, it has also been known as battle fatigue and shell shock.

Many veterans were shunned by society, rejected as a reminder of a war that the United States failed to win. As Gloria Emerson observed, 'Vietnam is now our word, meaning an American failure, shorthand for disaster... a loathsome jungle where our army of children fought an army of fanatics' (Gloria Emerson, foreword to the 1985 edition of *Winners and Losers: Battles retreats, Gains, Losses and Ruins from the Vietnam War*, New York: Norton 1985, p. vii).

It was only with the dedication in 1982 of the Vietnam Veterans Memorial in Washington that old wounds began to heal.

Today, the young girl in Nick Ut's photograph, Kim Phuc Phan Thi, has forgiven and publicly pardoned the person who had launched the napalm bombing of her village and has dedicated her life to promoting peace. Her foundation helps children who are victims of war, providing medical and psychological aid to help them overcome their traumatic experiences.

10 THINGS TO REMEMBER

1 *During the late 1950s, China and Russia's close friendship led to the USA forming SEATO, an alliance of non-communist countries.*

2 *Relations cooled by 1963 and the Sino–Soviet split was made public by Mao.*

3 *Washington's domino theory stated that if one country in South-East Asia fell to communism others would follow.*

4 *Communist North Vietnam used Vietcong guerrilla troops to terrorize non-communist South Vietnam. This led the USA to send military advisers to train South Vietnamese counter-insurgents.*

5 *Instability increased following the assassination of South Vietnam's leader in 1963, and America's military presence in Vietnam increased.*

6 *The 1964 Gulf of Tonkin resolution gave President Johnson the authority to pursue the war in Vietnam. American forces entered Vietnam officially.*

7 *In 1965 Operation Rolling Thunder began dropping bombs, napalm and herbicides on military targets and the Ho Chi Minh trail, and helicopters were deployed on search and destroy missions against the Vietcong.*

8 *The difficulty in distinguishing between Vietcong and Vietnamese from a helicopter, the inexperience and youth of the American GIs and the widespread use of drugs meant that atrocities such as the massacre of villagers at Mi Lai in 1968 were inescapable but indefensible.*

(Contd)

9 *The Vietcong Tet offensive in January 1968 led to peace talks and Nixon's policy of Vietnamization, i.e. that South Vietnam should increasingly conduct its own war.*

10 *American soldiers left Vietnam on 29 March 1973 and Vietnam became Communist in April 1975.*

10

Czechoslovakia

In this chapter you will learn about:
- *the coming of the Prague spring following the Soviet winter*
- *the effects of the early spring on the Cold War*
- *the Brezhnev Doctrine.*

In August 1968, a vintage 1908 tram was lifted onto a low
loader in Prague and began its journey to the National Tramway
Museum in Crich, Derbyshire. Within 36 hours of its departure
Czechoslovakia had been invaded and virtually sealed off by
Warsaw Pact armies. In Prague, the tram system had been
brought to a halt by Soviet tanks. Western governments did
little in response to the invasion for fear that delicate détente
manoeuvres would be affected, but there was much sympathy
in the West for Czechoslovakia's plight and in Britain old
memories of Chamberlain's description of the country as 'a
faraway country' inhabited by people 'of whom we know
nothing' pricked many a conscience. The tram became a symbol
of Czechoslovakia's resistance to the Soviet invasion, a rolling
anti-Soviet propaganda campaign moving through Germany
and Holland, across the Channel to Britain. The British media
christened it the 'freedom tram' or the 'refugee tram'; one
newspaper even went so far as to say 'Czech tram triumphs over
tanks' – wishful thinking perhaps, but the psychological effect of
the tram's arrival in the West was tremendous. The inhabitants
of Crich organized an extravaganza to welcome the tram and its
engineers; as one organizer later recalled, 'We all wanted to cock

a snook at the Russians' (Ian Yearsley, organizer and transport historian). What had caused this vignette to achieve such importance?

The Prague spring

In spite of their country having been a Soviet satellite state since 1948, many Czechs still remained opposed to control from Moscow and wanted to see political changes in their country. Primarily they wanted more freedom of expression, a choice of political parties rather than a one-party state, an end to the use of secret police and, in the economic field, an end to the Soviet exploitation of the Czech economy. The Czech economy had not only failed to grow but, from 1962 to 1963, national income had actually fallen. In 1966 the government of Antonin Novotny implemented the 'New Economic Model' which began tentively to decentralize the economy by giving some power to local managers and by placing more emphasis on the production of consumer goods and profits rather than quotas. The model was never fully established because of apathy and obstruction from local bureaucrats. These attempts at economic reform were too slow for the vast majority of Czechs, and Novotny's hardline attitude towards Slovakia led to scenes of protest and student rioting in the streets of Prague.

In January 1968, the Czechoslovak Communists decided more far-reaching reforms were needed, removed the unpopular President Novotny and elected Alexander Dubcek as their new Party Secretary, General Ludvik Svoboda as President and Oldrich Cernik, war hero and the Leader of the Free Czechs, as Premier. Novotny had attempted to organize a coup against his critics but was stopped by his own security forces. The new leaders were welcomed by Brezhnev, the Soviet leader. Dubcek had spent much of his youth in the USSR and was a committed supporter of the Soviet system: no doubt Brezhnev believed he would be a compliant ally.

The new government's programme of reform was dubbed 'the Czechoslovak road to socialism' and their aim was 'socialism with a human face'. The tight control of the Communist government had already been loosened slightly before their advent to power, but under Dubcek this relaxation of control increased even though he was less enthusiastic about this than Cernik. He naively assumed that the Communist Party could be genuinely popular in Czechoslovakia once the political and economic system had been 'tweaked' a little. His primary aim was to improve the standard of living of the Czech people; for too long Moscow had controlled the economy, forcing Czech industry to produce raw materials for the Soviet economy and preventing Czech factories from producing consumer goods, and living standards in Czechoslovakia were low as a result. Politics were discussed and debated in an atmosphere of freedom not seen since the 1930s. Dubcek's government's 'Action Programme' went so far as to suggest that the party's role should be strictly limited. This programme stated, 'we must have an end to delayed, distorted and incomplete news' and new newspapers were published which criticized previous Communist leaders.

Insight

Dubcek's programme focused entirely on political, economic and cultural domestic problems. It declared an end to censorship and guaranteed freedom of assembly, association and movement. No attempt was made to take an independent line on foreign policy or to relinquish socialism.

During the spring of 1968, Czechoslovakia was allowed unusual liberties by Moscow as the government attempted to improve living conditions by introducing freedom of speech in the media, developing trade with the West, permitting religious freedom and generally lessening the hold of the government over people's lives. These policies became known as 'the Prague spring'. Czechoslovakia remained a Communist country, but as Dubcek said, 'We want to set new forces of Socialist life in motion in this country, allowing a fuller application of the advantages of socialism.'

There was no attempt by Czechoslovakia either to break away from the Warsaw Pact or to make changes in its foreign policy; the lessons of the Hungarian uprising 12 years earlier were still within living memory. In June 1968 most Czech newspapers published 'The Two Thousand Words Manifesto' in which writers and intellectuals called for democratic reforms within a Socialist framework; in the same month government censorship was abolished.

Fear of reform in the Eastern bloc

Czechoslovakia's neighbours were unimpressed and feared a gap developing in the iron curtain which would imperil the security of the Eastern bloc. Ulbricht in East Germany was particularly worried as he felt under pressure from West Germany as contact between the two Germanys was increasing. By July 1968, with the exception of Romania, other Warsaw Pact countries were sufficiently concerned to send Czechoslovakia a formal warning stating that the developments in the country had caused them deep anxiety and that they felt the Czech media was anti-socialist and attempting to divert Czechoslovakia from the path of socialism.

Brezhnev, too, was concerned: after all it was from this direction that Russia had been invaded twice before during the twentieth century. There was also the fear that should Dubcek proceed to dismantle the country's 'internal security system' (namely the secret police), the KGB would be evicted from the country. He reminded Dubcek of the need for discipline and uniformity and that a lack of these elements in Czechoslovakia might endanger the whole of the Soviet bloc. If further demands for freedom were granted to Czechoslovakia, other Eastern European states might demand similar freedoms and this in turn might destroy the rule of the Communist parties, and thus Soviet control, in these countries.

The Soviet military also expressed its concern. During the early 1960s, the USSR had made agreements with members of the Warsaw Pact to station nuclear missiles in Eastern Europe, weapons which were to remain under Soviet military control. While Soviet troops were stationed in Hungary and Poland, no such military presence existed in Czechoslovakia. Indeed, when Prague began to liberalize its regime in 1968, the deployment of nuclear missiles in Czechoslovakia was delayed for fear they could not be closely controlled by Moscow.

In July a meeting was convened between Brezhnev and other Warsaw Pact leaders. A few days later the senior Soviet leaders met Dubcek and pressurized him to reimpose censorship and to rein in the media. In spite of what seemed to be reconciliation between Prague and Moscow in Bratislava, all was not well and the warm welcome given to Tito by Czechoslovakia worried Moscow that Dubcek was about to lead his country down the same independent road Tito had trodden in the 1950s.

The invasion of Czechoslovakia

Russia decided the only way to put a stop to this dangerous undermining of socialism was to invade Czechoslovakia. On 20 August 1968, Soviet paratroopers captured Prague airport and Warsaw Pact forces flooded into Czechoslovakia with 400,000 troops that were mainly, but not exclusively, Soviet. This move was not only condemned in the West – Yugoslavia, Albania and Romania expressed their concern, but a UN motion of censure was vetoed by the Soviets.

In the face of such military force the Czechs decided to fight back, using 'passive resistance'.

Insight

Rather than defending themselves militarily against the invading Soviet forces, the Czech people chose non-violence, using inventive means to bamboozle the troops. Graffiti mocked the invasion, troops found potable water scarce,

(Contd)

> Soviet trains were diverted, signposts were removed and
> clandestine radio stations broadcast resistance.

There were many pockets of resistance led by Czech citizens such
as the playwright Vaclav Havel but by and large the Soviet tanks
moved against unarmed civilians. The Soviets arrested Dubcek and
other Czech leaders and took them to Moscow where they were
persuaded to end the Czech flirtation with democracy.

Insight

Because of Havel's actions during the Soviet invasion of
Czechoslovakia, when he broadcast commentaries on events on
Radio Free Prague, his plays were banned in his own country.
He was a fervent adherent to non-violent resistance and played
a key role in the non-violent Velvet Revolution of 1989.

Dubcek had been swept along on a tide of reform which he was
unable to control and most historians now believe he was naive,
out of his political depth and incapable of resisting Brezhnev's
bullying tactics. Whatever the reality, he became a figurehead for
the 'Prague spring'. Throughout the crisis, Czech radio stations
urged people to remain calm and not to co-operate with the troops
rather than to engage them in armed conflict as had happened in
Hungary. These radio stations represented the independent voice
so feared by the Soviets who promptly tried to shut them down.

Were the Soviets invited in to seize control in Czechoslovakia?

Troops, surprised by the hatred of the Czechs that they
encountered on the streets, certainly believed they had been invited
into Czechoslovakia to help the people at the request of key
Czechoslovak party officials, but the reaction of the Czech people
must have caused them to question the veracity of such a belief.
Enough Czechs spoke Russian to be able to constantly question
the Soviet troops why they were there and rumours of Czech
complicity in the invasion began to spread.

These rumours were found to be correct when, after the fall of communism in Russia in the 1990s, secret files in the Kremlin were opened. On 3 August the Slovak Communist Party chief, Vasil Bilak, who was staunchly anti-reform, had written to Brezhnev inviting him to use all the means at his disposal to curtail the threat of counter-revolution in Czechoslovakia, which he believed was endangering socialism in the country. He sent a further letter on 17 August asking the Soviets to act quickly and decisively and offering to form an alternative government. These letters certainly provided a pretext for the Kremlin to claim they were acting on behalf of a legitimate alternative government. However, Bilak was unable to deliver and the USSR was forced to reinstate Dubcek who governed for several months until he was replaced by Gustav Husak in April 1969 and then, finally, expelled from the party in 1970. The people of Czechoslovakia were once more under Soviet rule and early in 1969 Jan Palach, a student, set fire to himself in a public protest at the Soviet intervention in Czechoslovakia and died in Wenceslas Square.

Insight

Palach was one of three Czech students who burned themselves to death in 1969. The twentieth anniversary of his death was marked in Prague by a week-long protest against communism. 'Palach week' is considered to be one of the catalysts which led to the Velvet Revolution in November 1989.

Why did the West once again fail to act?

China was quick to condemn the Russian invasion and expressed its view that force should not be used against a fellow Communist nation; perhaps they too felt vulnerable as they refused to toe Moscow's line following the Sino–Soviet split. Unlike the situation in Hungary in 1956, the Soviets did not consult China before invading Czechoslovakia.

The West did nothing but protest at Soviet actions because détente between the United States and Russia was just beginning to bear fruit – intervention on behalf of the Czechs could stall détente.

Czechoslovakia returned to strict Communist rule and the possibility of liberal reform within the Communist bloc disappeared. However, some Communist countries distanced themselves from Moscow; Romania had refused to send troops to invade Czechoslovakia in 1968 and continued to pursue a more independent line throughout the 1970s. Albania went further and left the Warsaw Pact in protest at Brezhnev's statement of policy known as the Brezhnev Doctrine.

Brezhnev Doctrine

Leonid Brezhnev justified his invasion of Czechoslovakia thus:

> **When forces that are hostile to socialism try to turn the development of some Socialist country towards capitalism... it becomes not only a problem of the country concerned, but a common problem and concern of all Socialist countries.**

This doctrine emphasized the unity of Eastern Europe and the interdependence of Eastern European states with the USSR. However, in spite of Soviet influence in Eastern Europe being more direct than that of the United States in Western Europe, Eastern Europeans retained their own identities and every so often would remind the Soviets that their fellow Socialists were not merely subservient puppets of Moscow.

In 1969 there was much celebration in Prague; the national ice-hockey team had defeated the Soviet team. It was to be another 20 years before a Soviet leader was to encourage the Czechs to demand greater freedom and by so doing ignited the 1989 'Velvet' revolution. In 1989 the Soviet leader Gorbachev was asked what the difference was between his reforms in the Soviet Union and those of Dubcek. He replied, 'Nineteen years.'

10 THINGS TO REMEMBER

1 *By the 1960s Czechoslovakia had turned against Russia, particularly since the Czech economy was deteriorating because of Russian exploitation of Czech resources.*

2 *In spite of Novotny's tentative attempts to reform the economy, most Czechs demanded more far-reaching reforms.*

3 *A new government under Dubcek proposed reforming socialism and placing a greater emphasis on producing consumer goods and improving the standard of living.*

4 *The Prague spring of 1968 saw more freedom of expression and even trade with the West being permitted by the Socialist government.*

5 *The liberalization of the Czech regime caused consternation among its more traditionally Socialist neighbours and the Soviet military, who feared a 'tear' in the iron curtain.*

6 *Russia invaded Czechoslovakia on 20 August 1968 and was met by passive resistance – later evidence showed that the Slovak Communist Party chief had 'invited' the Soviets to restore the political status quo.*

7 *In spite of consternation from the West and China, no country intervened on behalf of the Czechs.*

8 *Strict Communist rule returned to the country and by 1970 the man responsible for the Czech flirtation with democracy, Alexander Dubcek, had been expelled from the Communist Party.*

9 *The Brezhnev Doctrine issued as a direct result of the Prague spring emphasized that Eastern Europe should be united and dependent on the USSR.*

10 *Romania and Albania, both Communist countries, began to distance themselves from Moscow, particularly after the publishing of the Brezhnev Doctrine.*

Détente 1971–9

In this chapter you will learn about:
- *the different motives for détente on the part of the superpowers*
- *the SALT talks in 1972*
- *why détente failed.*

The first step towards détente in the late 1960s and early 1970s came in Europe when the West German leader, Willy Brandt, wanted to improve relations with East Germany and Eastern Europe. His policy was known as Ostpolitik and achieved some success between 1969 and 1973 when agreements on frontiers were made and treaties signed between West Germany and Warsaw Pact nations. At first Brandt's initiative was greeted with some enthusiasm in the West but with suspicion in the East. In 1970 Brandt signed the Treaty of Moscow with Brezhnev – a non-aggression pact. With Poland he signed the treaty of Warsaw – an agreement to respect existing frontiers in Central Europe including the frontier between the two Germanys. His policy took a more lenient line towards the East than previous West German governments and served to cool down the 'German problem'. East Germany may have been concerned that an improvement in relations between West Germany and the Warsaw Pact countries would lead to the isolation of East Germany within the Warsaw Pact and this may, in turn, have provided a spur to the improved relations between East and West Germany.

By the time that Brandt retired in 1974, not only had the two Germanys reached a *modus vivendi*, but Berlin, divided by the wall, had also achieved some stability. In 1972 the Basic Treaty was signed between West and East Germany which stopped short of full recognition of each other's sovereignty since both believed there was only one German nation. However, the Treaty did stipulate that the two countries 'shall develop normal good-neighbourly relations with each other on the basis of equal rights'. Further trade, cultural, sporting and personal contacts followed and the East had made concessions on Berlin. The Four-Power Pact of June 1972 had permitted the West garrisons in West Berlin and access to them, but at the same time prevented West Berlin becoming part of West Germany. Brandt can therefore be credited with creating an atmosphere of goodwill which helped along the process of reaching agreement on European frontiers discussed so frequently in the past.

Ostpolitik had rid Europe of many of the problems that had contributed to strained relations between East and West and had caused the Cold War to remain frozen. The 'German problem' now appeared to have little further relevance and other problems took its place. Yet there arose the belief that as the seemingly insoluble German Problem had been 'solved', then other problems might also be overcome; it was in this atmosphere that a relaxing of tension between the Great Powers came about and a thaw began.

Motives of the Great Powers

The United States, China and the USSR had all learned lessons about the limit of their powers during the 1960s – the United States in Vietnam, China in its relations with the USSR and the USSR in Cuba. Both East and West were aware of the dangers and cost of the nuclear arms race and in many quarters the time seemed right for a change in relations between East and West. The ten years from 1969 to 1979 became the decade of détente, or a relaxation of tension between the states. During these years the United States and the USSR made efforts to reduce the areas of tension between them and the United States and China worked hard to create a friendlier atmosphere following 20 years of downright hostility. The United States was keen to follow a policy of détente in order to drive a wedge between the USSR and China and force them even further apart. In addition, the United States faced increasing hostility towards its policy in Vietnam, from the American people and from American allies; détente was a popular policy and one which not only drew attention away from Vietnam but also fitted in with the wider strategy of developing better relations with China. This would be to America's advantage in the fight against communism in Vietnam, as both the Soviets and the Chinese were supplying arms to North Vietnam.

In the USSR Brezhnev was keen to extend Khrushchev's idea of peaceful coexistence in order to decrease defence spending, since by this time the USSR had caught up with the United States in the arms race, and as West Germany had agreed with East Germany not to acquire nuclear weapons, this removed another potential threat. Détente was a means of increasing trade with the West, and thus of developing the Soviet economy, and raising the standard of living within the USSR. It was also a way of avoiding being the odd one out in a two against one scenario between the United States, China and the USSR and there was a possibility it might persuade the USA to accept the post-war situation in Eastern Europe. The USSR was keen to consolidate its influence in Eastern Europe following the invasion of Czechoslovakia and the declaration of the Brezhnev Doctrine.

Both the United States and the USSR were worried about the situation in the Middle East: supplies of oil were vital to both the East and the West, and the Suez Canal was a vital link in sea routes. The conflict between the Arabs and the Israelis therefore involved both Communists and non-communists.

China's motives for détente had been forced upon it to a large extent by the actions of the other two powers. Ever since the

Sino–Soviet split in 1960, China had been suspicious of and intimidated by the USSR, and the Chinese press constantly referred to the USSR as 'China's most dangerous enemy' or as 'more treacherous than America'. China therefore looked to the United States for détente in order to isolate the USSR. China's leaders were anxious to modernize the country, especially in the areas of agriculture, industry, science and technology. Increased trade with the West would aid and speed up this modernization process.

Relations between the USA and China

In 1971, the US table tennis team was in Japan for the world championships. One day an American player boarded the Chinese team's bus by mistake. Talking to foreigners was considered a crime in China, therefore most of the team kept their distance from the American foreigner. The Chinese team captain, Zhuang Zedong, felt that this attitude was alien to the Chinese tradition of hospitality and offered the American a gift; this broke the ice and the next day the American captain approached Zhuang Zedong and asked that the American team be invited to Beijing to compete in the forthcoming table tennis competition there. The request was enthusiastically passed on but it was soon realized that this simple sporting request had hidden political implications. No American teams or official delegates had visited China in years, and no one in the Chinese government was willing to take responsibility for the invitation to the American team. Eventually the request went all the way to the top, to Chairman Mao himself, who did not hesitate to issue a personal invitation to the American team. The slogan for the tour? 'Friendship first, competition second.' This example of sport crossing all boundaries began an exciting period of détente in Sino–American relationships and has passed into history as 'ping-pong diplomacy'.

During the 1960s it seemed unlikely that relations between the United States and the People's Republic of China would improve. Both sides had continually denounced each other since the 1950s and China was opposed to US involvement in Vietnam and other areas in Indo-China. However, the Sino–Soviet split changed the situation as many in the United States saw that cultivating China's friendship might succeed in driving the USSR and China still further apart. President Nixon 'played the China card' and began changing America's policy towards China, hinting to *Time* magazine in October 1970, 'If there is anything I want to do before I die, it is go to China.' In April 1971, the United States lifted its 21-year-old trade embargo on China and in the same month the table tennis team made its astounding contribution to Sino–American diplomacy.

America's support of Taiwan's claims to represent China remained a sticking point, but as more and more Third World states entered the United Nations, each with a vote in the General Assembly, it became increasingly difficult for the United States to block the admittance of the People's Republic of China to the UN. On 25 October 1971, there were hysterical scenes at the United Nations Headquarters in New York as delegates screamed, sang, shouted, danced in the aisles and banged on desks. The reason for this hysteria? China had been admitted to the UN and Taiwan expelled. In Britain *The Times* noted that, 'A wrong done to the world's largest country has at last been righted.' Later in October 1971, the delegate from Communist China took the China seat at the UN. Kissinger had prepared the way for an official visit to China by the American President by visiting China secretly in July 1971. In February 1972 the trip went ahead; amid great fanfares and media coverage Nixon and Mao shook hands and toasted each other, taking plenty of time for photo opportunities in the Great Hall of the People in Beijing's Tiananmen Square and on the Great Wall of China.

Insight

Nixon and Kissinger adopted an almost sycophantic stance towards Mao: Kissinger called him a 'colossus' and Nixon praised his humour and vision. Mao on the other hand was not so impressed with Kissinger, calling him a 'funny little man ... shuddering with nerves ...'.

Trade and travel agreements followed: Chinese leaders visited the United States in 1979 and American firms were set up in China. In the same year the United States recognized Communist China as the legal government of China. The visit of 1972 was of great symbolic value to both sides and, although few concrete achievements were made, it did serve to lessen the tension between the two countries and brought new pressure to bear on the Soviet Union.

Insight

The giant pandas found in China were traditional diplomatic gifts even before the Communist regime but these gifts gained special significance when Mao Zedong gave President Nixon two pandas following Nixon's visit to China in 1972. In February 2010 two American-born pandas were returned to China.

The United States and the USSR

In this atmosphere, where the powers actively sought to defuse tension, both the United States and the USSR made great efforts to achieve progress in the problematic areas of arms control, limiting the expansion of nuclear and conventional arsenals and, the ultimate objective, disarmament. The period of détente was characterized by a series of long, drawn-out negotiations in these fields since getting agreement between the United States and the USSR on any military matters was inevitably going to be problematic. Limited co-operation in military affairs had begun after the 1962 Cuban Missile Crisis, and throughout the 1960s a variety of agreements were signed, some between the United States and the USSR, others involving other nations such as Britain in the Test Ban Treaty of 1963; most had loopholes and weaknesses.

The nuclear arms race was continuing to escalate, with the USSR gradually taking the lead in certain areas, and in conventional weapons the Warsaw Pact forces outnumbered NATO forces in Europe. In January 1969, following the inauguration of Richard Nixon as

President of the United States, the Soviets declared they were willing to enter into discussions regarding arms limitations. In November 1969, the United States and the USSR began SALT (Strategic Arms Limitation Talks) with the aim of slowing down the arms race by limiting the stock of long-range nuclear weapons. These talks took place in Helsinki and Vienna and lasted until 1972.

The background to the talks was interesting, with non-military pressures building up on both sides, encouraging the negotiators to reach an agreement for economic as well as military benefits. The USSR was suffering food shortages as a result of a severe winter in 1971–72 followed by a poor harvest; the US dollar was weakening and an economic deficit looming – the Soviet bloc could prove to be a lucrative market for American goods. While negotiations on military matters progressed, the two powers issued a list of 12 basic principles outlining their responsibilities to each other and to the international community. A US–USSR commercial commission was established to organize a trade agreement in October 1972.

Arms limitation discussions

The military aspect of SALT included discussions on ICBMs (intercontinental ballistic missiles – the long-range missiles), SLBMs (submarine launched ballistic missiles) and ABMs (anti-ballistic missile defences). The two powers eventually signed two treaties. In SALT 1 (1972) they agreed to reduce the number of anti-ballistic missile systems and to limit the number of offensive missiles and bombers. Generally the USSR was allowed to have more missiles than the United States because many American missiles were capable of carrying several warheads, each aimed at separate targets. Each side was allowed to have only 100 ABMs on each of two sites, thus reducing defence expenditure for both sides since a complete shield of ABMs was almost impossible to construct and prohibitively expensive. In order to ensure that these conditions were being maintained, both countries were permitted to use spy satellites.

Both sides connived at ambiguity and vagueness in certain parts of the treaty – there was no mention of modernization of weapons or replacement of older weapons with new, more sophisticated technology. Almost as soon as the ink on SALT 1 was dry, new Soviet MIRV missiles had been built, and on the American side the Cruise missile, a sonic speed flying bomb with deadly accuracy over ranges of 3,200 kilometres (2,000 miles).

The SALT 1 agreement was to last for five years, therefore further talks began (SALT 2) first with President Nixon then Ford and then Carter. These talks were more complicated as they covered weapons not covered by SALT 1 and were therefore less successful than had been hoped. Negotiations for SALT 2 opened in the winter of 1972–73 and it was hoped that they would be a complete review of the needs of the world as a whole. The Watergate scandal and Nixon's resignation in 1974 shook the process, but it was the rapid technological advances which really put paid to any meaningful agreement. There were some hopeful indicators: Brezhnev and Nixon signed the Agreement on the Prevention of Nuclear War in 1973; in 1974 underground testing of nuclear weapons with yields of 150 kilotons or more was banned; by 1976 agreement was reached on PNEs – peaceful nuclear explosions – used, so the Soviets claimed, to build harbours or excavate canals, but which the West believed to be ways of avoiding the Test Ban Treaty of 1963.

In 1979 SALT 2 agreed further limits on missiles. The new agreement gave a precise definition of the weaponry available to the United States and the USSR based on the number of such weapons possessed by the powers on 1 November 1978. In spite of President Carter's insistence that SALT 2 was 'the most detailed, far-reaching, comprehensive treaty in the history of arms control', the American Senate was becoming more and more uneasy about Soviet violation of existing agreements and its disregard of the Helsinki accords. In addition there was an increasing 'hawkish' tendency on the part of the American public as the USSR extended its influence in Africa and Asia. The response of the Senate was to refuse to ratify the SALT 2 treaty, a caution which seemed well founded when the USSR invaded Afghanistan in 1979.

In the early 1970s Henry Kissinger, the American Secretary of State, had claimed that it would be possible to spin a 'web of interests' which would make countries such as the United States and the USSR more interdependent, and from this would develop a climate of better understanding which would lead to more stable relations between East and West. Once SALT 1 had been signed, Kissinger arranged a series of trade agreements and cultural and scientific exchanges between the United States and the USSR. He was convinced that by helping to raise their standard of living and level of expectation, the Soviet people would push for democracy and reform. Cultural exchanges would provide many Russians with a glimpse of the Western shop window which might lead to a desire to change the USSR itself. Economic benefits for the West could also follow since the West would have to supply technical know-how and probably equipment for technological advances required in the USSR. In March 1972, President Nixon became the first American president to visit Moscow; in the same year the USSR purchased 400 million bushels of American wheat worth $700 million – nearly the entire US surplus grain reserve, a move which many Americans still refer to as the 'great grain robbery'.

Insight

In 1972 the USSR suffered a severe drought and disastrous harvest. In order to buy up grain from the West at low prices, they bought from several companies and succeeded in getting an export subsidy from the US government which was anxious to increase exports at that time.

European firms helped to build the natural gas pipeline from Siberia to the West and on 17 July 1975, three American Apollo astronauts met two Soviet Soyuz cosmonauts in space. In the West professional space travellers are called astronauts (from the Greek word *astron* or star) while in the Eastern bloc they were called cosmonauts (from the Greek word *kosmos* or universe).

However, Kissinger had his critics: some attacked his policies by claiming they led to over-dependence on the USSR by the West. By 1980 West Germany's trade with the Soviet bloc amounted to more than $200 per head of population and by 1990 France obtained one-third of its natural gas supplies from Siberia. Critics noted that while the USSR was prepared to sign arms control agreements and to develop trading links there was no let-up in the ideological struggle.

Human rights on the agenda but ignored

During the SALT negotiations the Soviets had sought a European Security Conference but other issues were given priority until the completion of SALT. In July 1973 following the signing of SALT 1 the previous year, the Conference on Security and Co-operation in Europe (CSCE) opened in Helsinki and continued until the 'Final Act' was signed in Helsinki in 1975. Representatives from 32 European countries, Canada, the United States and the USSR signed the Helsinki Accords which had been negotiated by multinational teams who had worked together for 22 months. It was not a legal document, it had no force in international law, but the signatories did agree to adopt its terms, although there was no means of enforcement nor of monitoring the degree to which the accords were 'adopted' by the participants. In part, the Accords followed up Brandt's Ostpolitik in that they recognized the existing frontiers of Eastern Europe and Soviet control over the region. They agreed to co-operate through trade links, cultural exchanges and the exchange of technological information – the 'web of interests' which Kissinger believed would lead to political agreement.

The one aspect which caught the attention of the general public was 'Basket Three' of the Accords – ten principles to be adopted as guidelines for relations between the signatories, including the promise to respect human rights, to co-operate in humanitarian fields and to allow people to travel freely across Europe. Supporters of the Accords saw them as a significant milestone on the road to détente: the USSR had signed a document which could be held up before them in future disputes involving human rights and the economic links between East and West would bring benefits to both sides. The cynics noted there was nothing new in the 'third basket' and that the USSR was hardly likely to conform to an agreement which had no associated means of enforcement. Critics claimed that the USSR had achieved formal recognition of their European gains to the detriment of America's promise to 'roll back' the frontiers of communism.

In the years following the Helsinki Accords the cynics were proved right. In the USSR and other satellite states, dissidents were harassed and imprisoned. The dissident Anatoly Sharansky was accused of being a CIA agent. The Soviet government halted the work of the eminent scientist Andrei Sakharov, a vocal critic of the Soviet government who called for an end to the Cold War, the introduction of democracy to the USSR and a worldwide ban on nuclear missiles. His book *My Country and the World* (1975) opened with a shattering indictment of Soviet society and the accusation that Soviet science had been strangled. This, coming from the man who is generally regarded as the person who did most to develop the Soviet hydrogen bomb and who was awarded the Order of the Red Banner, must have come as a bitter blow to the Soviet government. Many other critics and dissidents were arrested on charges of passing state secrets to foreigners, and were imprisoned or exiled. Others were sentenced to labour camps or diagnosed insane and imprisoned in mental hospitals where they were kept drugged or tranquillized.

In Czechoslovakia, members of a group known as Charter 77 were suppressed; this group of 242 Czech intellectuals and former government officials issued a charter demanding that the Helsinki Accords and the UN declaration on human rights be put into practice in Czechoslovakia. The Charter was smuggled into the West where it received considerable publicity. The Czech authorities clamped down hard on the signatories and imprisoned many of them. Among them was Václav Havel, a playwright who later became President of the Czech Republic. The promise to allow freedom of movement through Europe was constantly

ignored by the Soviet authorities. One distinct group pressing
for this right were the Soviet Jews, known as refuseniks, who
campaigned for the right to emigrate to Israel or the United States.
The publicity this group received all around the world saw the
numbers of Jews permitted to emigrate rise from 14,000 in 1975
to 51,000 in 1979, although the number went down following the
invasion of Afghanistan.

The end of détente

The period of détente came to an end at the end of the 1970s for
several reasons, perhaps the most basic of which was each side's
definition of the term and the purpose of détente. As seen above,
the Soviets were prepared to come to agreement on arms control
and to develop trading links, but they never compromised on
their commitment to the ideological struggle between capitalism
and socialism. At Helsinki the Soviets accepted the contents of
the 'third basket', among which was the need to recognize human
rights, but to them this was merely a 'scrap of paper'. The Soviets
defined détente as having very narrow limitations. To them it
consisted almost exclusively of military matters, the lowering of
spending on arms production which would have economic and
social benefits for the Soviet leadership. The remainder issues of
détente, human rights and trade, were merely peripheral features,
acceptable only if they were of benefit to the USSR and disposable
if they required any deviation from the status quo on the part of
the Soviet government.

To many, Brezhnev's 'programme for peace' was a mirage, a tactic
which the USSR employed as part of the ideological struggle. By
the end of the 1970s, the West became increasingly concerned
that the USSR was continuing to increase its military forces and
consequently it too began to spend more on its own forces and to
station American Cruise and Pershing missiles in Europe – a move
which shook the Soviets.

During the 1980s, Western leaders appeared who criticized the
USSR openly. Margaret Thatcher of Britain and President Ronald
Reagan of the USA refused to contemplate concessions on the part
of the West unless they were made from a position of strength.
The Soviet invasion of Afghanistan and the attitude to dissidents in
the USSR and the satellite states fuelled fears of Soviet intentions
and seemed to support the view of the USSR as 'the evil empire'.
In keeping with the Hollywood imagery came President Reagan's
Strategic Defence Initiative, or 'Star Wars' project, which had the
idea of creating a defensive shield against Soviet missile attack and
locating it in space. This destabilized the whole arms race since
such a defensive shield might encourage a US attack on the USSR
safe in the knowledge that 'Star Wars' would protect the USA.
Other incidents, such as the shooting down of the Korean airliner
KAL 007 when it strayed into Soviet airspace, harmed relations
between East and West and ensured that détente was placed on the
back boiler.

Insight

Reagan gave evidence to the House Un-American Activities
Committee during the McCarthyite witch-hunts and, because of
his support of McCarthyism, continued to work in Hollywood
during the 1950s. It should be no surprise that he was
vehemently anti-communist as President.

10 THINGS TO REMEMBER

1 *Ostpolitik succeeded in improving relations between East and West Germany and 'cooling down' the German problem.*

2 *The USA welcomed détente to keep the USSR and China apart and to distract the American public's attention from Vietnam.*

3 *Russia viewed détente as a means to reduce spending on arms, increase trade with the West and consolidate its influence in Eastern Europe.*

4 *China improved relations with the West in order to modernize and as a means of isolating the USSR.*

5 *Table tennis played an important part in Sino–American diplomacy when Mao Zedong invited the American team to a table tennis competition in China – Chinese admittance to the UN and Nixon's visit to China soon followed.*

6 *During the 1970s, economic problems paved the way for a deceleration of the arms race and the beginning of the Strategic Arms Limitation Talks.*

7 *Some progress was made in limiting nuclear weapons by the SALT1 agreement, but SALT2 was scuppered by rapid technological change.*

8 *Names and terms such as Sharansky, Sakharov, Havel, Charter 77 and refuseniks became familiar in the West as human rights behind the iron curtain became a cause célèbre.*

9 *Soviet détente was almost exclusively confined to military matters – trade and human rights were optional extras and there was no compromise on ideological matters.*

10 *The 1980s saw détente dead and buried as President Reagan and Prime Minister Thatcher took a firm stance against the USSR's 'evil empire'.*

12

The Middle East

In this chapter you will learn about:
- *superpower involvement in the Middle East*
- *clashes between the Arabs and Israelis and how these affected the Cold War*
- *the Soviet invasion of Afghanistan.*

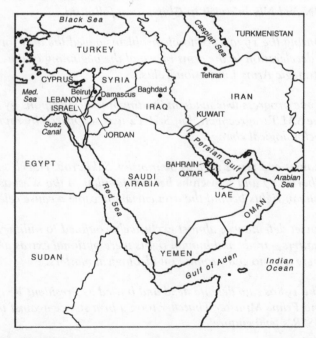

Figure 12.1 Map of the Middle East.

The Middle East has been a major area of conflict for centuries, but since the end of the Second World War and the founding of the state of Israel in 1948 there has been renewed conflict in this area.

The strategic position of the Middle East as a land linking three major continents – Asia, Africa and Europe – made it an area of such importance that it could not escape the Cold War. Its geographical position as a link with the oil-producing areas of the Gulf made it inevitable that it would be of interest to the major powers involved in the Cold War.

As the Middle East's old imperial masters, Britain and France, lost their influence in the area, the United States felt obliged to step into the power vacuum, in order to prevent the Soviet Union extending its influence in the area. The United States also felt that by forming alliances with Middle Eastern countries, it could complete the 'containment of communism'; equally the USSR believed that alliances with Middle Eastern countries would break America's encirclement of their country. American oil supplies from the Persian Gulf being shipped via the Suez Canal had to be protected; any Soviet influence in the Middle East was therefore a potential threat to the West should an East–West conflict develop in the future, as Russia could disrupt the Middle East oil supplies to the West. The USSR was not slow to realize that since the USA and its allies were so dependent on Middle Eastern oil the area was a potential Western weak spot.

The superpowers first became involved in the Middle East when they co-operated in producing the UN partition plan for the area. By the 1950s the West was relying more on oil supplies from the Middle East. Without this oil the economic and military power of the West would collapse since Europe and North America had become very dependent on it as a source of power for industry and transport. It was vital that supplies of oil should not be disrupted and the Suez Canal, which provided a short cut from the Mediterranean to the oil-producing areas of the Middle East, was a vital supply route for the West. The conflict over Israel dominated the Middle East, and had already caused one bitter war in 1948. During the 1950s the West became increasingly worried that future

Arab–Israeli conflicts might not only upset world peace but also threaten vital oil supplies.

United States interests

Since the early 1950s, the USA had been attempting to extend its influence in Middle Eastern countries. When the British Iran Oil Company was nationalized by the Iranian government in 1951, and later threatened to sell out to the USSR, the United States came to a secret agreement with the Shah of Iran to supply him with military aid in order to overthrow the Iranian government, and Iran signed an agreement to supply the United States and Western Europe with oil. In 1955, the United States persuaded Britain, Iran, Turkey, Pakistan and Iraq to sign the Baghdad Pact which attempted to limit the USSR; henceforth the Soviet Union was surrounded by hostile countries and American bases. The Pact actually led to increased Soviet involvement in the area in an attempt to undermine the treaty. By this time the new leaders in the Soviet Union were prepared to play a more active role in the area; this was noted by the American Secretary of State who warned that the Soviets were ready to play an active role in the Middle East, an area where two-thirds of the world's known oil reserves were located.

As the United States increased its military aid to pro-Western governments in Jordan, Lebanon and Iraq, the USSR increased its aid, in the form of loans and military advisers, to Egypt and Syria, the two Arab states which most objected to American influence in the Middle East. Middle Eastern nations were reluctant to become involved in the Cold War rivalry between the United States and the USSR, and in 1958 the Arab states and Israel voted to ask the UN to arrange the withdrawal of foreign troops from the area in an attempt to remove the Cold War influence.

For a time the influence of the two superpowers declined, but revived in the late 1960s and early 1970s because of Western dependence on Middle East oil and its concern that the supplies should not be interrupted by war in the region. During the early 1960s the United States invested heavily in Egypt, Iran, Saudi Arabia, Jordan and Israel; in order to offset America's increasing influence in the region, the USSR gave aid to Egypt, Syria and Iraq.

Throughout the 1970s and 1980s both superpowers continued their involvement in the conflict between Israel and the Arab states. The United States was politically a major supporter of Israel, although it did endeavour to work closely with both the Arab and Israeli governments in an attempt to find a solution to the area's problems. The Soviet Union was also politically involved through its support of Syria which became the main Soviet client state in the area. In the military field, both powers were involved in the supply of weapons and the training of troops during the war in Lebanon, and the United States became directly involved for a time when US marines formed part of the multinational peacekeeping force.

Insight

In 1975 a civil war broke out in the Lebanon which lasted for 15 years. Although the two warring factions were often portrayed as Christian versus Muslim, their individual composition was far more complex.

Attempts to find a lasting peace in the Middle East during the Cold War were faltering and largely unsuccessful. When President Sadat of Egypt made his 'Sacred Mission' to Israel in November 1977, hopes were high that real progress was being made towards a settlement of the Middle East conflict. Events after that meeting, especially the Arab reaction to the Camp David agreement, the assassination of Sadat and the conflict in the Lebanon, ended those hopes. A solution to the major problem in the area – the fate of the Palestinians – was no nearer at the end of the Cold War than it was in the 1940s. Recent events suggest that the Middle East is likely to remain an area of conflict for many years to come.

Insight

Camp David, the country residence of the American President, was also the setting for President Carter's negotiation of the
(Contd)

accord between Egyptian President Anwar Sadat and the
Israeli Prime Minister Menachem Begin, which led to the
1979 Israel–Egypt peace treaty.

Conflicts in the Middle East

During the post-war era there have been three main areas of
conflict: the Arab–Israeli conflict, the Gulf War between Iran and
Iraq, and the Soviet invasion of Afghanistan. These three areas
share one common element – the close interest of the USA and the
USSR which developed at some stage into the threat of involvement
or indeed direct involvement of one side or the other.

Arab–Israeli conflict – the background

The main cause of the conflict in the Middle East in the post-war
era was the refusal of the Arab countries to acknowledge the
existence of the state of Israel because of the way it was created
in 1948.

Since Biblical times, the Jewish race had been scattered throughout
the world but many dreamt of returning to their original homeland
in the Middle East. During the First World War, Britain had
captured Palestine from Turkey and was given a mandate to rule
the area for a period of 30 years and to set up a Jewish homeland
in the area. During the 1920s and 1930s, thousands of Jews settled
in Palestine but these settlers were not welcomed by the Palestinian
Arabs and violence frequently broke out. By 1947 Britain had
decided the violence was too great and it could no longer accept
responsibility for the area, which was handed over to the United
Nations. The UN drew up a plan to partition Palestine, creating
the new state of Israel which included parts of Palestine in the
north-east, on the coast and in the south. The rest of Palestine was
divided among the neighbouring Arab countries.

Many Palestinian Arabs, approximately 750,000 of them, were expelled from their lands and forced to reside outside of Israel; a great number of these fought as fedayeen (militants) to regain their homeland. Full-scale war has erupted in the Middle East five times since 1948, the first war commencing on the very day that the new state of Israel came into existence, in May 1948, as Arab forces invaded from the north, south and east. The new state of Israel inflicted a remarkable defeat on the forces of Egypt, Jordan, Lebanon and Syria and captured much of the land that had been allocated to the Arab countries by the UN partition plan. By 1949 the Arabs admitted defeat, although the agreement which ended this outbreak of war was only a ceasefire, not a peace settlement, as the Arabs refused to sign one. As a result of the war, Israel had grown larger but it was clear that the end of the war was only temporary, with existing borders policed by a UN commission. In 1950 a Tripartite Declaration on the part of Britain, France and the USA guaranteed the existing frontiers but failed to address the Palestinian problem, causing the Arabs to look elsewhere for a champion; from 1954 they found one in President Nasser of Egypt.

The Suez crisis 1957

War broke out again in 1956. This time it was not a simple case of Arab versus Israeli. Oil entered the equation which was further complicated by the involvement of British and French forces. In 1954 Gamal Nasser became President of Egypt and seemed intent on making his country the leader of the Arab world. In order to increase Egypt's strength, Nasser set about modernizing the country and planned to build a huge dam across the River Nile at Aswan; this would provide electric power and would aid irrigation of the crops. Such a huge project would require more money than Egypt could afford, therefore Nasser sought loans from overseas. Khrushchev promised the USSR would provide the capital for the project whereupon the United States, worried about Russian influence in Egypt, outbid the Russian offer. Without warning, the

United States withdrew its offer on the grounds that Egypt could not afford the interest payments. This was a humiliating blow to Egypt's national pride but Nasser soon found a solution. He proposed to nationalize the Suez Canal, which at that time was owned by a British/French company. The revenue from the canal came from tolls on shipping and was around £30 million a year; with this Egypt could build the dam without external grants.

> ### Insight
> Britain and France had controlled the Suez Canal since the nineteenth century and Britain had gained the right to protect the neutrality of the canal. However, in 1956 President Sadat nationalized the waterway to fund the building of the Aswan Dam, and by 1957 all British troops had been withdrawn.

Britain and France were furious and feared that Nasser could now put pressure on their shipping and oil supplies whenever it suited him. As Anthony Eden, the British Prime Minister, said, 'A man with Colonel Nasser's record cannot be allowed to have his thumb on our windpipe.' The United States, which had supplied Egypt with arms in the past, refused Nasser's request for American weapons. Nasser promptly turned to the Warsaw Pact countries and reached agreement with Czechoslovakia, which would supply arms in exchange for Egyptian cotton and rice.

Further surprises were in store for the United States when Israel attacked Egypt across the Sinai Desert in October 1956 and quickly captured the whole of the Sinai Peninsula. In accordance with the secret agreement Britain and France had made with Israel, British and French forces attacked Egypt, supposedly to separate the Israeli and Egyptian armies and to keep the Suez Canal open as an international waterway. Egypt refused to 'withdraw' from her own territory and, on 31 October, Britain bombed Egypt and dropped paratroopers to drive the Egyptians away from the Canal. Nasser retaliated by closing the Suez Canal and cutting the West's economic lifeline. Russia saw a chance to increase its prestige in the Middle East and threatened Britain, obliquely referring to the use of 'rocket techniques' which could 'crush any aggressor'. International pressure on Britain and France grew: the United States threatened not to supply them with oil from South America and the UN ordered the countries to withdraw from Egypt. After the intervention of the UN, Britain and France withdrew, and the Israeli forces left Sinai. A United Nations Emergency Force was sent to preserve peace in the area and remained there until requested to leave by President Nasser in 1967.

Britain and France had lost out in every respect. The Canal was blocked for months and was eventually taken over by the Egyptians and run without British and French involvement. NATO had been shaken by the invasion and the majority of its members disapproved of the British–French action; it took some time to rebuild the former trust between the Western powers.

One result of the war was the confirmation of Soviet support for Egypt; the USSR now financed the building of the Aswan Dam and the towering structure became a symbol for Soviet aid to developing countries. President Nasser's reputation as a leader who had stood up to bullying by the superpowers and finally got what he wanted was confirmed, and for a brief period Egypt and Syria formed a mutual defence pact, the short-lived United Arab Republic. The United States was all too aware of growing Soviet influence in the area and wanted to limit Soviet expansion, contain Arab radicalism and shore up regimes which were pro-Western. In March 1957, the United States announced the 'Eisenhower Doctrine' which promised both military and economic aid to those countries that required it to ward off communism. This was accepted by Lebanon and Jordan but refused by Syria which sided with the USSR. In the USA there was a growing commitment to Israel that increasingly came into conflict with America's other interests in the Middle East. To some in Washington, Israel was America's natural ally in the region, a bulwark against the further expansion of Soviet power; to others, support for Israel might drive Arab nations into the arms of the USSR and could encourage militant Islamic ideals which could destabilize the region further.

The Six Day War

After 11 years of uneasy peace, in May 1967 President Nasser demanded the withdrawal of the UN peacekeeping force in Sinai, closed the Gulf of Aqaba to Israeli shipping and moved Egyptian troops into positions near the Israeli army. Syria was under the impression that it was about to be attacked by the Israelis and shelled Israeli settlements from the Golan Heights, while skirmishing on the Syrian–Israeli border led to clashes in the air. Tension increased between Israel and the Arab countries in the region until Moshe Dayan, the Israeli Minister of Defence, decided that attack was the best form of defence and suddenly launched an attack on Egypt, destroying the Egyptian air force and defeating the armies of Egypt, Jordan and Syria in quick succession. The Israeli jets used in the attack had been supplied by the United States and destroyed over 300 Russian-built Egyptian aircraft in the attack on Egyptian airfields. From Egypt, Israel captured the Sinai Peninsula and Gaza; from Jordan a large stretch of territory along the West Bank of the Jordan, and from Syria the strategically important Golan Heights. The Israeli victory was shattering to Egypt. The Suez Canal was once again blocked and remained so until 1975, becoming a frontier between the Arabs and Israelis. In November 1967, UN Security Council Resolution 242 required the 'withdrawal of Israeli armed forces from territories occupied in the recent conflict', but the Israelis failed to comply in the same way the Arabs ignored the demand in the Resolution for 'acknowledgement of the sovereignty, territorial integrity and political independence of every State in the area'.

Although the Middle East states had voted unanimously to stay out of the Cold War at the UN in 1958, it became increasingly clear which sides the two Great Powers would back. The Israeli victory during the Six Day War had strengthened the voice of those advisers in Washington who supported Israel; they believed a special relationship existed between the United States and Israel based on shared values such as a pioneering spirit and a belief in democracy. The powerful Jewish lobby in Washington made sure that this special relationship developed into a strategic alliance; under President Nixon and Henry Kissinger the United States offered diplomatic support and economic and military assistance to Israel.

The Arab states in turn approached the Soviets for further military supplies. Iraq left the Baghdad Treaty (now called the Central Treaty Organization) and signed a treaty of friendship and co-operation with the Soviets. New regimes came to power in Sudan and Libya and they too looked to Moscow for support. Increasingly the Middle East became an armed camp divided between those who supported the Soviets and those who supported the United States.

In May 1972, as part of the process of détente, Nixon and Brezhnev signed the Basic Principles of Relations; in it they agreed not to take advantage of each other in the Third World. Anwar Sadat, the Egyptian leader following Nasser's death in 1970, feared he could no longer depend on the USSR for support in winning back the territory lost to Israel in 1967. This fear was confirmed when Moscow refused to provide Egypt with advanced military technology, whereupon Sadat expelled 15,000 Soviet military advisers from Egypt together with Soviet reconnaissance aircraft based in the country. Sadat then proceeded to play the superpowers off against each other, conducting secret talks with the United States even after the USSR resumed supplying him with arms. Sadat and Hafez Assad, the Syrian leader, met in April 1973 and came to the conclusion that the only way to win back their land lost in 1967 was to prepare for war.

The October War

On 6 October 1973, the Jewish Day of Atonement, an Arab attack took Israel by surprise. The first attacks were on Israeli positions which were under-strength because many soldiers had been allowed leave to celebrate the religious holiday of Yom Kippur. In the north, Syrian commandos stormed the radar surveillance post on Mount Hermon while 800 Syrian tanks, among them the latest Soviet T-62s, and three infantry divisions poured into the Israeli-occupied Golan Heights. In the south, the Egyptian armed forces backed by 2,000 tanks, 160 SAM missile batteries and 2,300 artillery pieces attacked across the Suez Canal, overran Israeli defences and pressed forward into Sinai. The Israelis regrouped and the whole nation was placed on a war footing, pleas were made to the USA for military assistance. The Israelis concentrated on defending the Golan Heights where fighting was intense; the defences held and Egypt began to dig in.

The second week of the war has been called the 'week of the airlift' as both sides were openly supplied with arms from the two superpowers.

Soviet Antonov-12 aircraft began to airlift supplies to their allies in Damascus and Cairo, delivering thousands of weapons and tons of ammunition. The USA responded by supplying Israel with arms in order to turn the tide of the war, repulse the Soviets and gain enough political leverage with which to influence the peace negotiations.

Phantom jets were sent to Israel and C-130 and C-5 cargo planes began to fly in arms, ammunition, tanks, helicopters and other technology of war. This swung the military balance in Israel's favour, and the country launched a huge offensive against Syria and advanced towards Damascus before halting on the outskirts to consolidate its forces.

In the south the biggest tank battle since the Second World War was raging with the Israelis inflicting heavy losses. Intense diplomatic activity on the part of Kissinger and Kosygin, the Soviet representative, led to a ceasefire agreement in an emergency session of the UN Security Council on 22 October. This ceasefire prevented Israel from inflicting a resounding defeat on Egypt, but within hours of the ceasefire taking effect, it collapsed and Israel began an all-out attack on the Egyptian Third Army – it seemed the Egyptian army would be wiped out. At this point the Soviets warned Israel of the 'gravest consequences' if it did not halt its advance, and the United States became increasingly aware that here was a strong possibility that Russia would send in troops to help Egypt. Indeed Brezhnev hinted in a letter to the USA on 24 October that if the United States did not agree to act jointly to impose the UN ceasefire, the USSR would consider acting unilaterally.

Kissinger did not inform President Nixon of Brezhnev's letter; the President had just been informed that the House Judiciary Committee was going to proceed with impeachment proceedings against him because of presidential involvement in the Watergate scandal – Nixon had been drinking heavily that night and was in no fit state to discuss the situation in the Middle East. Kissinger proceeded alone to hold a meeting of security advisers and to issue a DEFCON 3 military alert, whereby American forces were placed on a worldwide nuclear alert to show the Soviets that the USA meant business. It seemed the Middle East would draw in the superpowers to a direct conflict.

The Kremlin did not respond to the American alert in a confrontational way and within two days the alert had been lifted. A few days later the USA compelled Israel to accept the ceasefire and Sadat agreed to accept a UN multinational force to monitor the ceasefire rather than insisting on a joint US–Soviet force. The United States had achieved a resounding diplomatic victory – both sides in the Middle East now looked to the USA to resolve their differences by negotiation and the Soviets seemed excluded from influence in the area.

However, other Arab countries stepped in to remind the United States that its offer of a $2.2 billion arms deal with Israel was unacceptable to the Arab world. The eight Arab members of OPEC (the Organization of Petroleum Exporting Countries), inflamed by the outcome of the Yom Kippur War, resentful of the low prices paid to them by the West for their oil and conscious of fast-diminishing reserves of oil, imposed cut-backs in oil supplies to the United States from the Middle East. From 1971 to 1981 oil prices rose almost 20-fold, which played havoc with national economies heavily dependent on oil. The developed countries experienced a strange combination of inflation and recession as production costs and unemployment rose. In the peace talks following the Yom Kippur War, America's need for oil outweighed its support for Israel and the result was a more favourable settlement for Egypt.

Insight

Although the United States still produces a large amount of oil it increasingly relies on imported oil. As America's economy is oil-based it doesn't need to deplete its entire reserve of oil before it begins to falter – a shortfall between demand and supply of 10 to 15 per cent could adversely affect it.

Following four wars between the Arabs and Israelis in only 25 years, the United States believed the only way to safeguard Middle East oil supplies was to end the hostility between Egypt and Israel. If the United States was able to persuade Egypt to sign an agreement with Israel this would split Egypt from other Arab countries, help safeguard Israel by dividing Arab opposition and very likely deflect Egypt from Russia because of her probable isolation among the Arab nations. In 1975 Sadat moved closer to the USA, visiting the country in that year. In the same year at Geneva agreement was reached regarding demarcation lines around the Suez Canal, and the Canal was reopened. In 1976 a treaty of friendship between Egypt and the USSR was cancelled. US–Egyptian relations improved still further when Jimmy Carter became US President in 1977.

Sadat's 'sacred mission'

In 1977 Sadat announced he was prepared to go to Israel to pursue peace, and in November he duly addressed the Knesset (the Israeli parliament) – the peace process had begun. Menachem Begin, the Israeli leader, visited Cairo and both leaders went to Camp David at the invitation of President Carter in September 1978. Here a framework for an Egyptian–Israeli settlement was agreed. Sadat offered full recognition to Israel and Begin agreed to return Sinai to Egypt. Russia believed this separate peace treaty would make a full settlement of all the Middle East's problems more difficult to find and TASS (the Soviet news agency) proclaimed it a 'betrayal of the Arab cause'. Again Moscow had been marginalized.

The peace treaty was signed in March 1979 and Sinai evacuated and returned to Egypt in 1982. Sadat's peace initiative won him, jointly with Begin, the Nobel Peace Prize in 1978 but it cost Egypt most of its allies in the Arab world and probably cost Sadat his life: he was assassinated in October 1981 by Muslim fundamentalists who disliked his ties with Israel and the West.

Following the Six Day War in 1967, Israel had taken control of the West Bank and the Gaza Strip. Years of discrimination against the Arabs followed: land was confiscated for Israeli settlements, taxes raised from the Arab population and Palestinian rights, such as holding press conferences and flying the Palestinian flag, were curtailed. On 8 December 1987, an Israeli taxi driver driving carelessly careered into a crowd of Palestinian labourers killing four of them. This proved to be the spark which ignited a powder keg of anger and resentment and launched an Intifada – an Arabic word meaning 'uprising' or 'shaking off'. This mass uprising involved the whole Arab population in a spontaneous outbreak of violence against the occupying Israeli forces. Having few firearms, the crowds made use of petrol bombs and stones during violent street fighting involving both women and children. The response of the Israeli troops shocked many of their own people as well as the outside world. During the first four years of the Intifada over 1,000 Palestinians were killed; 25 per cent of these were under 16 years of age. These reprisals, far from quelling the Palestinian resistance, intensified the hatred and led to more extreme means, such as suicide bombers, being employed. The first approaches to peace were made by Yasser Arafat, the leader of the Palestinian Liberation Organization (PLO), in November 1988 when he officially recognized the existence of Israel, yet the conflict still continued.

Iran

When President Carter went to the Middle East in March 1979 to intervene personally in the peace process, it was generally considered a risk which could damage American prestige. The success of his intervention was hailed as a real triumph of statesmanship and one which had lessened the possibility of Soviet gains in the area should it become unstable in the future. The instability of the region soon manifested itself in a new form – Iran.

The Shah of Iran had been America's closest ally in the Persian Gulf for 25 years. He had ruthlessly modernized the country and had undertaken vast engineering and construction projects using oil revenues earned by Iran from American and British oil companies. The fruits of this modernization benefited only a narrow section of society and opposition to the Shah's policies grew within the Islamic clergy hostile to Western policies which seemed to ride roughshod over traditional Islamic values. In 1971, to celebrate 2,500 years of monarchy in Iran, the Shah held a party in Persepolis, the ruined capital of ancient Persia. $200 million was spent on providing the 500 guests with food especially flown in from Maxim's in Paris, vintage champagne drunk from exquisite crystal goblets and accommodation in tents each containing several rooms, including two bathrooms. All this extravagance, in a country where the poor had little access to the basics in life such as clean water, electricity, hospitals and roads, naturally caused resentment. Protests against the Shah grew and he increasingly became more tyrannical, depending on the army and the CIA-trained secret police to keep him in power.

In January 1979, the Shah was forced to abdicate and fled the country to the United States where he sought medical treatment. The fundamentalist religious leader the Ayatollah Khomeini returned to Iran, denounced the United States as 'the Great Satan' and proclaimed an Islamic republic. Hundreds of the Shah's supporters were arrested and executed and the process of Westernization reversed with the institution of the Sharia (sacred law of Islam).

The changes following the success of the Islamic revolution were profound. Street names were changed, bars, cinemas, cabarets, casinos and liquor stores were all closed down and Western music banned. Women still had the right to work but were encouraged to stay at home and read the Koran. Outside the home the veil became a compulsory garment and women were expected to cover themselves with the chador. This caused much resentment among some middle-class women who had benefited from the Shah's rule, but others argued that wearing the chador enabled women to be seen as a human being, not as a sex object. Modesty and conservatism were encouraged in women and, for example, when travelling on buses they were expected to use separate doors and sit at the back.

The Iranian revolution unsettled the whole region. Not only had the United States lost an important ally, but religious fundamentalism alarmed both the USSR and Iran's neighbour, Iraq. OPEC reacted to the chaos by raising the base rate of petroleum by 24 per cent, precipitating another fuel crisis and economic recession in the West.

On 4 November 1979, militant Iranian students captured the American Embassy and took hostage 66 Americans. The students refused to release the hostages until the deposed Shah was extradited from the USA. The United States responded by suspending Iranian oil imports, freezing official Iranian assets in the USA and warning of military action. The regime refused to compromise and 52 American hostages remained captive for 14 months. An abortive attempt on the part of the American government to release them in April 1980 only served to destroy President Carter's credibility as a leader. During their captivity the pop song 'Tie a Yellow Ribbon' became a symbol for the American hostages and on their release in January 1981, on the day of Ronald Reagan's inauguration as President, the entire country seemed festooned in yellow ribbons.

The Gulf War – Iran v. Iraq

The neighbouring countries of Iran and Iraq were traditional
enemies with deep-rooted ethnic and ideological differences.

> ### Insight
> Khomeini called for Islamic revolutions throughout the Muslim
> world including in Iraq, Iran's neighbour, which – like Iran – had
> a majority Shia population. The leader of Iraq, Saddam Hussein,
> was anxious to avoid this happening but at the same time was
> eager to annex the oil-rich region of Khuzestan.

In September 1980, the Iraqi President Saddam Hussein attempted
to topple the Ayatollah Khomeini. The result was a war which had
worldwide implications: the Gulf states supplied around 40 per cent
of the West's oil and interruption of supplies from the two warring
countries and surrounding states would cause severe economic and
industrial problems; the area was also strategically important to the
United States and the USSR. The war lasted longer than expected,
gravely damaging the oil industries of both countries. By 1985
Iraqi dead were estimated to be in the region of 70,000 and 50,000
prisoners had been taken. In 1986 Iran estimated the cost of the
damage it had suffered to be over $200 billion.

The war was fuelled not only by fierce hatred but also by the ease
with which both sides obtained weapons. By 1986 the United
States seemed to be supplying both sides, and secret dealings
between Washington and Tehran emerged in the Irangate scandal
which involved the secret sale of arms to Iran and the diversion
of profits to help the Contras in Nicaragua. There was always
a danger that the war might escalate, and Washington became
alarmed when spy satellites revealed Saudi Arabia to be stockpiling
Chinese missiles. The horrific use of cyanide and mustard gas by
the Iraqis against Kurdish civilians during the bombing of the Iraqi
town of Halabjeh gave weight to Tehran's complaints that Iraq
was using chemical and biological weapons against the population
and led to renewed international efforts to bring about a ceasefire

in the area. The first ceasefire of summer/autumn 1988 was generally regarded as untenable since it had been brought about by stalemate.

Afghanistan: the Soviet Vietnam

During the nineteenth century, Afghanistan had been a field of interest for Britain and Russia; the Russian Tsars tried to annex northern Afghanistan while the British Raj took control of parts of southern and eastern Afghanistan. The country remained fiercely independent in spite of these links with Russia and the West, but in 1973 Afghanistan came into the sphere of Cold War politics as the new leader Daoud Khan turned away from Soviet influence, expelling Soviet advisers and outlawing the Communist Party, and turning instead to the West with their offers of economic aid to develop the country.

In 1978 Daoud was murdered by Soviet-trained Afghan officers who appointed Nur Mohammed Taraki President of the new pro-Soviet regime. The Afghan leaders were divided among themselves on both tribal and party lines, but the reforms introduced by the new left-wing regime soon provoked opposition from Islamic clerics. The Ayatollah Khomeini supported Islamic fundamentalist rebels in Afghanistan; the Mujahideen, or soldiers of God, were soon fighting against the 'godless' regime. In an armed uprising in the city of Herat they killed hundreds of national advisers together with Soviet advisers and their families. Taraki appealed for help from Moscow, but the Politburo, while fearful of Islamic fundamentalism, was also fearful that Soviet intervention would not solve anything but rather turn the Soviets into the aggressor. It was decided not to intervene directly.

In 1979 Hafizullah Amin seized power as President and Taraki was suffocated with a pillow by Amin's agents. Although a Communist, Amin was not on good terms with the USSR and rumours reached Moscow that he was approaching the United States with a view to striking a deal. The Kremlin was in a difficult position. Détente was breaking down and a new arms race with the West was on the horizon as NATO introduced Cruise and Pershing missiles into Europe. The Islamic fundamentalists in Afghanistan might overthrow Amin and draw in the Soviet Muslim population from the area near the Afghan border that might then break away from the USSR. Amin might make an alliance with Pakistan and China. It seemed that the Soviets had little to lose.

The decision to use Soviet troops to overthrow Amin and establish a more pro-Soviet Afghan regime was made under strange circumstances: Brezhnev was drunk, his health was failing and he left the meeting early; Kosygin who was opposed to intervention was not present; Andropov was won over by the argument that the collapse of the Afghan revolution would endanger Communist regimes everywhere. On 22 December elite KGB troops flew into Kabul and were followed by additional air troops and equipment, while over the border came hundreds of Soviet tanks and tens of thousands of motorized infantry. These deposed and murdered Amin and installed a new government led by Babrak Karmal.

Washington believed the invasion was part of a plan to dominate the area as far as the Persian Gulf and so denounced it and suspended grain sales to the USSR. In his State of the Union address on 23 January 1980, President Carter called the Soviet invasion the most serious threat to peace since the Second World War. He warned that any Soviet intervention in the area of the Persian Gulf would be considered an attack on US interests and would be met with military force which might include nuclear weapons. The United States made arrangements to supply the Afghans secretly with weapons through Pakistan, having made a deal with President Zia of Pakistan offering him economic aid to prop up his regime. Carter's view of the USSR had been changed completely by the invasion of Afghanistan and he took several anti-Soviet measures: SALT 2 was now dropped and American arms spending increased; US athletes were ordered to boycott the 1980 Olympic games held in Moscow, however not all Western countries conformed with the American lead – the British Olympic Association ignored Margaret Thatcher's call for a boycott and defiantly sent a team.

The invasion put an end to superpower détente, but not all of Washington's allies saw a need for this. Helmut Schmidt visited Moscow and, although Thatcher pledged support, nothing more was forthcoming. Indeed, as US trade with the USSR dropped, other nations stepped in. It seemed that the United States was powerless to reverse Soviet aggression and equally powerless to force its allies into line.

The war in Afghanistan dragged on during the 1980s and by the end of 1987 around 12,000 Soviet troops had been killed there.

The hatred felt by the Afghan people was fuelled by atrocities committed by the Soviet troops. One eight-year-old boy, who had fled to a refugee camp over the border in Pakistan, recalled how the Soviet troops had killed his father with three bullets. His brother tried to fight the soldiers who had killed his father but was finally overpowered. The soldiers cut off his fingers with a bayonet and beat him. Finally, he was shot through one ear with a bullet which exited through the other ear, an image which has haunted the younger boy ever since.

One young Soviet soldier recalled how the Afghan children loved fireworks and how some Soviet soldiers had deliberately filled a firework with explosives and given it to some children to play with. All the children gathered round to watch the firework – none survived the explosion when it was lit.

The Mujahideen were equally cruel to captured Soviet soldiers and many soldiers carried personal poison capsules and grenades for use should they be captured – a quick death was preferable to the torture which frequently followed capture by the Afghan guerrillas.

Moscow, under its new leader Mikhail Gorbachev, realized the war could never be won and was eager to find a way to withdraw the Soviet Army without endangering the position of Najibullah, who had replaced Karmal in 1986. As *glasnost* (a Russian word for 'openness' used by Gorbachev to signify greater tolerance and freedom of expression in Soviet public life) spread in the USSR, the media began to report events in Afghanistan accurately and even to call for a Soviet withdrawal. Without US support the Afghan rebels might be forced to come to terms with Najibullah but Reagan had privately approved $300 million of covert military assistance to the Mujahideen and by 1987 the United States was spending $630 million per year in Afghanistan.

Gorbachev offered a timetable for withdrawal in exchange for US support for a coalition in Kabul with the PDR (Communist Party) sharing power with the rebels. Washington was unwilling to let Moscow off the hook and was unsure such a coalition would work. However, in March 1988 the rebels in Peshawar made Hekmatyar their new leader which signified they were open to compromise.

On 14 April 1988, a series of accords on Afghanistan were signed in Geneva by the USSR, Afghanistan and Pakistan and witnessed by the USA. The Soviet Union agreed to withdraw its troops from Afghanistan over a ten-month period but there was no agreement by the signatories on ending military support for the various factions inside Afghanistan. The last Soviet troops left Afghanistan in February 1989 but the legacy remained and affected not only the USSR but also the rest of the world. The Soviets had spent billions of roubles and lost 20,000 soldiers during the ten-year war which had caused great damage to the Soviet economy. As many as 1 million Afghans had been killed in the fighting; millions more fled as refugees to Pakistan or Iran and the Afghans who remained suffered food shortages caused by the destruction of farmland. The United States had spent over $2 billion on covert operations in Afghanistan and, by arming Islamic fundamentalist forces, had left a legacy of terrorism. For example, although the CIA attempted to buy back some of the hand-held Stinger anti-aircraft missiles it had supplied to Afghan rebels, hundreds were left unaccounted for. A long civil war between rival groups would drag on for years.

10 THINGS TO REMEMBER

1 *Oil and its strategic position drew the Middle East into the Cold War as the USA attempted to contain communism and the USSR strove to extend it.*

2 *Both superpowers invested heavily in the economy of the area and became involved in the conflict between Israel and the Arab states.*

3 *Britain and France invaded Egypt in 1957 in an attempt to keep the Suez Canal link to the Gulf open.*

4 *Egypt turned to the USSR for support, so the USA offered military and economic aid to other countries in the area.*

5 *The Israeli victory in the Six Day War against Egypt in 1967 led to many Arab states seeking military aid from Russia since the Israelis had a 'special relationship' with the USA.*

6 *The October War, or Yom Kippur War, of 1973 could have escalated into a direct clash between the superpowers had Henry Kissinger not compelled Israel to agree to a ceasefire and Egypt not accepted a UN force to monitor it.*

7 *Because of the huge rise in oil prices imposed by OPEC, US relations with Egypt improved.*

8 *The overthrow of the Shah of Iran in 1979 led to an Islamic republic, the loss of American influence in the area and another fuel crisis and economic recession in the West.*

9 *Both sides of the Iraq–Iran war 1980 were supplied with weapons by the superpowers.*

10 *Russia invaded Afghanistan in 1979 but US support for the Mujahideen rebels continued the war until 1989.*

13

The Cold War in Africa and Latin America

In this chapter you will learn about:
- *the reasons why the superpowers were interested in Africa*
- *Cuba's role in Third World revolutions*
- *the United States' attitude towards communism in its own backyard.*

To many people the word Africa conjures up images of children. Not the usual carefree pictures the West associates with childhood but pictures which hint at a poverty few can begin to comprehend: starving children with distended stomachs; tiny bodies wrapped in cloth awaiting burial; children carrying rifles and sub-machine guns not as part of a playground game but for real. Sometimes the rest of the world reacts in a positive way as it did when the 'Live Aid' concert raised millions of pounds for famine relief in Ethiopia during the 1980s; too frequently the world looks on helplessly.

During the 1950s the 'winds of change' blew through the African continent sweeping away years of colonial rule by the European powers and leaving in their wake a clutch of newly independent states.

Insight
The phrase 'winds of change' was first used by Harold Macmillan in 1960 to warn of the British government's

intention to decolonize Africa and make many African states that were under British rule at that time independent.

During the 1950s and 1960s more than 30 African states declared their independence, some achieving their self-government by peaceful means, such as Ghana in 1957, others through years of struggle. In Algeria the French fought a bloody eight-year war until 1962 in an attempt to keep the North African country under French rule; Belgium left the Belgian Congo to its own devices and a violent civil war which claimed thousands of lives including the Secretary General of the United Nations, Dag Hammarskjold, whose plane was shot down in 1961 while he was on a peace mission to the Congo on behalf of the UN.

Insight

Controversy surrounds Hammarskjold's death and some, including Archbishop Desmond Tutu, have claimed that there is evidence of the involvement of the CIA, MI5 and the South African secret service. There is even a 'confession' by a CIA hitman that he assassinated Hammarskjold on the orders of the CIA.

By the 1970s only a few white minority governments remained in power, one of these being the apartheid regime in South Africa which was engaged in a struggle with the outlawed African National Congress (ANC). The years of the Cold War were years of crises for Africa for a variety of reasons. The most serious problem Africa faced (and still faces) was poverty caused by natural disasters such as drought and by non-natural disasters, such as war. Governments in some recently independent states, lacking in experience, faced great difficulties in trying to solve such problems, and in some cases, such as Angola, Ethiopia and the Sahara, the problems were exacerbated by rebellions within the countries themselves, border disputes and guerrilla raids.

During the Cold War the USA, the USSR and several European countries became involved in African disputes predominantly in Angola, the Horn of Africa and Chad. The USSR saw its role in Africa as helping to overthrow the colonial powers, giving aid to black nationalist liberation movements, giving support to governments sympathetic to communism and aiding African forces which were in any way anti-West. It supplied aid to both Angola and Mozambique and military equipment including tanks, aircraft, missiles and guns (particularly the AK-47 Kalashnikov automatic weapon) to both Somalia and Ethiopia. Few Soviet advisers accompanied this massive military aid. In fact Cuba supplied the manpower. In Angola, Ethiopia, Guinea, Libya, Mozambique, Tanzania and Uganda, Cuban troops, instructors and technicians trained and advised the armed forces. Many African nations were prepared to accept aid from the USSR in spite of their reluctance to support Soviet influence in their countries; in fact some countries preferred to receive support from the USSR rather than from the West since they remained rather suspicious of the West's intentions in Africa.

The USA and several Western European countries had major trading links with many African countries and supplied aid, both humanitarian and military, at different times and sometimes to both sides involved in a conflict. The USA supplied weapons and tanks to both Somalia and Ethiopia during their conflict in the Horn of Africa, and provided air transport to ferry Moroccan troops into Zaire to replace French and Belgian units fighting pro-Communist guerrillas in the south of Zaire. France retained military bases in Gabon, the Ivory Coast and Senegal, and gave aid and military assistance to Chad to fight on the government's side against Libyan-backed guerrillas. British and American companies completed important trade deals in Nigeria during the 1980s; the USA bought 47 per cent of Nigeria's oil and sold goods and services worth $1,000 million a year to Nigeria. However, following the war in Vietnam, the USA was unwilling to become involved again in a major overseas conflict; the American Congress refused to vote additional funds to President Ford in order to counter Soviet aid in Angola and in 1978 President Carter refused to give military aid to Somalia in spite of the fact that the USSR was giving aid to Ethiopia at that time. Some advisers in Washington became increasingly concerned that the Soviets were spreading their influence in Africa by sending humanitarian and military aid to the country, and they felt that the United States could be doing more to counter this growing Soviet menace. In the early 1980s the United States did extend aid to African countries and aimed to speed the withdrawal of Cuban troops from Angola.

Angola

Portugal retained control over its African colonies for longer than most European imperial nations. In 1974, a military coup in Lisbon removed the Portuguese dictatorship of Marcello Caetano 'to save the nation from the government'. Democracy returned to Portugal and the new regime announced its intention to grant independence to Portugal's colonies, willingly shedding what had become a burden with 40 per cent of the government's income being spent on the armed forces needed to keep the colonies under control.

In the former Portuguese colony of Angola there were three main groups vying for power: Agostinho Neto, the leader of the Popular Movement for the Liberation of Angola (MPLA), wanted to establish a Marxist state; Holden Roberto headed an anti-communist group, the Front for the National Liberation of Angola (FNLA) – this group had received some backing from the CIA; finally there was the National Union for the Total Independence of Angola (UNITA) led by Jonas Savimbi which was a breakaway group from the FNLA with a power base in the south of the country.

Each of these groups received at least some of its support along tribal lines but their ideologies also attracted support from countries outside of Angola itself, and in this way what was essentially a civil war became part of the Cold War.

Following the coup in Portugal in 1974, the three groups had agreed to hold elections and to pave the way for total independence from Portugal in November 1975; this was known as the Alvor Accord. Unfortunately external interests soon complicated the situation.

The FNLA had received aid not only from the CIA but also from the Chinese government. On the other hand, the MPLA received arms from the Soviets. Following the Alvor Accord the United States' secret intelligence and covert operations committee (known as the 40 Committee) agreed to fund the FNLA to the tune of $300,000. This had the same effect as lighting the blue touch paper on a firework. The FNLA decided to ignore the Alvor Accord and make a bid for power immediately, by attacking and killing MPLA forces. The Soviets, who until then had given only modest aid to the MPLA, increased their arms provision. The MPLA also revived its connections with Cuba and requested further aid from Fidel Castro. A military delegation from Cuba arrived in Angola in August just as the fighting grew fiercer, and promptly increased their military commitment to the MPLA by sending three ships of Czech rifles, food and clothing and approximately 500 military instructors.

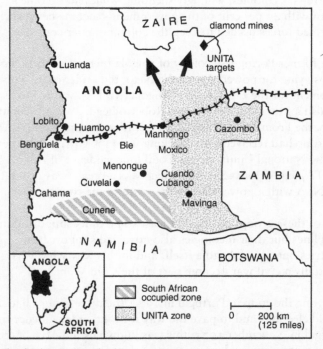

Figure 13.1 The political situation in Angola 1984.

To further complicate matters, the CIA now decided to fund the UNITA forces as well as the FNLA; President Ford agreed to send arms and supplies to the tune of $41 million by August 1975. These supplies arrived in Zaire where they were distributed to both the UNITA forces and the FNLA; the President of Zaire, Mobuto Sese Seko, was the brother-in-law of Holden Roberto, the leader of the FNLA, and he contributed several commando battalions to aid the FNLA cause. Thus equipped, the FNLA marched towards the capital of Angola, Luanda.

In the meantime, South Africa had become increasingly concerned that a left-wing government in Angola might provide a base for the banned African National Congress (ANC) from which to launch attacks on South Africa's apartheid regime. In order to prevent this South Africa had begun to give aid to the UNITA forces. However, having been prompted by the United States, Pretoria sent several thousand South African regular troops together with a group of European mercenaries into Angola. This group began to move rapidly north towards Luanda.

The MPLA, aware of the build-up of their opponents' forces, appealed to Cuba for increased aid. Cuba sent their elite troops directly from the Caribbean into battle against the South African forces, and succeeded in halting the South African advance. Moscow sent further arms shipments of tanks, missiles and other weapons to support the Cubans. In the bush south-east of Luanda a well-armed brigade of Cubans clashed with the South African troops and won a resounding victory, inflicting heavy losses on the South Africans. These battles at Ebo proved to be the turning point. The administration in Washington had exhausted its CIA funds and had to approach Congress for more aid for its allies in Angola. There was widespread opposition to this request and it was turned down by both the Senate and the House of Representatives. Although President Ford believed that this denial of funds would lead to a Communist victory in Angola, Congress refused to budge as the United States had no national interest in that area. Within three months the fighting by proxy was over; South Africa and Cuba both withdrew their troops.

The MPLA declared an independent People's Republic of Angola and this government was recognized by the USSR and several African states. In 1976 the USSR signed a 20-year treaty of friendship with the new Marxist government. In 1978 a Russian plan had been uncovered which revealed that the USSR was building up weapons and military advisers in South Angola in order to back a coup by SWAPO (South West African People's Organization).

By 1980 Angola was in difficulties in spite of the presence of 20,000 Cuban troops and advisers and the millions of dollars' worth of Soviet aid. SWAPO from Namibia had several training camps in the south of Angola where guerrillas were being trained to attack the South African military forces occupying Namibia using weapons supplied by the Russians and Cubans. South African military units made many devastating raids into Angola in order to destroy these bases. The rebel group UNITA also reappeared, and with South African aid was able to make raids in northern Angola until well into the 1980s.

Insight

South Africa had ruled Namibia by mandate from the League of Nations but refused to relinquish that mandate in 1946. The extension of apartheid to Windhoek ignited the Namibian war of independence in 1959 but it was not until 1990 that full independence for Namibia was achieved.

The United States 'lost' the battle to prevent the advance of communism in Angola but what is interesting is the role played by the Cubans in the extension of the Cold War to Africa in the 1970s. There is a tendency in the United States to view the Cubans as the mercenaries of the USSR, however, in the case of Angola, it is clear that Cuba acted out of revolutionary zeal rather than as the minion of the USSR. Fidel Castro's ambition had always been to spread the Communist revolution around the world: in Angola this ambition happened to coincide with nationalist struggles in that country.

The Horn of Africa

In North-East Africa is an area known as the 'Horn of Africa'.
Ethiopia, which forms part of this area, had once been a Western
outpost, but in 1974 the Emperor Haile Selassie was defeated by
the Marxist Colonel Mengistu Haile Mariam. The new Communist
government ended American aid and sent home 4,000 American
advisers and technicians, replacing them with the equivalent from
the USSR and Cuba.

Somalia, Ethiopia's traditional enemy in the same area, had also
signed a treaty of friendship with the USSR and now saw an
opportunity to swap sides and gain the support of the United
States. In spite of the Soviets' efforts to keep Somalia within the
Socialist camp, the Somali leader, Mohammed Siad Barre, marked
his departure by attacking the Ogaden region of eastern Ethiopia in
July 1977 and capturing the greater part of it within three months.
Mengistu appealed for help and within four months approximately
15,000 Cuban troops and tons of Soviet arms had been flown
into the region and had expelled the Somalis. Washington accused
Moscow of using the Cuban troops to extend its power in Africa
'by proxy'. Certainly, the Ethiopian revolution opened up new
opportunities in East Africa for Moscow which saw the possibility
of opening a seaport base for its naval ships in the area thus
giving the Soviet fleet supervision of shipping between the Indian
Ocean and the Mediterranean Sea. This in turn caused concern
in Washington as there was a potential threat to oil supplies and
at the cost of some $150 million the United States built a huge
naval base on the island of Diego Garcia to give it supervision of
shipping in the Red Sea and the Indian Ocean.

Despite the involvement of the superpowers, a drought from 1983
to 1985, combined with long-term soil erosion, brought about
famine in Ethiopia and the problems were made worse by crop
diseases in the north and disorder in the south as the Eritreans and
Tigreans struggled for independence from Ethiopia. It is impossible
to estimate the number of deaths in this region during this period;

relief workers struggled to cope with the millions of sick and starving. The West was quick to make political capital from the emergency, criticizing the Marxist government but being slower to condemn the Eritrean rebels who destroyed trucks carrying food to the starving. Universal relief operations were instigated but the wave of public concern was tremendous having been stirred up by the heart-breaking television coverage. There was anger too at the governments who failed to use the resources they alone could command. In July 1985, Bob Geldof mobilized show business personalities, pop stars and the youth of nations to raise funds for famine relief in Ethiopia by holding a 16-hour televized pop festival. Live Aid succeeded in raising over £50 million in the United Kingdom and the United States but today famine still remains a huge problem in Africa.

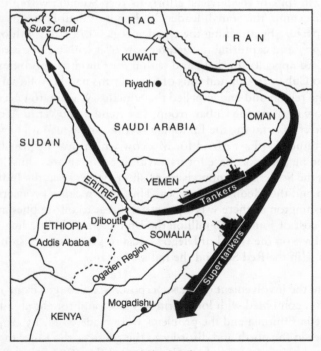

Figure 13.2 Position of Horn of Africa in relation to oil fields in the Gulf.

Latin America

Latin America, situated on the doorstep of the United States, has always been a matter of concern to Washington, fearful that any instability in that area might affect North America.

Insight

As long ago as 1823 the United States had voiced its opposition to any European nation colonizing independent nations in North or South America. This was the Monroe Doctrine and its influence can be clearly seen in Cold War relations between the USA and Latin America.

During the Cold War, instability came to mean the appearance of a Communist or left-wing government in any of the countries of Latin America since these could look to the USSR for aid or military assistance as Cuba had done in 1962. Such governments could also provide a base from which Soviet subversion could spread to all areas in the Americas. The Cuban revolution caused much anxiety in Washington which at times became almost obsessed with schemes to oust Fidel Castro, Cuba's leader, by means which seem laughable today – how could the CIA have imagined that the loss of Castro's beard would lead to Cuba turning once again to the United States?

It could be argued that Cuba did indeed represent an indirect threat to the United States as the country continued to export its own brand of revolution to Latin America and to Africa, but often the threat was more perceived than real. In 1965, a coup in the Dominican Republic was believed to have been inspired by Cuba and resulted in the United States sending 23,000 marines to the island. It was discovered that there was no Cuban involvement, and the United States had to withdraw from what was in reality a civil war. Yet there were attempts by Cuba to stir up revolution. In 1965 Che Guevara, one of the heroes of the Cuban revolution, went to Bolivia with the intention of stirring up a rising which would spread through Latin America and overthrow American imperialism. It failed to materialize. He was eventually captured and executed without trial. The USSR remained fairly impassive in Latin America, perhaps regarding the area as the preserve of the United States in much the same way as it believed the Eastern bloc to be its preserve. Much of the Socialist activity in Latin America was 'home grown' and developed out of circumstances peculiar to each country in which it appeared, a fact which the United States chose to ignore.

Chile

The Second World War had boosted the Latin American economies because of the increase in the Allies' need for raw materials and foodstuffs as the war progressed. In the wake of this prosperity came fuller employment and expectations among the people of higher standards of living, but so too did involvement in the conflicting ideologies of the era. For a time there was a growth in Marxist influence both in the labour movements and in some governments such as Chile and Ecuador, but the advent of the Cold War had the effect of weakening communism's hold on the area since it seemed to be directly linked to a threat from the USSR, a threat which the United States could not ignore as it strove to keep the Americas free of any Soviet intervention as the Cuban Missile Crisis had shown in 1962.

Chile had a long history of democracy: the army interfered far less than in other Latin American countries and a wide spectrum of political ideas was usually tolerated. In spite of improving literacy rates, declining death rates and a growth in cities and towns, problems remained. Copper dominated the economy and many of the copper companies had been funded by foreign capital. Indeed the United States had extensive interests in Chile's copper and silver mines and the American conglomerate ITT controlled the telecommunications system. Land distribution remained unequal and inflation was rising. Socialist and capitalist ideas competed to solve Chile's problems but when it seemed likely that the Socialist

Salvador Allende Gossens would win the 1964 general election with a coalition of Communists and Socialists, Washington decided to intervene by using a secret fund to influence the outcome of the election.

How could the world's 'greatest democracy' justify the use of such tactics to undermine the democratic process in another country? It was simple. They argued that the Soviets spent money to support other countries' political parties and trade unions, therefore the United States was justified in doing the same in the name of fairness. The next election in 1970 saw the United States preoccupied with events elsewhere and in 1970 Allende topped the polls but failed to win an outright majority which would confirm his position as leader.

President Nixon was determined to 'save Chile from communism' and in the 50 days before the Chilean Congress would select the President from the two leading candidates (Allende and the conservative Jorge Alessandri), the United States came up with a two-pronged approach. The first prong was a programme of covert operations conducted by the CIA with the purpose of persuading the Chilean Congress not to vote Allende into office. The second prong was top secret; it involved CIA agents gaining access to the country, linking up with right-wing military officers and staging a coup. The first prong included rumours in the press, posters, leaflets, slogans and anti-Allende graffiti. The second prong caused even the CIA agent in charge of the operation to wonder if the agency was doing the right thing in a country which had such a strong democratic tradition. The CIA failed to persuade the Commander in Chief of the Chilean army, General Rene Schneider, to lead a coup but eventually found a disaffected retired general, Roberto Viaux, with whom the CIA conspired to kidnap General Schneider. At the last minute, the CIA decided Viaux was too unreliable and called off the coup. Viaux decided to carry on but botched two attempts to abduct General Schneider. In a shoot-out following a third attempt, General Schneider was killed, but rather than having the effect the CIA desired, his death led to the Christian Democrat Party supporting Allende rather than his right-wing opponent. Salvador Allende became the first democratically elected Marxist president in the world.

Allende's government faced obstructions from the start as the United States did all it could to destabilize the Chilean government, spending over $8 million in the process. Allende's radical economic programme proved too much for some supporters of private enterprise with American backing. Chilean land was redistributed to 40,000 families and the banks, copper, iron, textiles and some fisheries firms were nationalized. Chilean interests in these nationalized businesses received compensation, American interests did not. Pressure from the United States resulted in loans to Chile being cancelled and American aid was not forthcoming; some industrial assistance came from the USSR but not the amount needed to prop up the Chilean economy. Inflation began to spiral out of control, industry slumped, farming stagnated, unemployment grew but Allende ignored pressure by Castro to move further to the left and was determined, as the head of a democratically elected government, to pursue his own path to socialism. The CIA encouraged strikes among the lorry drivers; teachers and doctors went on strike; rebels began to create chaos and it seemed as if socialism was not working in Chile.

In August 1973, General Augusto Pinochet took control of the army and plotted Allende's downfall. On 11 September he conducted a military coup and in the fighting in the presidential palace, President Allende was killed. In the military takeover which followed, 50 years of Chilean democracy and respect for human rights was laid to rest. Thousands of Allende's supporters and sympathizers, Communists, Socialists and Liberals, were arrested and taken to the national football stadium for 'processing', a euphemism for torture and execution. Many, like folk singer Victor Jara, were never seen alive again. His widow, Joan, in a television interview said, 'I know that he was a sort of a source of strength to his fellow prisoners. I know that he sang there. I know that they beat him down. I know that they broke his hands and his wrists. And I know that after two days they killed him off.' Many people simply disappeared, without a word to their families, never to be heard of again. The killings went on for years and it is estimated that as many as 800,000 people were arrested – there are no exact figures of the numbers murdered.

In its obsession with ridding the 'Americas' of a Marxist president, the United States had unleashed a torrent of human rights abuses, precisely the type of abuse they were so quick to condemn in the Eastern bloc. It was not until 1986 that the United States found Pinochet an embarrassment and sponsored a United Nations resolution condemning his abuses of human rights. Some of his international supporters remained true to the end. While receiving medical treatment in Britain during 1998, Pinochet was placed under house arrest while extradition proceedings against him were conducted. He was visited and defended in the press by Margaret Thatcher whose government had always preferred Chile's generals to those in Argentina. Pinochet never faced trial; he was eventually released on medical grounds in 2000 by the then Labour Home Secretary Jack Straw.

Nicaragua

Nicaragua had been ruled by the Somoza family since 1936. They had kept the country on a right-wing path and became the richest family in Latin America by exploiting the country mercilessly and amassing a huge fortune. The government was brutal and corrupt, as its reaction to the country's major earthquake proved, and its record on human rights was abysmal.

Insight

In 1972 an earthquake measuring 7.5 on the Richter scale destroyed the capital city Managua. More than 25 countries sent aid totalling several millions of pounds but government failings meant that little of this reached the people most affected by the earthquake.

They were, however, generally acceptable to the United States in spite of their despotic nature and President Franklin D. Roosevelt is alleged to have said of General Somoza, 'I know he's a son of a bitch, but he's our son of a bitch.' The main priority of the United States was to maintain stability in the region and when hostility to the dictator Anastasio Somoza Debayle grew in the 1970s, President Ford increased American military aid to him. Somoza's record on human rights became an embarrassment to President Carter who tried to distance his administration from this tyrannical regime by reducing American aid to Nicaragua.

On 10 January 1978, an opposition politician, Pedro Joaquin Chamorro, was murdered and this event precipitated weeks of rioting and strikes in protest against Somoza. This soon escalated into civil war and Somoza was forced to flee in 1979 from the Sandinista National Liberation Front – a left-wing resistance movement founded in 1961. The new left-wing government, led by Daniel Ortega Saavedra, quickly seized Somoza's personal properties, began a policy of land reform and nationalized the key industries. Nicaragua faced acute social and economic problems and thousands of Cuban doctors, teachers, agricultural experts and military advisers flooded into the country to aid recovery. Some progress had been made by 1981 when Ronald Reagan became President of the United States, and in the same year another civil war began in Nicaragua when the paramilitary *contrarevolucionarios* (known as the Contras) launched an attack from neighbouring Honduras. They sought support from other countries and found a natural ally in Ronald Reagan. The United States now accused the Sandinistas of conspiring with Cuba and the USSR to aid the Communists in El Salvador, imposed trade sanctions against Nicaragua, laid mines in Nicaraguan waters and supplied weapons and advisers to the Contras in their fight against the Sandinista government. The National Security Council of America which authorized these steps aimed to 'eliminate Cuban/ Soviet influence in the region'. Reagan seemed to have found a new mission, although he did encounter some opposition in the American Congress.

> The Reagan administration viewed the El Salvador military
> government as a bulwark against communism in that area
> and substantially increased military and economic aid. This
> was challenged by Congressman Moakley of Massachusetts
> who revealed the injustices of the US-backed government and
> paved the way for the UN peace accords of 1992.

The Sandinistas, led by Daniel Ortega, made progress within the
country: Nicaraguan output increased; polio was eliminated;
literacy and housing were improved; and economic aid was
forthcoming from European countries. In 1984 multi-party
elections were held and neutral observers declared them to be
acceptably democratic and fair. The United States refused to accept
this verdict and Reagan still believed that there was a Cuban–
Soviet conspiracy afoot to destabilize the area. Soviet support for
Nicaragua was cool and the number of Cubans in the country by
the mid-1980s was put at 6,000 workers and fewer than 1,000
military advisers. US support for the Contras continued and
increased Nicaragua's economic difficulties with inflation rising by
300 per cent and austerity measures being introduced by Ortega.
In spite of this the Contras seemed to be nearing defeat, especially
when the American Congress blocked the funds President Reagan
wished to send them. The news that he had found new sources of
finance by selling American arms to Iran illicitly and passing the
proceeds to the Contras scandalized international journalists and
led to the whole affair being called 'Irangate', recalling another
American President who had not acted in complete accordance
with the American constitution.

In 1987 President Oscar Arias Sanchez of Costa Rica attempted
to bring a ceasefire and reconciliation to Nicaragua and publicly
condemned US interference. However, political changes in the area,
when right-wing governments gained ground in El Salvador and
Panama, made the Arias peace initiative seem unlikely to succeed.
Suddenly the Nicaraguan government and the Contras agreed to
a two-month truce on 25 March 1988. Arrangements were made

to free prisoners and to allow the Contras a role in Nicaragua's political life, and national elections were scheduled for 1990. President Arias' plea that each Latin American country should be allowed to work out its own future without external interference seemed more likely to be heard with the demise of the Cold War in Europe.

USSR involvement in left-versus-right conflicts in Latin America seemed to be peripheral, although several American Presidents believed that Soviet and Cuban involvement was at the heart of the rise of left-wing politics in the area. It was as though what was actually happening in Latin America was less important than what the United States believed was happening. Certainly Cuba was involved in attempts to spread its own brand of revolutionary fervour to other countries in the Caribbean and Latin America, but rarely did the Soviet Union become involved to the same extent as it had in 1962.

In El Salvador, Cuba supported leftist fighters against a right-wing military regime by supplying them with small arms. Ronald Reagan then increased aid to El Salvador's military junta from $36 million in 1981 to $197 million in 1984 which led to the military junta sending death squads into the countryside to look for peasants who might have given aid to the rebels. One in five of the population fled abroad for refuge and tens of thousands of people were killed or simply went 'missing' – to this day these are known as the 'disappeared'. Their families still wait for news. Neither side was able to defeat the other in El Salvador but Washington preferred to aid a right-wing military junta with a scandalous record on human rights rather than allow a left-wing government to come to power. El Salvador remained free from communism as the Cold War in Europe drew to a close, but the human price was horrific.

10 THINGS TO REMEMBER

1 *The US became concerned about Russia's growing influence in Africa.*

2 *In Angola the CIA gave financial backing to the anti-communist FNLA and to UNITA, the Soviets and Cuba financed the MPLA, South Africa gave aid to UNITA and China aided the FNLA – a recipe for chaos!*

3 *In 1975, the MPLA established a Marxist government which nurtured SWAPO guerrillas attacking Namibia, but simultaneously the MPLA suffered UNITA rebel raids in North Angola.*

4 *America worried that a proposed Soviet naval base in Somalia and Ethiopia would threaten US oil supplies.*

5 *Several 'home-grown', democratically elected Socialist governments appeared in Latin America during the 1960s and 1970s.*

6 *Chileans and Nicaraguans suffered human rights abuses tacitly condoned by America because of its fear of growing left-wing influence.*

7 *In Nicaragua the left-wing Sandinista government progressed in solving social and economic problems, but the US backed Contra rebels and tried to undermine the democratically elected government.*

8 *Reagan tried to pass funds illegally and unconstitutionally to the Contra, but the main players in Nicaragua came to a truce in 1988.*

(Contd)

9   *Cuba spread its own brand of communism to other countries including Bolivia, Chile and El Salvador.*

10   *El Salvador's military junta received millions of dollars of aid from the USA to ward off left-wing rebels, but often this aid was used against the Salvadorian people. Tens of thousands simply 'disappeared' without trace.*

14

The second Cold War

In this chapter you will learn about:
- *Ronald Reagan's attitude towards the Soviet Union*
- *'Star Wars' – Reagan's obsession?*
- *Poland 1980–90 and the appearance of the Solidarity movement.*

In 1980 Ronald Reagan replaced Jimmy Carter as President of the United States. He firmly believed that détente had caused the USA to lose ground to the USSR and returned unequivocally to an anti-Soviet policy. Included within this policy were initiatives such as expanding America's armed forces, developing the neutron bomb and new missiles such as the MX Peacekeeper missile, basing nuclear missiles such as Cruise and Pershing 2 in Europe and developing the Strategic Defence Initiative (SDI), a programme to develop anti-missile weapons using laser beams which would form a defensive shield in outer space.

The tone of the language used in the early 1980s was hostile. True to his background in Hollywood movies, Reagan used terms borrowed from cinema to describe the USSR as an 'evil empire' and SFI as 'Star Wars'. Reagan's talk of the possibility of fighting a limited nuclear war which could be contained in Europe did not endear him to many Europeans either. He was joined on the world stage by other leaders who were strongly anti-communist: Margaret Thatcher, the British Prime Minister, known as the Iron Lady for her uncompromising stance on a variety of issues; Pope John Paul II who had been the Archbishop of Krakow, who was also anti-communist and whose following in Poland was so huge that it alarmed Moscow; in West Germany, Helmut Kohl, who continued his predecessor's policies of allowing medium-range missiles to be based in West Germany; and François Mitterrand who, although the first Socialist to become President of France, was one of the most staunch supporters of the Western Alliance. The advent of these anti-communist leaders to power, at the same time as the revolution in Iran and the Soviet invasion of Afghanistan, led to the dawn of a second Cold War and the end of détente. Once again the principal aim was to rearm the West and 'roll back' the influence of the USSR.

Poland

In the early 1980s the first major threat to Soviet control in Europe came not from the West but from within the Eastern bloc itself. The Poles had always disliked being ruled as a Soviet satellite state; there was a strong feeling of national identity which resented the country being run by external forces and which yearned to be free to make its own policies even if this was in conjunction with a close alliance with the USSR. The USSR had tried to suppress the Catholic Church in Poland but in spite of Soviet efforts, the Church remained as strong as ever and pushed for greater freedom of worship and the right to run Catholic schools in Poland; living standards were poor, there were constant shortages of food and consumer goods and the government-imposed censorship made discussion and freedom of expression impossible.

During the 1970s Edward Gierek, the Polish Communist Party leader, had succeeded in introducing some economic reforms, which saw some improvement in living standards, and he sought a *modus vivendi* with the Catholic Church, allowing religion to be taught in Polish schools. Economic problems, however, continued, and in 1976 a 60 per cent rise in prices was announced. Naturally this was met with protests, demonstrations and strikes by the Polish people. The police angered the people further when they caused deaths and injuries while cracking down on these strikes.

This pattern of price rises followed by strikes was repeated during the 1980s and increasingly the focus for the strikes fell on the Lenin shipyards in Gdansk, an electrician named Lech Walesa and a union named *Solidarnosc* ('Solidarity').

Insight

The Solidarity union was founded in 1980 to challenge the Communist government during strikes in the Gdansk shipyards. It became the first opposition movement to take part in free elections in a Soviet satellite in 1989. Solidarity formed a coalition government with Poland's United Workers' Party, and its leaders dominated the national government.

LECH WALESA

Walesa was an electrician in the shipyards and poorly paid at a time of high bread prices. His colleagues had elected him to the strike committee at the shipyard and he was frequently in trouble with the authorities for his trade union activity. In the late 1970s and early 1980s he rose to prominence as the leader of Solidarity. Walesa was able to appeal to a mass audience in Poland and abroad and was also able to negotiate with the authorities, making compromises when necessary.

Insight

As one of the leading members of Solidarity, Lech Walesa symbolized the political struggles leading to the collapse of the USSR. Awarded the Nobel Peace Prize in 1983, he was elected as President in 1990. His argumentative style alienated voters and embarrassed the government. He failed to be re-elected in 1995.

In 1980 there were more shortages of food and price rises and once more the workers in the Baltic shipyards went on strike. The government seemed unsure how to respond, fearing that a crackdown would lead to massive social unrest and a general strike. Eventually Gierek decided to negotiate with Solidarity, which became the first independent self-governing union in the Communist world. The Polish Communist Party signed an agreement with Solidarity whereby the workers agreed to accept the Socialist economic system, the role of the Communist Party and Poland's links with the USSR. In turn, the government accepted the right of the Polish people to form independent trade unions with the right to strike, the need for higher wages and better working conditions and for a relaxation of censorship thus permitting more openness of discussion. It seemed amazing to the rest of the world that the USSR had permitted this agreement to be made; certainly Solidarity was a threat to Soviet control not only in Poland but also in other countries in the Eastern bloc.

Following its victory, Solidarity created problems for itself by expanding its branches all over Poland, and in-fighting about whether or not to become a political movement putting pressure on the government for reform, rather than a traditional trade union working for the rights of its workers. At this the USSR encouraged the Polish armed forces to seize control of the government and ban Solidarity. General Jaruzelski became the new Polish leader and sent tanks to impose the declaration of martial law on 12 December 1981, arrested Solidarity's leaders and suspended trade union activity. He had been pressurized by the hardliners within the Polish Communist Party and the USSR which had shown him army manoeuvres taking place on Poland's borders and impressed upon him that Moscow could not accept what was happening in Poland. Solidarity was formally abolished in 1982 but many millions of its members continued to work 'underground'.

Henryka Krzywonos was a tram driver who represented her co-workers at the Gdansk shipyards during the strike. She was convinced the massive support for Solidarity would unify the Poles as a nation and that intense worldwide media interest in the Polish events would protect the strikers from reprisals by the Polish authorities. She was wrong. In December 1981 Jaruzelski imposed martial law, banned Solidarity, imprisoned many members of the trade union and intimidated others. Henryka was one of the latter. The authorities broke down the door to her flat, searched the premises and beat her up, ignoring the fact that she was pregnant. She lost the baby. Despite the harsh repression Solidarity survived as an underground movement to re-emerge six years later.

Insight

Following this incident, Henryka was unable to have children and was persecuted by the Communist regime. In the late 1980s she established a family orphanage in Gdansk and adopted 12 orphans.

This crushing of Solidarity inspired a strong anti-Soviet backlash in the West which was deliberately confrontational. Reagan pushed through Congress huge increases in the defence budget as if trying to outspend the Soviet bloc to the point where it could no longer compete; the protests of Europeans were ignored and Cruise and Pershing missiles sited in Europe and military aid heaped upon anti-Communist guerrillas in Afghanistan and Nicaragua.

Confrontations

There were confrontations reminiscent of the 1950s. For example, the shooting down of the Korean airliner KAL 007 by Soviet fighters on 31 August 1983 caused an international outcry in a similar way to the shooting down of the U-2 spy-plane in 1960. The tragic loss of KAL 007 came at a particularly tense moment in the Cold War increasing each side's suspicions of the other and enabling Reagan to exploit the anti-Soviet sentiment generated by the incident to increase American military spending.

Insight

Some websites cite a conspiracy theory – that KAL 007 landed safely and that the passengers were taken prisoner by the Russians and remain imprisoned to this day.

A NATO war game code-named 'Able Archer' caused panic in the USSR to such an extent that all Soviet forces were placed on full nuclear alert.

By the time Brezhnev died in 1982 it seemed the Cold War would continue to the bitter end. The appointment of Mikhail Gorbachev in 1985 ensured that it did not.

Mikhail Gorbachev – change in the USSR

In 1985 Mikhail Gorbachev was appointed Secretary General of the Soviet Communist Party. He was 54, young to be a Soviet leader, and committed to reforming the USSR. He faced many internal problems: the standard of living in the USSR was even lower than in many of the satellite states and already low standards of health care and housing were declining; food shortages in the USSR meant that the Soviet government had to import grain from the United States and Europe; defence spending had got out of control as the USSR tried to keep pace with the increased spending of the United States. It was imperative that Gorbachev restructured the Soviet economy to allow more competition and provide more incentives to produce goods. It would also mean the reduction of Party control of the economy, an end to the command economy so beloved by the old-style Communists, and encouraging Western companies to invest in the USSR. He called this economic reform *perestroika*. His other famous reform was *glasnost*, or openness about government policy. This saw the once censorship-obsessed government permitting freedom of expression. Many individuals who had been imprisoned for being critical of Communist policies were released and others, such as Andrei Sakharov, were permitted to return from exile.

On 26 April 1986, an explosion destroyed the 'No. 4' reactor at the Chernobyl nuclear power plant in the Ukraine. Radioactive debris was scattered over a wide area – more radioactivity was blown up into the atmosphere than at Hiroshima and Nagasaki. Thousands of kilometres away on a farm in Llanarmon-yn Ial, North Wales, hill-farmer Mrs Florence Jones had just delivered twin lambs, the second set that day. Little did she know that the sheep and lambs in her fields would never get to market as they would be contaminated by the fallout from that nuclear explosion near Kiev. It was two days before a Swedish monitoring station picked up high levels of radioactivity in the atmosphere and forced the Soviet authorities to admit publicly what had happened. There was several days' delay before the scale of contamination was assessed and evacuation of the area organized and in July it was finally decided to entomb the reactor under a mountain of concrete. In spite of this, the emergency work had been too little and came too late; today the incidences of thyroid cancer, leukaemia and other radiation-related diseases are higher than normal among the population in that area. The accident showed how obsolete Soviet technology was and it illustrated how incapable the old system was of responding to and reporting information of a disaster of this size. It was no longer tolerable that an industry such as the nuclear industry should be so secretive. In this sense the Chernobyl accident was a spur to *glasnost* and reform within Gorbachev's Russia.

It is interesting to note that in the Ukrainian language, Chernobyl is the name of a grass, wormwood, which is mentioned in the Bible in the book of Revelation (8:10–11) that foretells the end of the world.

> *And the third angel sounded, and there fell a great star from heaven, burning as it were a lamp, and it fell upon the third part of the rivers, and upon the fountains of waters.*

> *And the name of the star is called Wormwood: and the third part of the waters became wormwood; and many men died of the waters because they were made bitter.*

Détente

Clearly Gorbachev's internal policies could have no chance of success unless the excessive spending on defence was brought to an end, and he became determined to end the Cold War in order to save the Soviet Union. His first dramatic gesture came at the Reykjavik Summit in 1986 when he offered the West massive reductions in Soviet arms leading to a 'Zero Solution', completely eliminating nuclear weapons within ten years. Reagan's obsession with his 'Star Wars' project was the only thing which prevented this becoming a reality. The Washington Summit in 1987 was a media success, but it was Gorbachev's speech to the General Assembly of the United Nations in New York which spelled out the end of the Cold War. He renounced Communist ideology, the Brezhnev Doctrine and the arms race. Although the West was uncertain about his intentions at first, the events in the Soviet satellite states in 1989 made it clear that Gorbachev was 'for real' – the Cold War was at an end.

10 THINGS TO REMEMBER

1 *The Western leaders of the 1980s – Reagan, Thatcher, Kohl and Mitterand – ended détente as they attempted to roll back Soviet influence and rearm the West.*

2 *The Polish Solidarity union successfully negotiated with the Polish Communist Party for certain civil rights.*

3 *General Jarulzelski, the new Polish leader, was pressurized by Communist hardliners. He arrested the leaders of Solidarity and abolished the trade union.*

4 *America became more confrontational and increased spending on arms and funding for anti-communist groups.*

5 *Flashpoints such as the shooting down of the airliner KAL 007 by the Soviets and the NATO war game 'Able Archer' deepened the Cold War.*

6 *Gorbachev's advent as Secretary General of the Soviet Communist Party brought* perestroika *and* glasnost *to the USSR.*

7 Perestroika *brought an end to the command economy, while* glasnost *saw an increased openness and freedom of expression about government policy.*

8 *The nuclear accident in Chernobyl, Ukraine and the ensuing radioactive fallout demonstrated the shortcomings of the Soviet system and contributed to reform.*

9 *Gorbachev wanted to curb defence spending and in 1986 proposed to eliminate nuclear weapons within 10 years, a proposal greeted with scepticism by the USA.*

10 *Gorbachev's speech to the UN in 1987 renounced Communist ideology, the Brezhnev Doctrine and the arms race – it seemed the Cold War was over.*

15

The collapse of Soviet influence in Eastern Europe

In this chapter you will learn about:
* *the changes in East Germany 1989–90 which led the way to freedom*
* *the Velvet Revolution in Czechoslovakia 1989*
* *Hungary's liberalization 1988–90*
* *Romania – a bloody episode in the end of communism 1989*
* *events in Bulgaria.*

'Have you heard Frank Sinatra's song "My Way"? Hungary and Poland are doing it their way.' This was the view of one Soviet spokesman, Gennadi Gerasimov, on the changes taking place within Eastern Europe in the late 1980s. To him it seemed as if the Brezhnev Doctrine was dead and had been replaced instead by the 'Sinatra Doctrine'!

During the late 1980s the Soviet grip on the countries of Eastern Europe was finally loosened because of the changes within the USSR itself and because of the growing opposition to Soviet control within the countries of Eastern Europe. Détente had encouraged greater opposition to Soviet control and Communist governments as it had led to an increase in trade with the West with many Western companies investing in Eastern European business or, as in the case of Pizza Hut and McDonalds, opening branches of their companies in the Eastern bloc. This had, in turn, encouraged an interest in capitalist methods and the free market. Increased contact with the West had made the citizens of Eastern Europe more aware of the higher standards of living in Western Europe in marked contrast to those in Eastern Europe. The scarcity of consumer goods even led to rubbish bins in tourist hotels becoming a source of tights and cosmetics, while there were many stories of tourists being approached and asked to sell their jeans! It was clear that most Eastern bloc countries no longer felt threatened by the West and no longer saw the need for Soviet military protection.

Mikhail Gorbachev's reforms within the Soviet Union had encouraged demand for similar changes within the countries of Eastern Europe. His attitude towards these countries was far removed from those of his predecessors. Gorbachev envisaged a more equal relationship between the USSR and its satellite states, not one that depended on Soviet military might to enforce the Soviet party line. This, naturally, created problems for the Communist parties in Eastern Europe and their leaders: they could no longer depend on Soviet military aid; they could no longer justify their policies by referring to Marxist doctrine, after all Gorbachev had declared Marxism to be a failure; they now had to accept that the Communist Party was not always right.

Within the countries of the Eastern bloc there was growing opposition to the 'Communist way'. Communist rule meant that no other political parties were allowed, yet many of the people wanted a choice of political parties for whom they could vote in free elections following political campaigns where free and frank discussion could be held. Every country in the Eastern bloc had its own secret police which used torture and terror to halt any criticism of Communist governments. This intimidation and the censorship of the media meant that there was no freedom of expression; state-controlled radio, television and newspapers parroted the party line rather than giving unbiased reporting of events.

Increasingly the state-controlled economy was seen as inefficient, unable to produce sufficient food or consumer goods for the people.

There were an increasing number of individuals who wanted to run their own businesses without state interference, who relished the thought of producing what the market wanted rather than what the government dictated. The 1980s had seen the standard of living decline in Eastern Europe: prices and unemployment had risen and there was a shortage of housing, food and consumer goods. Working conditions were a danger to health and safety as the accident in Chernobyl had proved.

In certain Eastern European countries, such as Poland, many people were strongly religious and had been persecuted for their religious beliefs by the Communist governments. These people now pushed for freedom of religious worship.

Nationalism also played a part in the downfall of Soviet influence. The Communist Party expected loyalty to an international concept of communism rather than loyalty to individual nations; if national loyalty were to be given at all it should be given to the USSR as the birthplace of the Communist revolution. More Eastern European nations wanted a government that would act in the interests of its citizens rather than some external power.

Hungary 1988

In 1988 the Hungarian leader Kadar was replaced by Imre Pozsgay, a more liberal Communist, and the pace of reform quickened. Pozsgay accepted the need for reform in Hungary and led the way by arranging 'round table talks' with other parties. During the talks free travel was permitted to Austria and the West and attracted many East German 'tourists' supposedly holidaying in Hungary but in reality fleeing to the West. In 1989 Gorbachev agreed to withdraw Soviet troops from the country. In October 1989 the Communist Party renamed itself the Hungarian Socialist Party leaving only a small rump of diehard Communists. The first completely free elections were held in Hungary in March and April 1990; there was no decisive result but a coalition government between the

Smallholders and the Christian Democrats was formed – the first post-war non-communist government in Hungary.

Insight

The Smallholders' Party was supported primarily by peasants. Its leaders were middle-class and had a variety of political views. Post-war, the party dominated the Hungarian parliament until there was a coup d'état in 1947. The Communists forced Smallholder leaders to leave the country or be arrested.

East Germany 1989–90

When Mikhail Gorbachev came to power in the USSR it seemed that Erich Honecker, leader of the German Democratic Republic (DDR), would follow his lead in reforming East Germany. On the Olof Palme Peace March in September 1987, the unofficial peace groups were allowed to march alongside the official state representatives.

Insight

Olof Palme was a Swedish politician. In 1980 he had been the UN mediator in the Iran/Iraq war and was renowned for his efforts to bring peace to the region. He was re-elected as Swedish Prime Minister in 1982 and was assassinated in 1986 while returning from the cinema.

By the autumn of 1989 thousands of people were fleeing from East Germany through Austria and Hungary and it became clear that Honecker's government was resorting to repression. The secret police (Stasi) raided newspaper offices and smashed their printing presses and even the Soviet magazine *Sputnik* was censored as being too liberal. It was estimated that there were 86,000 Stasi agents and at least another 100,000 informers who watched and reported on any deviation from the party line by their friends, family or work colleagues. The Stasi kept files on over 6 million of the 18 million citizens of East Germany.

When Gorbachev visited the country he was greeted by massive
demonstrations which encouraged him to put pressure on Erich
Honecker to permit reforms. Honecker's uncertain handling of the
refugee crisis gave rise to the belief that peaceful demonstration
would bring results and from 25 September thousands of protesters
paraded around Leipzig each week expressing their wish for
reform. There were clashes between the police and demonstrators
but the lack of will on the part of the regime to pursue a hard
line against the demonstrations showed that the party leadership
was losing control. On 17 October Honecker was replaced by
Egon Krenz who attempted to win support for his government by
opening up crossing points through the Wall. On 10 November
1989, thousands of East Germans marched to the Berlin Wall and
the guards joined the protesters in pulling it down. Chaos ensued,
Krenz was sacked and Hans Modrow was appointed as General
Secretary. Modrow made far-reaching concessions including free
elections to be held on 18 March 1990. In these elections the
Communists were defeated and East and West Germany were
reunited on 3 October of that year.

Visitors to East Germany shortly after the fall of the Berlin
Wall were able to see the utilitarian ingenuity of the population.
Many car owners had adapted the 'DDR' signs on their vehicles
by the careful use of two pieces of masking tape to cover the
first 'D' and the 'R' leaving only the central 'D' visible. They
were all Germans now. However, some resisted the prospect of
buying a shiny new BMW on the basis that it was a 'foreign' car!
Some people were at pains to point out to their visitors that not
everything about the old East German system was bad and that
they wished certain elements, particularly in the area of social
care, to remain.

The changes in East Germany following the events of 1989 were tremendous. One British businessman, Hugh Williams, recalls a business visit to Saxony in 1990:

> *We climbed out of the car after several hours' drive. We were at an airfield close to the Polish border. Our guide told us to stretch our legs while he checked whether the restaurant was open. It was cold and the snow was falling as I walked through a stand of pine trees. I emerged into the open and was amazed to see 43 MiG fighters standing in a line along the edge of an airfield. It could have been a scene from a novel by John Le Carré.*

Six months earlier he would have been arrested or even shot simply for being there. The guide returned; the restaurant which had been opened in the control tower of the former Russian air base was open, and the menu included second-hand MiG fighters, one careful owner at a bargain price of $4,500!

Czechoslovakia – the Velvet Revolution 1989

In 1987 Gorbachev visited Prague to be greeted with chants of 'Gorbachev, Gorbachev!' He encouraged many Czechs to demand greater freedom but the Czech government held out against reform for as long as it could. In January 1989 crowds gathered in Wenceslas Square to honour the memory of Jan Palach, a Czech student who, 20 years previously, had burned himself to death in protest at the Soviet invasion of Czechoslovakia. The Czech security police broke up the meetings using great brutality.

News of the reforms in Poland and East Germany encouraged the demonstrators to continue and they were supported by Gorbachev himself who urged the Czech government to respond to the people's demands for reform. News of the breaching of the Berlin Wall acted as a spur and demonstrations in favour of reform broke out in several Czech cities. The restrained nature of these protests – the demonstrators used jingling keys, candles and cigarette lighters as a sign of protest – earned the demonstrations the name 'the Velvet Revolution'.

Two groups set themselves up in opposition to the regime: The Civic Forum led by Vaclav Havel in Prague, and the Public against Violence group in Slovakia. In total 23 parties fought the General Election of 1990; Civic Forum and Public against Violence won convincingly. Vaclav Havel of the Civic Forum was elected President of the National Assembly, and Alexander Dubcek returned to be its chairman.

Romania

Romania was one of the last of the Eastern bloc countries to experience change in the late 1980s, but when it came it was the most violent. The Romanian people suffered years of tyrannical rule under Nicolae Ceausescu in spite of the fact that many in the West, including Margaret Thatcher of the United Kingdom, regarded him as a liberal because of his attempts to throw off Soviet control.

Little was known about the harsh domestic policies inflicted upon the Romanian people. Censorship was extreme; contact with foreigners was prohibited; faxes and photocopiers were banned and even typewriters had to be registered. The state secret police (the Securitate) terrorized the population and it was claimed that every telephone was bugged and that over 25 per cent of the population were informers. Nothing was sacrosanct; even women's fertility was strictly controlled by the state. As the birth rate dropped, contraception and abortion were made illegal and all women younger than 45 were expected to have at least five children. This legislation was enforced by compulsory regular gynaecological inspections. Naturally, since the legislation took no account of women's health, income or personal opinions, many illegal abortions were performed and thousands of babies were abandoned in overcrowded, squalid orphanages. These institutions were inadequately staffed and resourced and the traditional practice of injecting newborn babies with extra blood coupled with the lack of sterile medical supplies and trained staff meant that the HIV virus quickly took hold among the children.

The spark which ignited a variety of long-standing grievances against the Communist dictator Nicolae Ceausescu was the attempted deportation of a priest from the town of Timisoara.

Insight

Minister Laszlo Tokes was ordered to leave his church in Timisoara. He chose to remain there, protected by 5,000 people surrounding the building. On 17 December the army began firing on the crowds, killing around 97. News of the crackdown spread, sparking more protests which led to the overthrow of Ceausescu.

In the demonstrations which accompanied this event the Securitate killed 71 demonstrators. Four days after the events in Timosoara the Ceausescus appeared in front of a huge crowd of people outside the Central Committee building in Bucharest. Usually such appearances were accompanied by an organized ovation from the crowd. This time the crowds booed and shouted, 'Down with the murderers.' It was unprecedented. Television coverage was immediately suspended in spite of the fact that Ceausescu was in the middle of a speech, and this more than anything else alerted the Romanian people to the fact that a revolution was underway in their country. The television studios were soon seized by the people and for five days Romanian television stayed on the air with live coverage of the fall of the Communist regime. One principal newscaster had sworn only to wear a navy suit on the day that Ceausescu was overthrown, he hurriedly changed and began his broadcast with the words 'Romanian television is free!'

The protests grew and the army sided with the people against the Securitate. Ceausescu fled from the capital but was captured and, together with his wife Elena, was executed on Christmas Day.

In 1990 the National Salvation Front was set up, led by Ion Iliescu, but many Romanians felt the Communists were still in charge. Some attempt at economic reform was made but price increases led to strikes and demonstrations. In September 1991 a new constitution was approved: this overhauled the political system and created a powerful presidency and a two-house parliament. The transition from communism to democracy was not an easy one and the real process of economic reform was not begun until 1995.

Bulgaria

Todor Zhivkov was the party leader in Bulgaria and fiercely loyal to the USSR, as can be seen by his participation in the invasion of Czechoslovakia in 1968. In Bulgaria he was not a radical Communist and even had the support of the Orthodox Church. Bulgaria's economy encountered difficulties in the 1980s and Zhivkov's position became untenable as Gorbachev's reforms in Russia undermined much of his regime's credibility. In November 1989, after the fall of the Berlin Wall, the Communist leader resigned and free elections were held the next year which resulted in a win for the Bulgarian Socialist Party. Zheliu Zhelev was elected President but strikes and general confusion continued. In July 1991 a new constitution was approved and in November 1991 Bulgaria's first non-communist government was formed.

Yugoslavia

Yugoslavia had been created at the end of the First World War and comprised seven main nationalities. In most areas the nationalities were intermingled forming a hotchpotch of races and religions.

Insight

Yugoslavia was made up of a variety of ethnic groups including Albanians, Bulgarians, Croats, Hungarians, Macedonians, Montenegrins, Muslims, Serbs, Slovaks and Slovenes. Tito succeeded in keeping these groups united but after his death Yugoslavia plunged into political and economic chaos.

Under the rule of Josip Broz, later known as Tito, the Communist Party took control after the end of the Second World War. Tito's first priority was to eliminate all domestic opposition and enforce his authority. He formed a federal republic which consisted of six republics and two autonomous regions. Communist authority was enforced by the State Security Administration which had powers to arrest and even to execute political opponents. Although Tito broke with Stalin in the late 1940s, he implemented many Stalinist policies such as forcible agricultural collectivization and rapid industrialization. The main effect of Tito's break with Stalin was to turn Yugoslavia towards the West for military and economic aid. Political changes took place in 1950 and local committees were given extensive governing powers. In 1963 the republics gained more independence at the expense of the federal government, but Tito maintained his supremacy over the republican leaders. Who would take over the reins of powers on his death?

When Tito died in May 1980, there was genuine grief at his passing. He had ruled pragmatically through a type of 'democratic socialism'. However, Yugoslavia had not progressed uniformly: there had been economic change but political change lagged behind and the late 1970s had seen growing political fragmentation. Tito had planned for a collective leadership to ease the country through the years following his death. The elections to determine the leader of the party and the President of the country were to be held separately by members of a nominated panel for specified periods of time. Disagreement surfaced almost immediately regarding the structure of the state: the Serbs wanted a strong federal government while other leaders wanted power to remain with the republic in a weak confederation. Although the system bequeathed by Tito worked during the early 1980s in spite of inflation, unemployment and separatist agitation, his death left a power vacuum which was filled by republican leaders adept at playing the ethnic card.

Renewed ethnic tensions in 1988 culminated in a mass seizure of the state parliament by aggrieved Serbs. A series of serious ethnic disturbances and political squabbling soon led to civil war which the party was unable to prevent. In Eastern Europe regimes broke free of Soviet power and Communist one-party rule with relatively little bloodshed but in Yugoslavia there was the added ingredient of ethnic rivalries. Economic dissatisfaction in the Soviet bloc was channelled into demands for political reform and an end to Communist rule – in Yugoslavia it was channelled into ethnic rivalry.

Communist Eastern Europe had ceased to exist in 1989 but this did not mean Eastern Europe entered peacefully into a new age. In January 1993, Czechoslovakia split into two separate states – the Czech Republic and Slovakia. The worst problems arose in the former Yugoslavia where a number of areas tried to win independence following the collapse of Communist control in 1990. Both Croatia and Slovenia declared their independence in 1991. There followed a civil war which spread through the area and led to the horrors of ethnic cleansing.

10 THINGS TO REMEMBER

1 Glasnost *and* perestroika *in the USSR led to demands for similar reforms within the satellite states.*

2 *The Hungarian Communist leader negotiated with other parties, permitted free travel to the West and reinvented the Communist Party as the Hungarian Socialist Party.*

3 *East Germany was reluctant to reform but popular demonstrations culminated in the demolition of the Berlin Wall on 10 November 1989.*

4 *Following peaceful pro-reform demonstrations in Czechoslovakia – known as the Velvet Revolution – Vàclav Havel, a former dissident, was elected President.*

5 *Three years later, Czechoslovakia split into two states – the Czech Republic and Slovakia.*

6 *Romania's transition to democracy was hampered by the powerful Securitate police, but by Christmas Day 1989 the Communist dictator Nicolae Ceausescu had been deposed and executed.*

7 *In Bulgaria Todor Zhivkov resigned in November 1989, opening the way for free elections which were won by the Bulgarian Socialist Party.*

8 *Under Marshal Tito the disparate collection of races and religions that made up Yugoslavia was ruled effectively by his 'democratic socialism'.*

9 *Tito's death left a power vacuum which resulted in ethnic tensions erupting into civil war following the collapse of Communist control in 1990.*

10 *The end of communism in Eastern Europe in 1989 heralded a series of events which altered the political and ethnic map of Europe still further.*

16

Cold War spies

In this chapter you will learn about:
- *spying and espionage and their role in the Cold War*
- *individual spies and their stories*
- *spies in fiction and in film.*

In 1959, Leonore Heinz, 31, a secretary in the Foreign Ministry of the West German government, answered her doorbell to find an attractive young man bearing an enormous bouquet of red roses. He was looking for someone else and he had the wrong address. By way of an apology for having disturbed her, the man thrust the roses at Leonore. She was naturally delighted and invited him in for coffee. Over coffee she discovered his name was Heinz Sutterlin, that he was a photographer, that they had many interests in common and it seemed quite natural when Heinz invited her out for dinner a few nights later. Over the next few months they attended concerts together and he showered her with gifts, visits and delicious dinners 'à deux'. Leonore was overjoyed – not only had she found romance, but the man in question was handsome and attentive. They married in December 1960.

As Heinz's work was freelance and unpredictable, Leonore continued to work as a secretary at the Foreign Ministry. One day, Heinz asked her to bring home some papers from her office, and although she was shocked at this request, Leonore was fearful that he might leave her. Faced with the prospect of losing her handsome husband and returning to her former lonely existence, Leonore ignored her feelings of guilt and succumbed to his request. For the next five years, Leonore would bring home documents every lunchtime which Heinz would then photograph while she cooked the lunch. Each afternoon she returned the documents and Heinz passed the photographs – many of them top secret – to his contact, a man called Runge, an agent for the KGB based in Moscow but working undercover in West Germany. Unfortunately, in 1967 Runge defected to the West and surrendered his list of agents to the CIA. Heinz and Leonore were promptly arrested by the authorities in West Germany and put on trial as spies.

During the trial it emerged that Heinz Sutterlin had trained as a spy for the East German Ministry of State Security. As his 'handler', Runge had ordered him to marry a secretary from the West German Foreign Ministry with a view to obtaining state secrets. Leonore, unable to face the reality that her romance and marriage had been part of a Soviet KGB plot, hanged herself with her nightdress in her cell – just one victim of the shadowy world of espionage. Markus Wolf, an East German spymaster, summed up the whole episode when he denied that spying was romantic: 'It's dirty; people suffer.'

This story shows three main features of a spying operation during the Cold War. First, the collection of intelligence data from the opposite side was a routine affair: Leonore's documents were passed to Heinz (the agent), who then passed them to his handler Runge, who in turn passed them to his superiors. The documents were closely studied by intelligence agents in the USSR in order to ascertain what West Germany was doing or planning to do. Runge had boasted that the KGB had read reports even before the West German foreign minister!

Secondly, counter-intelligence was extremely important as both sides strove to protect their own agents by laying false trails in an attempt to confuse the opposition and even expose the enemy agent by this subterfuge. In the story above, the CIA was able to expose the Sutterlins only when Runge defected to the West.

Finally the Sutterlin episode shows the importance of covert operations – where both sides used their intelligence agencies to put pressure on their enemies and to support their allies.

Spies and spying came to epitomize the era of the Cold War. Winston Churchill described the process of spying as 'the battle of the conjurors', a particularly apt parallel with the intelligence agents practised in the art of deception, slipping in and out of the shadows with their codes and microdots, risking their lives to collect and pass on information. Yet, spying was nothing new, as the USSR had spies in place before the Cold War began. Two scientists working in Los Alamos on the atomic bomb project enabled the Soviet Union to take an early lead in the espionage stakes. Klaus Fuchs and Ted Hall passed detailed drawings of the atomic bomb's trigger device to their Soviet handlers thus enabling the USSR to detonate its own atomic bomb in 1949 – two years earlier than anticipated by the West.

From the very early years of the Cold War secrets played an important part, each side trying to gather information about the other side's secrets while keeping their own firmly under wraps. Most espionage missions and electronic surveillance attempted to discover the secrets of the arms race and the developments in new weapons. Berlin was probably the main centre of espionage. Its geographical position 160 kilometres (100 miles) behind the iron curtain and the fact that, although it was a divided city, Berliners crossed sector boundaries daily for work and pleasure prior to 1961, made it ideal for both sides to conduct covert operations and to introduce spies easily. By the early 1960s the city probably had the highest concentration of both technological and human spies the world had ever seen. It became increasingly difficult to do anything without the other side knowing. Innumerable diplomats, businessmen and journalists were involved in espionage, passing on jigsaw pieces of information which gradually formed the whole picture. In 1954 the CIA dug a tunnel under the Soviet sector with a view to tapping telephone wires; the KGB had been informed about this by its spy George Blake, but allowed it to continue for 11 months! Berlin was also the setting for several of the Cold War's most potent symbols including the Berlin Wall and the Glienicke Bridge, where many captured spies were traded back and forth.

Why spy?

The motives of Cold War spies varied. Early in the period spies tended to act out of political conviction. Kim Philby, Guy Burgess and Donald Maclean, Communist spies within British intelligence and the Foreign Office, sincerely believed that what they were doing was right. Burgess and Maclean passed a variety of information to Moscow during the 1940s including Britain's intentions regarding the Marshall Plan. Philby, as a member of the British Intelligence Service, passed information about Sigint (a means of intercepting signals) to the KGB and also betrayed agents in the Balkans, many of whom were captured and executed. By 1951, Burgess and Maclean had defected to the Soviet Union to be joined in 1963 by Philby. The effect of this treachery on Western intelligence was devastating, morale was undermined and the American agencies refused to trust British intelligence for many years to come.

Insight

Philby, Burgess and Maclean were part of what became known as 'the Cambridge five'. All had become Communists while at Cambridge. Philby (Stanley), Burgess (Hicks), McClean (Homer) and Blunt (Johnson) are generally better known than the Fifth Man John Cairncross (Liszt), however it is now believed that the spy ring consisted of more than five members.

In the later years of the Cold War, spies' motivation became increasingly monetary. Aldrich Ames, an officer in the CIA, was also the KGB's 'mole' (undercover agent); he acted only for money. He was paid $2.7 million and had $1.9 million owing to him when he was arrested in 1994. He had been in the employ of the KGB for ten years and had betrayed some 25 CIA agents, ten of whom were shot. Among these was Dmitri Polyakov, recruited as a CIA 'mole' in 1961. Polyakov was considered to be one of the most productive double agents the CIA had in Russia. It was the search for the mole who had betrayed him that led the CIA to Ames in 1994.

Insight

'Mole' is a term used for a spy working for one nation but who is loyal to his or her own nation's government. The Cambridge five, who spied for Russia while working in quite senior positions within the British government, are the most famous British moles.

Technology and spying

Spying did not take place only on the ground. President Eisenhower realized that aerial intelligence and satellite photography were powerful tools, especially having received a picture of him playing golf at Camp David, taken from 21,300 metres (70,000 feet), in which he could easily identify himself and his golf ball! The U-2, a Lockheed aircraft especially developed for the CIA, was first used to gather intelligence in 1956. Its ability to fly at very high altitudes and long distances made it difficult to detect by Soviet fighters. Equipped with cameras and radio receivers the U-2 was able to detect Soviet long-range bomber bases and missile sites, and spying flights over Soviet territory became a regular occurrence. The U-2 incident just before the Paris Peace Summit in 1960 resulted in Khrushchev storming out in protest; it seemed that one spy flight had ended one of the best chances to end the Cold War. American forces went on worldwide alert immediately after the summit.

Gary Powers, the captured U-2 pilot, was put on trial in Moscow and sentenced to ten years' imprisonment; he was released in 1962 in exchange for Rudolf Abel, a Soviet spymaster operating in New York. Abel had been tracked down quite by chance. In 1957 a Finn had walked into the American Embassy in Paris, had admitted to spying for the Soviets and had backed up his story by producing a coin especially adapted for carrying microdots. His handler in the United States was a man called 'Mark'. The American Federal Bureau of Investigation (FBI) kept watch on an artist's studio in Brooklyn and observed an ordinary-looking middle-aged, balding man arrive, stay a few hours and then leave. In spite of their attempts to track him, he disappeared. Several weeks later they succeeded in tracking the man, whom they had by now named as Emil Goldfuss, a Brooklyn artist, to the Hotel Latham where he was arrested. Their searches revealed a panoply of spying devices: microfilm concealed in a hollow pencil; radio receivers and transmitters; thousands of dollars and many other items which enabled the FBI to track down other Soviet agents. Emil Goldfuss was in fact Colonel Rudolf Abel of the KGB, the Soviet secret service, an experienced agent who had worked inside the German army during the war and had even been decorated with German military honours! In the United States he had become the chief of operations and had run an entire network of spies throughout North America while all the time keeping up his cover as Emil Goldfuss. It was his trial more than any other which convinced the United States of the efforts being made by the USSR to uncover US defence secrets as it came at a particularly delicate time in the Cold War. The USSR had just shown that it was ahead of the United States in the field of technology by sending Sputnik into space.

Technology played an increasingly important role in espionage. In Alaska the Dew Line, 40 American radar stations, watched and waited for any surprise attack by the Soviets, while only a few kilometres away Soviet 'weather stations' undertook a similar task in anticipation of an American attack. Listening stations all over the world intercepted and decoded radio traffic; satellite stations in space photographed military installations in fine detail; Soviet and Western nuclear submarines played a deadly game of cat and mouse fathoms under the sea; Star Wars became a reality when the USA developed the Strategic Defence Initiative which was a programme to develop anti-missile weapons using laser beams to create a huge laser shield in space.

Spies in literature and the movies

So important an element of the Cold War were spies and espionage that it was natural that these aspects would be seized upon by authors and film-makers of the later twentieth century. Films such as *The Ipcress File* (1965) and *The Spy Who Came in From the Cold* (1965) took a laconic view of both sides and were based on British novels, though produced in Hollywood. Often, the literary characters in the books of John Le Carré enjoyed the luxury of being worried more about the ethics and morality of the Cold War whereas other literary spies seemed to be more concerned with getting results and thwarting the Communist menace.

Le Carré wrote about spies, spymasters and undercover agents who were totally anonymous and emphasized that much espionage was routine. One such intelligence officer was Ian Fleming – assistant to the Director of Naval Intelligence of the British Admiralty. From behind his desk in the Admiralty he rose to the rank of Commander in the Royal Naval Volunteer Reserve by interpreting intelligence from German and Soviet forces. A prosaic career when compared with that of his alter ego – James Bond – who made his first appearance in Fleming's book *Casino Royale* in 1954, and who continues to thrill audiences all over the world to this day. It is estimated that approximately 25 per cent of the world's population have seen at least one Bond film. One avid fan of the novels was John F. Kennedy and his enthusiasm for them assured their popularity, helping to make Fleming a top bestseller in the United States. Fleming not only dined with the Kennedy family in 1960, but according to some, also suggested ways the United States might rid themselves of Fidel Castro, the Cuban Socialist revolutionary. These included spreading rumours that Castro was impotent and flooding Cuba with fake US dollars. The assassination of JFK in November 1963 by yet another avid Bond fan, Lee Harvey Oswald, meant these plans were not put into practice.

James Bond movies are a fair indicator of the course of the Cold War although they deliberately dispensed with SMERSH, Fleming's

Russian terrorist organization, and instead made Bond's enemies part of a multinational terror network, SPECTRE – the Special Executive for Counter-intelligence, Terrorism, Revenge and Extortion. This allowed the producers Albert 'Cubby' Broccoli and Harry Saltzman to introduce a variety of evil megalomaniacs from a variety of racial and political backgrounds. Take, for example, the Teutonic Ernst Blofeld, who famously appears stroking a white Persian cat and dressed in a Mao Zedong-style suit. By using such simple devices the film-makers managed to pander to British prejudices against both Germany and communism. The films encouraged the public to draw parallels with contemporary events. *Dr No* (1962), for example, echoed the Cuban Missile Crisis – no wonder President Kennedy arranged a private viewing of it in the White House! Other 007 films developed more explicit Cold War themes and drew attention to areas of potential East–West confrontation. As the fear of nuclear war intensified in the 1960s, Bond films featured plots involving rockets and nuclear weapons, emphasizing their potential danger if they should fall into the wrong hands. *Thunderball* (1965) saw the theft of a NATO bomber carrying nuclear weapons; *Goldfinger* (1964) warned of Chinese attempts to use 'dirty' nuclear bombs to get their hands on US gold held in Fort Knox. As the Cold War thawed during the 1970s, the films tackled storylines about international problems such as the drugs trade (*Live and Let Die*, 1973), germ warfare based in space (*Moonraker*, 1979) and even British–Soviet co-operation (*The Spy Who Loved Me*, 1977). By the 1980s a second Cold War had developed and tensions between the superpowers had returned. Once again the Bond movies reflected this change. SPECTRE was mothballed and the emphasis placed on renewed British–Soviet hostility. In one film Bond, played by Roger Moore, destroys a computer which could render British nuclear forces useless; he observes to a senior Soviet spymaster watching him, 'That's détente, comrade. You don't have it and I don't have it.'

Since the events of 1989 and the disintegration of the Soviet Union, Bond movies have chosen to reflect other US foreign policy concerns such as Latin American drug barons (*Licence to Kill*, 1989) and North Korea (*Die Another Day*, 2002), perhaps because of the need to maintain North American viewing figures. Or is it because the world has changed, as Bond's now female boss (played by Dame Judi Dench) – perhaps mirroring the real-life former head of MI5, Dame Stella Rimington – suggests when she calls him a 'misogynist dinosaur, a relic of the Cold War'.

No doubt in future we can expect to see storylines which reflect the emergence of Al-Qaeda.

Ordinary people

Not all Cold War spying was as romantic or as exciting as the exploits of James Bond; it should be remembered that most successful spies passed themselves off as ordinary people and moved easily among their work colleagues and neighbours, as was the case in the Portland Spy Ring.

In 1959 the CIA received a sealed envelope from the American Ambassador in Berne. In it was a letter from a Polish intelligence officer offering details about Soviet spying operations in the West. One case this letter referred to was of a traitor within the Royal Navy who was passing naval secrets to the Soviets. The details provided enabled the British to pin down the individual concerned – one Harry Houghton who worked at the naval base in Portland, Dorset. He and his friend Ethel Gee, who also worked in Portland, seemed to be living beyond their means and were placed under surveillance by officers from MI5 (Military Intelligence, section 5) responsible for counter-espionage and security matters.

Insight

Gee, an unmarried filing clerk who cared for her elderly relatives, worked in the Admiralty Underwater Weapons Establishment, Portland, and passed secrets to her lover Harry Houghton. Houghton served in the Royal Navy before gaining employment as a clerk in the Admiralty Underwater Weapons Establishment. He passed secret information

regarding nuclear submarines to a KGB agent. Gee and
Houghton married in 1970 having served nine years for
spying.

In June 1960, MI5 watched Houghton meeting a businessman
called Gordon Lonsdale and handing over documents to him.
Lonsdale then deposited these together with a steel box, in a
safe deposit box in the Midland Bank in Great Portland Street,
London. On examination of this safe deposit box, MI5 found a
number of spying essentials – camera, film, a lighter with secret
compartments, timetables for the transmission of radio messages
and a 'one-time pad', a device for encoding messages. Lonsdale
was not an easy target to keep track of but he was followed several
times to a suburban bungalow in Ruislip, the home of a bookseller,
Peter Kroger, and his wife.

Insight

The Krogers were Morris and Lona Cohen, American
Communists who, acting for the USSR, acquired the blueprints
for the atomic bomb from Ted Hall. They were each awarded
the USSR's highest honour 'Hero of the Soviet Union'.

On 7 January 1961, Houghton and Ethel Gee caught the train to
London. In Gee's shopping bag were secret documents pertaining
to Britain's first nuclear-powered submarine. Once in London the
pair did a bit of shopping, met Lonsdale by the Old Vic theatre and
passed over the shopping bag. They were immediately arrested.
The next to be arrested were the Krogers. Their ordinary suburban
bungalow at 45 Cranley Drive, Ruislip, contained secrets worthy of
James Bond. Ordinary household objects had been adapted to make
secret hiding places for spying equipment. Large sums of money were
recovered, so too were a radio set, false passports and photographic
equipment. In Mrs Kroger's handbag three tiny microdots were
found; these were later enlarged and found to be letters in Russian.
This ordinary bungalow was a spy centre: when radio experts
listened in at the times given on the timetable found with the radio
set, they picked up coded messages which, when traced, were found
to have been transmitted from a location near Moscow.

All five spies went to prison although Lonsdale was later exchanged for a British spy, Greville Wynne, in 1964, and the Krogers were exchanged in 1969.

Real-life espionage, however, was as bizarre as any Bond movie. In the 1950s an elaborate plan, Operation Splinter Faction had been concocted to undermine the Soviet satellite states. It was a CIA disinformation campaign which attempted to drive a wedge between the Soviet Union and its satellites. Dulles allowed one of his operatives to be arrested and put on trial as a US master spy and delighted in the chaos it caused.

Its failure led to the deaths of many agents. In the 1960s President Kennedy had commissioned research into the production of deadly cigars, poisoned diving suits and explosive seashells with a view to ridding the United States of her dangerous neighbour, Fidel Castro. In the 1970s, Soviet-backed agents succeeded in killing Georgi Markov, a Bulgarian dissident living in London, by using a poisoned umbrella tip.

Insight

Markov was poisoned by ricin administered through the point of an umbrella. The name of the assassin has recently been uncovered in the Bulgarian archives – Francesco Gullino, code name Picadilly.

Soviet bloc agents too were implicated in the plot to assassinate Pope John Paul II in 1980. His firmly anti-communist stance had alarmed the Kremlin, particularly after his astoundingly successful visit to Poland in that same year.

10 THINGS TO REMEMBER

1 All Cold War participants spied and held covert operations to undermine and obtain information about their opponents' regimes.

2 Arms and weapons development were the main focus of spying, beginning with the atomic bomb project in Los Alamos during the Second World War through the Cuban crisis in the 1960s, to the Strategic Defence Initiative in the 1980s.

3 Berlin was the epicentre for espionage. Ideally situated geographically, its constantly shifting population made it easy to introduce and eliminate spies.

4 Early in the Cold War, spies such as Philby, Burgess and Maclean tended to be recruited by ideology. As time progressed, money proved a greater attraction.

5 Technology such as U-2 spy planes and satellites enabled the superpowers to spy from the air and from space.

6 Authors such as Le Carré and Fleming and films featuring James Bond (agent 007) led people to believe spying was a dangerous but romantic profession.

7 Unlike the debonair James Bond, most spies were nondescript and blended into the civilian population.

8 Many Soviet spies were 'sleepers', 'planted' after the Second World War and awaiting instructions from their handlers before being 'activated'.

9 Espionage could be as far-fetched as Hollywood films, as plans to poison Castro via a poisoned cigar demonstrate.

10 Since the end of the Cold War several spying 'mysteries' have been solved as official records have been released and spies identified.

17

The end of the Cold War

In this chapter you will learn about:
- *the end of the Cold War once communism had collapsed*
- *the effect the Cold War had on the lives of the people*
- *the cost of the Cold War.*

In 1988 Mikhail Gorbachev addressed the General Assembly of
the United Nations in New York with a speech which practically
brought the Cold War to an end. In this astounding speech,
Gorbachev announced the Bolshevik Revolution was in the past; he
renounced the Brezhnev Doctrine by saying that the Soviet satellite
states should be free to pursue their own destiny; most surprisingly
of all he announced the withdrawal of the Soviet Union from the
arms race which had been one of the main features of the Cold
War. To the new American President, George Bush, this had come
too quickly. His advisers warned him that Gorbachev's speech
might be a deliberate ploy to unbalance the West so that the
Soviets might strike a resounding blow to democracy in some way.
The massacre by the Chinese Communist government of political
protesters and students in Tiananmen Square in Beijing seemed to
confirm Western opinions that communism had no intention of
going quietly.

Insight

The student protests in Tiananmen Square had been timed
to coincide with Gorbachev's visit to Beijing. Troops were

used to break up the students in spite of the peaceful nature of the protests. Some suspect that Deng Xiaoping deliberately ordered the bloody attack to give his failing leadership more credibility.

Yet in Europe, apart from a few violent outbursts in Romania, Georgia and some of the Baltic states, the death of communism came swiftly and quietly. Perhaps the key to the swift demise of communism in the East European satellites lay in East Germany. As thousands of East Germans fled to the West through Hungary, which now had a reformist Communist regime and had opened its borders with Austria, Gorbachev had firmly warned Erich Honecker against trying a Tiananmen Square solution to his problems: how unlike Khrushchev's reaction to the refugees fleeing East Germany through Berlin. Just as the Cold War had 'kicked off' with the Berlin blockade and airlift in the 1940s, now it had come full circle with the fall of the Berlin Wall in 1989.

Less than two years after the events in Berlin, the USSR ceased to exist. In August 1989, disillusion with Gorbachev's reforms had set in and many Russians began to question whether the drift to capitalism was appropriate for Russia. Gorbachev struggled to appease both the Communist Party hardliners and the more radical reformers but failed to satisfy either. Boris Yeltsin began to become more prominent as his demands for faster reform became more vocal. He demanded that Gorbachev increase the pace of reform or resign. Yeltsin's popularity ensured his appointment as the first democratically elected President of the Russian Federation; however, the situation continued to deteriorate. On 20 August 1991, Communist hardliners decided to take matters into their own hands and instigated a coup. Tanks moved into the centre of Moscow and a self-appointed 'Emergency Committee' announced it was in control. The Russian population realized the seriousness of the situation when the usual television programmes were replaced by the ballet *Swan Lake* and when announcements were made that Gorbachev was 'undergoing treatment' in his dacha in the Crimea.

Rod Williams and his wife Margaret were on holiday in Russia when these events took place and they recalled how, suddenly, the tourists were surrounded by security men and gently, but firmly, taken away from Moscow to a place of safety outside the capital. They recalled too the atmosphere of tension and the overt carrying of arms by their bodyguards. Their minders were genuinely worried that this would be the end of the Westernization process in Russia to such an extent that one of them failed to show up for work – he had gone to Moscow to help the people surround the White House, home of the Russian parliament, in order to protect it from the troops of the 'Emergency Committee'.

Sasha Gorlov, then a student of economics in Moscow University, recalls talking to the soldiers who had flooded into Moscow, persuading them to read the resistance leaflets and to join the people rather than fight them. Perhaps the most memorable scene was that of Boris Yeltsin himself climbing onto a tank in front of the White House and urging the people to resist.

Insight

Yeltsin will be remembered as a colourful character as well as a staunch protector of democracy during the coup in 1991; while staying in the White House he was found one evening in his underpants trying to hail a cab in order to get a pizza.

Later on in 1991 Yeltsin disbanded the Communist Party in Russia and formally ended the Soviet Union which was replaced by the Commonwealth of Independent States (CIS).

Insight

The Commonwealth of Independent States was formed in 1991 as a successor to the USSR. It was open to all republics which had previously formed the Soviet Union and all members were to be sovereign, independent nations.

With the disappearance of the Soviet state and its ideology, the whole *raison d'être* of the Cold War had disappeared.

How did the Cold War affect the people?

There are several approaches to answering this question. One could concentrate on the toll the Cold War took on civilians' lives: millions in Korea, Vietnam and Afghanistan; hundreds of thousands in Africa; tens of thousands in Latin America; thousands in Eastern Europe. More civilians were killed in this 'cold' war than in any 'hot' war. It affected even the thoughts of people; millions felt stifled by the overbearing ideology of the state and that includes many American people during the McCarthy witch-hunts of the 1950s.

Insight

Senator Joe McCarthy whipped up anti-communist feeling within the USA during the 1950s when he began a witch-hunt to root out and prosecute Communists. He frequently made accusations without hard and fast evidence and ruined the careers of innocent people as a result.

FASHION

The Cold War affected more trivial and frivolous aspects of people's lives in the twentieth century. With the benefit of hindsight it can be seen that fashion played its part in the Cold War. It could be argued that uniforms featured strongly: corporate America dressed in grey suits; blue cotton suits in Maoist China; the black beret of Latin American revolutionaries; the trench coats worn by spies; the blue jeans worn by young people on both sides of the iron curtain. Western women were encouraged to aspire to high fashion while in the Hollywood film *Silk Stockings* (1957) it was imagined that any Russian female would swoon at the very sight of Paris fashion!

POPULAR MUSIC

Cold War anxieties, especially about nuclear war, worked their way into popular music. Bob Dylan was inspired by the Cuban Missile Crisis to write 'A Hard Rain's A-Gonna Fall' in 1965. The Clash released a double-sided single with nuclear annihilation themes in 1979 including 'London Calling'. By the 1980s, with a new military build-up under President Reagan, a German band, Nena, released '99 Luftballons', the story of a boy and a girl releasing a batch of balloons which are mistaken for missiles by the superpowers thus initiating a nuclear Armageddon. Sting wrote 'Russians' which noted, 'There's no such thing as a winnable war, it's a lie we don't believe any more' and concludes with the words, 'I hope the Russians love their children too.' The Beatles wrote the tongue-in-cheek 'Back in the USSR' in 1968. Vietnam had its share of high-profile protest songs such as Country Joe McDonald and the Fish with their 'I feel like I'm fixing to die Rag' (or 'Vietnam Rag', 1965) and many groups played concerts close to the Berlin Wall in the hope of reaching 'the other side'. One of the most ironic perhaps was Pink Floyd's 'Wall' concert in the early 1980s.

BOOKS AND THE CINEMA

Literature and films have both been influenced by the Cold War. Many literary works were smuggled out of Russia including some by Andrei Sinyavsky and Yuli Daniel who were put on trial and imprisoned in labour camps in 1966. Others were written openly, such as the works of Alexander Solzhenitsyn – including *Cancer Ward* (1968) and *The Gulag Archipelago* (1973) – the author consequently lost his Soviet citizenship and was exiled. In the West, spy thrillers by authors such as John Le Carré and Ian Fleming sold in their millions and confirmed the West's view that the 'good' guys came from the West and the 'bad' guys came from the East.

The Cold War enjoyed much success at the box office with such films as *Dr Strangelove (or How I learned to love the bomb)* (1963), a political satire which foresees nuclear Armageddon brought about by the accidental release of a nuclear missile by a crazy American commander. Spies and espionage feature heavily in the Bond movies and films such as *The Ipcress File* (1965) and *The Spy Who Came in From the Cold* (1965), the more jaundiced view of spying. The film *M*A*S*H* (1969) about the Korean War used comedy to show the horrors of war. Vietnam, of course, had a number of films of all genres – *Coming Home* (1978), *The Deer Hunter* (1978) and *Apocalypse Now* (1979) all emphasized the futility of war and the damage it inflicted on American society.

What was the financial cost of the Cold War?

During the Cold War confrontation between the superpowers, a balance of sorts had been struck. True, there had been moments of high drama: General MacArthur had nearly invaded China; the United States had considered using nuclear weapons on several occasions, as too had the Soviet Union; the United States and the Soviet Union had feared the effect of nuclear weapons while China's Mao Zedong had claimed China would welcome and win a nuclear war. A balance of power existed, but it was a balance that had been achieved at tremendous cost. The superpowers had equipped themselves with both nuclear and conventional weapons costing trillions of dollars, much of which could have been better spent on other needs in their respective societies. Did this spending actually protect the ideals of the two sides or did the cost undermine the ideology and the society that each side was trying to protect?

On the Soviet side it would seem that the huge expense of defence led to the regime's eventual demise, but in the United States the expense of the Vietnam War for example put paid to President Lyndon B. Johnson's ambitions for a 'Great Society'.

At the end of the Cold War there are those who would argue that there was only one superpower left – the United States – and that the values and policies of the USA had 'won' the Cold War. An American historian, Francis Fukuyama, in his book *The End of History* (1989) wrote that all the big ideological and historical questions of the twentieth century had been answered, therefore 'history' was at an end. Rather an optimistic and premature view – there is still the legacy of the Cold War to contend with, and new questions have loomed since the destruction of the World Trade Centre Towers in New York on 9/11, an event rooted firmly in the twentieth century.

> ## Insight
> The suicide attacks on the World Trade Centre in 2001 by al-Qaeda are known simply as 9/11. Two planes were flown into the Twin Towers causing them to collapse within two hours, a third plane crashed into the Pentagon, and a fourth crashed in a field on its way to Washington.

Since the break-up of the Soviet Union there is still the question of its nuclear arsenal which remains spread through the fractured states which succeeded the USSR, many of which may not be regarded as 'responsible'. There has been considerable press coverage about the threat of so-called 'dirty bombs' in recent years. These relics pose an increasingly difficult problem for Western governments both in terms of dealing with the nuclear components in a safe manner and preventing their falling into the hands of terrorist groups.

10 THINGS TO REMEMBER

1 *In 1988 the Chinese Communist government decisively limited political dissent, as demonstrated by the Tiananmen Square massacre.*

2 *The fall of the Berlin Wall in November 1989 brought the Cold War to a poetic end as people power tore down the 'iron curtain'.*

3 *In 1991 an attempted coup by Communist hardliners tried to 'turn back the clock' in Moscow.*

4 *Boris Yeltsin (later President of the Russian Republic) climbed onto a tank in front of the Russian Parliament and urged Russians to resist the coup.*

5 *The Communist Party in Russia was banned in 1991 and the Soviet Union was replaced by the Commonwealth of Independent States.*

6 *By 1992, the new Communist Party of Russia had been legally established, and won the largest bloc of seats in the 1995 parliamentary elections.*

7 *The financial cost of the Cold War was extortionate and led to the eventual demise of the USSR.*

8 *The civilian population paid a high price: millions died as a direst result of the fighting and millions suffered low standards of living as their governments spent on arms rather than social reform.*

9 *The break-up of the USSR created independent states, some of which suffered from political and economic instability while others were constrained by Russia's efforts to maintain control.*

10 *The Cold War legacy includes toxic pollution left by chemical and nuclear weapons, instability in regions such as Afghanistan, divided nations and poor diplomatic relations between the USA and some Arab nations.*

Glossary

arms race The competitive build-up of nuclear weapons between the United States and the Soviet Union.

atomic bomb The first nuclear weapon – an explosion is created by splitting atomic nuclei and this leads to a huge release of energy.

B-52 The strategic US heavy bomber that had the capacity to carry nuclear weapons and was the mainstay of US nuclear forces in the 1950s.

Baikonur Cosmodrome The Soviet missile-testing facility in Kazakhstan.

Bay of Pigs Where an American-organized invasion by Cuban exiles, 17–20 April 1961, landed and was defeated by Castro's forces.

Berlin airlift The response by the USA and Britain to a Soviet blockade of all land and canal routes to the city: 2.3 million tons of supplies were shipped by air to the Western sector from June 1948 to May 1949.

Checkpoint Charlie The border site between East and West Berlin – scene of a famous stand-off between American and Soviet tanks in October 1961.

CIA Central Intelligence Agency that conducts US intelligence and counter-intelligence.

COMECON The Soviet version of an economic community – the Council for Mutual and Economic Co-operation was Moscow's answer to the Marshall Plan.

containment The policy to contain Soviet influence to the extent it reached at the end of the Second World War.

Contras Counter-revolutionary forces backed by the USA – opposed to Nicaragua's left wing Sandinista government.

Cruise US missiles.

Cuban Missile Crisis October 1962 – the Soviet Union placed nuclear weapons on Cuba and the United States responded with a blockade.

DEFCON Indicates US defence conditions on a scale of five (the lowest state of alert) to one (war).

détente A thaw in relations between the United States and Soviet Union from 1969 to 1975.

glasnost Policy initiated by Gorbachev in the Soviet Union in the 1980s. It increased freedom of speech, association and the press.

Hungarian Revolution Mass uprising that was crushed by Soviet troops and tanks, 3–4 November 1956.

hydrogen bomb A nuclear weapon hundreds of times more powerful than the atomic bombs dropped on Hiroshima and Nagasaki.

ICBM Intercontinental ballistic missiles – nuclear weapons with a range of more than 5,600 kilometres (3,500 miles).

IRBM Intermediate-range ballistic missiles – nuclear weapons with a range of between 960 kilometres (600 miles) and 5,600 kilometres (3,500 miles).

iron curtain The term used by Churchill in 1946 to describe the East–West split between Communist and democratic nations becoming apparent in Europe.

MAD Mutual assured destruction, a theory which believed that the existence of nuclear weapons ensured that they would not be used since each side could retaliate thus ensuring complete destruction.

Marshall Plan The European recovery plan intended to bolster Western democracy in the years following the Second World War.

MIRV Multiple independently targeted re-entry vehicle – enabled missiles to carry several warheads each aimed at separate targets.

Mujahideen Islamic rebels opposed to the Soviet-backed 1979 coup in Afghanistan – received support and funding from the USA.

NATO North Atlantic Treaty Organization – established in 1949. A military and political alliance of European nations, the United States and Canada. Designed to protect the West from a Soviet attack.

Ostpolitik Chancellor Willy Brandt's 'Eastern Policy' of improving ties between Soviet bloc nations and West Germany.

peaceful coexistence The term used by Khrushchev in 1963. The USA and USSR would compete economically and politically but avoid starting a thermonuclear war.

perestroika Gorbachev's policy of economic restructuring in the Soviet Union during the 1980s.

Pershing US nuclear missiles deployed in West Germany in the 1970s and 1980s.

Politburo Executive committee of the Communist Party of the Soviet Union.

Potsdam Third wartime meeting of the Big Three Alliance leaders, Churchill, Truman and Stalin.

Prague spring Brief period of political reform and freedom in Czechoslovakia in 1968 under the leadership of Alexander Dubcek – ended by Soviet occupation.

Red Army Armed forces of the Soviet Union.

refuseniks Soviet Jews and others who were denied exit visas and were persecuted for trying to leave the USSR.

Rolling Thunder Bombing campaign against North Vietnam.

SALT Strategic Arms Limitation Talks in the late 1960s and 1970s. SALT 1 limited each country's ballistic missile defence and froze the deployment of ICBM launchers.

SALT 2 Set limits on the number of strategic missile launchers and other systems each country could deploy.

SDI Strategic Defence Initiative (1983), also known as 'Star Wars,' a land- or space-based shield against a nuclear attack.

Six Day War Israel's surprise offensive launched on 5 June 1967, to pre-empt a planned Arab invasion.

Solidarity The first autonomous labour union in the Soviet bloc – originated in mass protests at the Lenin shipyards in Gdansk, Poland, in summer 1980.

space race Competition between the United States and the Soviet Union to dominate outer space.

Sputnik The first artificial Earth satellite launched by Moscow in 1957.

START Strategic Arms Reduction Talks, 1982–91.

Stasi East German secret police.

Tet Offensive A series of attacks launched by North Vietnamese and Vietcong forces in South Vietnam in January and February 1968, during the lunar new year Tet.

38th parallel The dividing line between North and South Korea.

Tonkin Gulf Following the alleged incident when North Vietnamese patrol boats fired on the USS *Maddox* in the Gulf of Tonkin on 2 August 1968, Congress approved the Gulf of Tonkin Resolution which gave President Johnson authority to send troops to Vietnam.

Truman Doctrine Established in 1947 – it pledged to provide US military and economic aid to any nation threatened by communism.

U-2 US spy plane used for US intelligence gathering before the development of satellite reconnaissance in the 1970s.

Velvet Revolution Mass protests in Czechoslovakia that led to the fall of communism in that country in November 1989.

Vietcong Communist guerrillas in South Vietnam who strove to reunite the country with North Vietnam.

Vietnamization Nixon administration's decision to turn over control of the Vietnam War to South Vietnam while US troops withdrew.

Warsaw Pact Eastern European defence organization established in Warsaw, Poland, on 14 May 1955 – a counter to the US-led NATO.

Yalta Meeting of the Big Three leaders, Stalin, Churchill and Roosevelt in Yalta, 4–11 February 1945.

Zero Option Proposal by the Western German peace movement that all European intermediate-range nuclear forces be banned.

Taking it further

Websites

General history of the Cold War
www.thecorner.org/hist/europe/coldwar.htm

Russian archives online
www.pbs.org/redfiles/rao/archives/index.html

Life growing up in East Germany
www.ironcurtainkid.com

Primary sources on the Cold War:
www.wilsoncenter.org/coldwarfiles

Dedicated to education, preservation, and research on the global, ideological, and political confrontations between East and West:
www.coldwar.org

The British National Archives:
http://learningcurve.pro.gov.uk/coldwar

Kennedy and the Berlin crisis:
www.nsarchive.org

Museum in Berlin dedicated to Checkpoint Charlie:
www.checkpointcharlie.org

Dedicated to the Berlin Wall:
www.dailysoft.com/berlinwall

Audio files and descriptive notes of President Kennedy's Oval
Office conversations with his advisers:
www.hpol.org/jfk/cuban

Information on key political and military figures as well as major
events of the war:
www.spartacus.schoolnet.co.uk/vietnam.html

Portal to information about the Vietnam War:
www.vietnamwar.net

James Bond Site:
www.007.com

Bibliography

Christopher Andrew and Oleg Gordievsky, *KGB: the inside story
of its foreign operations from Lenin to Gorbachev* (HarperCollins,
1990)

Jeremy Black, *The Politics of James Bond* (Praeger, 2001)

Carl Friedrich and Z.K. Brzezinski, *Totalitarian Dictatorship and
Autocracy* (Harvard University Press, 1956)

John Lewis Gaddis, *The Cold War* (Penguin, 2007)

John Lewis Gaddis, *We Now Know. Rethinking Cold War History*
(Clarendon Press, 1998)

Mikhail Gorbachev, *Memoirs* (Doubleday, 1996)

Max Hastings, *The Korean War* (Michael Joseph, 1987)

Godfrey Hodgson, *People's Century* (BBC Books, 1995/1996)

Jeremy Isaacs and Taylor Downing, *Cold War* (Bantam Press, 1988)

Stanley Karnow, *Vietnam: a History* (Viking Press, 1983)

M.P. Leffler, Odd Arne Westad (eds), *The Cambridge History of the Cold War* (Cambridge University Press 2009)

Martin McCauley, *The Origins of the Cold War 1941–9* (Longman, 1995)

Angus Roxburgh, *The Second Russian Revolution* (BBC Books, 1991)

Ann Tusa, *The Last Division: Berlin and the Wall* (Hodder & Stoughton, 1996)

Films

*M*A*S*H* (1969)

Doctor Strangelove (1963)

The Spy Who Came in From the Cold (1965)

Any James Bond movie!

Index

007 (James Bond), *241–2, 251*
9/11 terrorist attacks, *252*

Abel, Rudolf, *239*
Able Archer wargame, *217*
ABM Treaty 1972, *95, 97–8*
Adenauer, Konrad, *36, 41*
aerial intelligence, *86–7, 90, 238*
Afghanistan, *189–92*
Africa, independence, *195–202*
Agent Orange defoliant, *138*
Agreement on the Prevention of
 Nuclear War, *165*
airlift, during Berlin Blockage,
 39–40
Albania, exit from Warsaw Pact,
 156
Allende Gossens, Salvador, *205–6*
America *see* USA
American Embassy siege,
 Tehran, *187*
Ames, Aldrich, *237*
Amin, Hafizullah, *189–90*
Anglo-Soviet Treaty, *12*
Angola, conflict, *197–200*
anti-nuclear movements, *101–3*
Arab–Israeli conflict, *176–7*
Arafat, Yasser, *185*
arms race
 accidents, *92–4*
 anti-nuclear movements,
  101–3
 détente, *94–6, 164–7*

development, *83–90, 91–2*
 expansion under Reagan,
  96–9
 influence of Gorbachev,
  99–101
 limitation talks, *95, 164–6*
 see also nuclear weapons
assassination attempts, *109–10,
 124–5, 135, 195, 244*
Aswan Dam Project, *72*
Atlantic Charter, *12*
atomic bomb *see* nuclear weapons
Axis forces, Eastern Front, *9*

Baghdad Pact, *174, 181*
Basic Treaty, East and West
 Germany, *159*
Bay of Pigs, *44, 110–12*
Berlin
 blockade, *39–41*
 centre of espionage, *236*
 East–West exodus, *44–5*
 position in Cold War, *39*
 stand-off at Checkpoint
  Charlie, *46*
 visit by President Kennedy,
  46–7
 Wall *see* Berlin Wall
Berlin Blockade, *39–41*
Berlin Wall
 concerts, *250*
 erection and escapes, *45–7*
 dismantling, *226*

Big Three
    meetings, *10, 12–15*
    see also Churchill;
        Roosevelt; Stalin
Bizonia, *38*
Bond movies, reflection of
    political change, *241–2*
Brezhnev, Leonid
    détente, *94–5*
    peace programme, *160,
        169*
    warning to Czechoslovakia,
        152
Brezhnev Doctrine, *156, 246*
brinkmanship, *66, 124, 129*
Britain
    agreement with Shah of
        Iran, *174*
    Berlin airlift, *39–40*
    Korean War, *54, 64–5*
    sector in Germany, *34, 35,
        36, 38*
    siting of US missiles, *90*
    Suez crisis, *177–9*
    war in Malaya, *52–3*
    see also Churchill; Thatcher
Broz, Josip (Tito), *24–5, 231*
buffer zone, USSR, *17–18, 21*
Bulgaria
    fall of communism, *230*
    loss of monarchy, *23*
    USSR influence, *12*
Burgess, Guy, *237*

Cambridge Five, *237, 238*
Campaign for Nuclear
    Disarmament, *101–2*
capitalism, *4, 6*

Carter, James (Jimmy)
    denial of Somalian aid, *196*
    Middle East intervention,
        185
    response to Kabul invasion,
        190
Castro, Fidel, *107–9, 120–1, 123–4,
    125, 200*
    assassination attempts,
        109–10, 244
Castro, Raul, *125*
CDU, *36*
Ceausescu, Nikolae, *228–9*
Central Intelligence Agency
    see CIA
Central Treaty Organization, *174,
    181*
Chernobyl nuclear explosion,
    218–19
Chiang Kai-shek, *50, 51, 128*
Chile, interference from US, *205–7*
China
    admission to UN, *162*
    attack on Formosa, *66*
    civil war, *50–1*
    communism, *49, 51–2*
    détente, *160–1, 161–3*
    Korean War, *55, 59–63*
    Mao's policies, *130–1*
    nuclear weapons, *92*
    support for North Vietnam,
        137
    and USA, *51, 162–3*
    and USSR, *51, 128, 129–31*
    war against Vietnam, *144*
    see also Mao Zedong
Christian Democrat party (CDU),
    36

Churchill, Winston S.
    discussions with Stalin, *10,*
      11–12
    iron curtain speech, *18*
    role in détente, *66–7*
    support for Greek
      monarchy, *26*
    view of Marshall Plan, *30*
    White Russian aid, *7*
CIA
    anti-Guatemalan guerrillas,
      106–7
    disinformation campaign,
      244
    effect of Soviet spying, *237*
    free radio station, *76*
    meeting over Grenada crisis,
      98
    moles, *238*
    operation in Cuba, *109–10, 112*
    and peace movements, *102*
    plans against Castro, *110, 112*
    tunnel under Berlin, *236*
    unrest in Chile, *206*
CIS, *248–9*
Civic Forum, *228*
Clay, General Lucius, *38, 39, 45–6*
CND, *101–2*
Cold War
    description, *2–3*
    effect of populations, *249–51*
    financial costs, *251–2*
    origins, *2, 5–8*
COMECON, *144*
Cominform, creation, *29, 38*
Comintern, *5, 38*
Commonwealth of Independent
  States (CIS), *248–9*

communism
    in China, *49, 51–2*
    in Eastern Europe, *34–41,*
      43–6, 47, 73–8
      fall, *222–32, 247*
    and Korean War, *55–65*
    in Latin America, *203*
    in Malaya, *52–3*
    style of government, *4, 5–6*
    under Tito, *24–5, 231*
communist threat, *6*
consumerism, in Eastern Europe,
  224
containment, *28*
Contras, *100, 208, 209*
cordon sanitaire (buffer zone),
  17–18, 21
Council for Mutual Economic
  Co-operation, *144*
counter-intelligence, *235–6*
counterpart funds, *31*
Croatia, *232*
Cuba
    and Africa, *196, 198, 199,*
      200, 201
    Castro's seizure of power,
      107–8
    CIA operations, *109–10, 112*
    and Latin America, *203, 208,*
      209, 210
    missile base crisis, *113–23*
    playground of the USA,
      107
    relationship with USSR, *109*
    support for El Salvador, *210*
Cuban blockade, *117*
Cuban missile crisis, *113–23*
Czech Republic, *232*

Czechoslovakia
    division, *232*
    economic reform, *150–1*
    human rights issues, *168*
    invasion, *153–5*
    Prague spring, *151*
    Velvet Revolution, *156, 227–8*
    Warsaw Pact influence, *152–3*

D-Day landings, *9–10*
Daoud, Muhammad, *189*
denazification of Germany, *34–6*
détente
    arms race, *94–6, 164–7*
    Basic Principles of Relations, *181*
    beginnings, *66–7*
    Brandt's Ostpolitik policy, *158–9*
    and Czechoslovakia, *155*
    end, *169–70, 213–14*
    and Gorbachev, *219–20*
    human rights, *167–9*
    motives for, *159–61*
    USA and China, *161–3*
    USA and USSR, *163–4*
Dew Line, *239*
Diem, Ngo Dinh, *132, 134–5*
Domino Theory, *65–6, 144*
Dubcek, Alexander, *150, 152, 153, 154, 155, 228*

East Berlin, escapes to West, *47*
East Germany
    advent of communism, *24*
    Basic Treaty, *159*
    establishment of Cominform, *38*
    government, *41*
    political groups, *36*
    reunification with West Germany, *225–7*
    see also Berlin
Eastern Europe
    effect of de-Stalinization, *73*
    elections, *13*
    expulsion of Germans, *16*
    fall of communism, *158, 222–32, 247*
    intimidation and censorship, *223*
    occupation by USSR, *21, 22*
    rebellion, *73–8*
    unity with USSR, *156*
    Velvet Revolution, *156, 227–8*
    Warsaw Defence Treaty, *42–3*
    see also Czechoslovakia; Hungary; Poland; Romania
economic aid, Marshall Plan, *28–31*
Egypt
    relationship with USSR, *72, 179, 181, 183, 184*
    Six Day War, *180–1*
    Suez crisis, *177–9*
Eisenhower, Dwight
    Domino Theory, *65*
    Korean War, *62*
    lack of response to Hungary, *77*
    policy on Cuba, *109*
    US spy planes, *87, 90*
El Salvador, conflict, *210*
Ethiopia, *201–2*
ExComm, *114–16, 118, 122*

Far East *see* China; Korea;
  Malaya; Vietnam
fashion, effect of Cold War, *249*
federal government, *36*
feudalism, *49–50*
films, *65, 241–2, 250–1*
Fleming, Ian, *241*
FNLA, *197, 198, 199*
Ford, Gerald, denial of Angolan
  aid, *196*
France
    control of Indo-China, *132*
    military aid to Chad, *196*
    Suez crisis, *177–9*
free elections promise, *14*
Front for the National Liberation
  of Angola (FNLA), *197, 198, 199*
frontier changes, Europe, *2, 14*
Fuchs, Klaus, *16–17, 82, 236*

Gagarin, Yuri, *91*
Gaza Strip, *185*
Geneva accords, Afghanistan,
  192
Geneva summit 1955, *70, 132*
German problem, *43, 158, 159*
Germany
    Berlin Blockade, *39–41*
    currencies, *38–9*
    democratization, *36–7*
    Denazification, *34–6*
    division post-war, *13, 15,
      33–4, 35*
    post-war condition, *33*
    reparations, *14, 15, 37*
    reunification, *226–7*
    see also Berlin; East
      Germany; West Germany

giant pandas, diplomatic gifts,
  163
glasnost, 218, 248
Glienicke Bridge, *237*
Gloster Hill battle, *65*
Gold, Harry, *16–17*
Goldfuss, Emil, *239*
Gomulka, Wladyslaw, *73–4*
Gorbachev, Mikhail
    and Afghanistan, *191–2*
    appointment, *98–9*
    and arms race, *99–101*
    attitude to Eastern Bloc, *223*
    demise of power, *247–8*
    détente, *219–20*
    and Reagan, *99–100*
    reforms, *218*
    response to protests, *226*
    United Nations speech, *220,
      246*
great grain robbery, *166*
Great Leap Forward, China, *130–1*
Great Powers, *3–5*
    see also China; USA; USSR
Greece
    British influence, *12*
    restoration of monarchy, *26*
Greenham Common, *102–3*
Grenada, invasion by USA, *98*
Guatemala, US support, *106–7*
Guavera, Che, *107–8*
Gulf of Tonkin attacks, *136*
Gulf War 1980, *188–9*

Hall, Ted, *82, 236*
Hammarskjold, Dag, assassination,
  195
Helsinki Accords, *167–8*

Hiroshima, nuclear bomb, *17*
Ho Chi Minh, *132, 133–4*
Honecker, Erich, *225*
Horn of Africa, *201–2*
human rights
    atrocities in S America,
      206–7, 207–8, 210
    détente, *167–8*
Hungary
    economic prosperity, *79*
    loss of democracy, *23*
    reform, *224–5*
    uprising, *75–8*
Hussain, Saddam, war with Iran,
   188
hydrogen bombs, *84–5*
hyper-inflation, *7–8*

ICBMs, *84, 88*
Ich bin ein Berliner speech, *46–7*
Indo-China, division, *132*
intercontinental ballistic
  missiles (ICBMs), *84, 88*
Intermediate-range Nuclear
  Forces (INF) Treaty, *100, 103*
Intifada, *185*
Iran, *185–9*
Irangate, *100*
iron curtain speech, *18*
Israel
    conflict with Arabs, *176–7,
      180–5*
    US support, *174–6, 177–8,
      180–1, 182–3, 184*

James Bond movies, *241–2, 251*
Johnson, Lyndon B.
    escalation of Vietnam war,
      135, 136–7, 138, 139

    peace initiatives, *142*
    social reform reduction,
      141, 145

Kadar, Janos, *78, 79*
KAL 007, *217*
Kennan, George, *18*
Kennedy, John
    arms race, *91*
    assassination, *124–5, 135*
    Bay of Pigs, *111*
    Berlin crisis, *44, 45, 46–7*
    and Castro, *244*
    Cuban missile crisis, *116–17,
      118, 119, 121, 124*
    Cuban trade embargo,
      110
    decisions on Vietnam, *134,
      135*
Kennedy, Robert, talks with
  USSR, *119, 120, 122*
KGB
    overthrow of Amin, *190*
    spies, *236, 237–8, 239*
    see also USSR, spies
Khomeini, Ayatollah
  Ruhollah, *186–7, 189*
Khrushchev, Nikita
    Cuban missile crisis, *113–14,
      117, 119, 120, 123*
    de-Stalinization of USSR,
      71–2
    exposure of US spy planes,
      87
    and Hungarian uprising,
      76–7, 78
    response to Berlin, *44, 45,
      46, 47*
    split with Mao, *130*

Kissinger, Henry
    agreements with USSR, *166*
    attitude to Mao Zedong, *162*
    October War, *183*
    peace with Vietnam, *143*
Korean War, *54–63*
    films, *65, 251*
    forgotten war, *64–5*
    global effect, *127–8*
    significance for Cold War,
        63–4
Krenz, Egon, *226*

Latin America
    communism, *203*
    see also Chile; Nicaragua
Le Carré, John, *240*
League of Nations, *5, 7*
    see also United Nations
listening stations, *239*
literature, influence of Cold War,
    240–2, 250
lithium bombs, *85–6*
Live Aid, *202*
Long Telegram, *18*
Lucky Dragon incident, *85–6*

MacArthur, General[N], *55, 58–9, 61*
McCarthy, Joe, witch-hunts, *249*
Maclean, Donald, *237*
MAD situation, *84, 95*
Malay Emergency, *52–3*
Malayan Communist Party (MCP),
    52–3
Mao Zedong, *49, 50–1, 92, 128*
    Great Leap Forward, *129–30*
    Khrushchev split, *130*
    meeting with Nixon, *162*

nuclear weapons, *92*
relationship with USSR,
    129–30
rise to power, *49, 50–1*
spread of communism, *128,
    131*
Markov, Georgi, *244*
Marshall, George C., *26–7, 28–31*
Marshall Plan, *28–31*
massive retaliation principle,
    63, 66
MCP, *52–3*
media
    effect of Vietnam coverage,
        145
    see also films
Middle East
    Afghanistan conflict, *188–92*
    Arab–Israeli conflict, *176–7*
    conflict in Iran, *186–8*
    Gulf War 1980, *188–9*
    importance of oil supplies,
        173–4
    October War, *181–4*
    Sadat peace mission, *184–5*
    supply of arms by USA, *174–6*
    see also Afghanistan; Egypt;
        Iran; Israel
Mohammad Daoud, Sardar, *189*
moles (espionage), *238*
Molotov-Ribbentrop Pact, *6*
Monroe Doctrine, *203*
movies, *65, 241–2, 250–1*
MPLA, *197, 198, 199–200*
Mujahideen, torture of captives,
    191
music, influence of Cold War, *250*
My Lai massacre, *140*

Nagasaki, nuclear bomb, 17
Nagy, Imre, 75, 76, 78
Namibia, independence, 200
NASA, 90–1
Nasser, Gamar, 72, 177–9, 180
National Union for the Total
  Independence of Angola
  (UNITA), 197, 199, 200
NATO, formation, 41–2
Nicaragua, conflicts, 207–10
Nixon, Richard
    attitude to Chile, 205
    relationship with China, 162
    Vietnam policies, 142–3
    visit to Moscow, 166
North Atlantic Treaty
  Organisation, 41–2
North Korea see Korean War
North Vietnam
    creation, 132–4
    final offensive, 143–4
    Russian military equipment,
    139
    see also Vietcong; Vietnam
novels, influence of Cold War,
  240–2, 250
Novotny, Antonin, 150
nuclear landmines, 103
nuclear weapons
    accidents, 93–4
    attacks considered by USA,
    45, 66
    cost, 251
    effect of threat, 62, 63, 66
    first explosions, 3, 16–17
    INF weapon elimination, 100
    missile bases, 90, 113–23,
    122, 152–3

spying operations, 236
test-ban treaty, 124
see also arms race
Nuremberg, war crimes trials, 35

Obama, Barack, relationship
  with Cuba, 125
October War, 181–4
oil, dependence of West, 173–4
Olof Palme Peace March, 225
OPEC oil prices, 183–4
Operation Mongoose, 112
Operation Rolling Thunder, 138
Operation Splinter Faction, 244

Pacific atom bomb tests, 84–5
Palach, Jan, 155, 227
Palestine, partitioning, 176–7
Palestinians, uprising, 185
Palme, Olof, 225
Paris Peace Accords, 143
Paris summit, 87
peace movements, 101–3
perestroika, 218
Philby, Kim, 237
ping-pong diplomacy, 161
Pinochet, General Augusto, 206
Poland
    loss of democracy, 22
    Nazi-Soviet division, 6
    post-war disagreements,
    13–14
    reforms by Gomulka, 73–4
    rise of Solidarity, 215–16
    USSR/USA pawn, 14
    Warsaw uprising, 11
    western frontier, 7, 8, 15
Polish Corridor, 12–13

Polyakov, Dmitri, *238*
Popular Movement for
  the Liberation of Angola
  (MPLA), *197, 198, 199–200*
popular music, influence of
  Cold War, *250*
post-traumatic stress disorder, *146*
Potsdam Conference, *15–16, 17, 37*
Powers, Gary, *238*
Pozsgay, Imre, *224*
Prague spring, *151*
Public Against Violence, *228*

Radio Free Europe (RFE), *76–7*
Rakosi, Matyas, *23*
Reagan, Ronald
    and Cold War, *96–8, 98–101,
      213–14, 217, 220*
    Irangate, *210*
    reluctance to compromise,
      170
    support for El Salvador, *210*
Red Army, *11, 14, 17, 21*
Roosevelt, Franklin D., talks with
  Stalin, *14*
refuseniks, *169*
religious freedom, *224*
reparation from Germany, *14, 15, 37*
Reykjavik Summit, *219–20*
RFE, *76–7*
Romania
    abdication of king, *23*
    communist regime, *228–9*
    distancing from Moscow, *156*
    fall of communism, *229–30*
    USSR influence, *12*
Romanian orphanages, *228–9*
Russian Civil War, *5, 7*

Sadat, Anwar, *175, 181, 184–5*
SALT, *95, 164–6*
Sandinista National Liberation
  Front, *208, 209*
SDI, *97, 170, 213*
SEATO, *128*
September 11th terrorist
  attacks, *252*
Shah of Iran, *186*
Sino-Soviet split, *129–31, 137, 162*
Six Day War, *180–1*
Slovakia, *232*
Slovenia, *232*
Smallholders' Party, *224, 225*
Solidarity, *215–17*
Solidarnosc, *215–17*
Solzhenitsyn, Alexander, *250*
Somalia, *201–2*
South Africa and Angola, *198,
  199, 200*
South East Asia Treaty
  Organization (SEATO), *128*
South Korea *see* Korean War
South Vietnam
    creation and development
      of conflict, *132, 134–5*
    military action by US, *138–9*
    Peace Accord arrangements,
      143
    US pacification programme,
      140
    see also Vietnam
South West African People's
  Organization (SWAPO), *200*
Soviet *see* USSR
space race, *88–9, 90–1, 91, 166*
spheres of interest document,
  11–12

sports
  boycott of Moscow games,
    190
  ping-pong diplomacy, 161
spying
  and arms race, 82
  atomic bomb programme,
    16–17, 82, 236
  Bond movies, 241–2, 251
  in fiction, 240–2
  motives, 237–8
  operations, 234–7, 244
  operatives' background,
    234–5, 242–4
  spy planes, 86–7
  by Stalin in Tehran, 11
  technology, 238–9
  see also CIA; KGB; Soviet
    spies
Stalin, Joseph
  discussions with Churchill,
    10–11, 11–12
  installation of communist
    leaders, 22
  Korean War, 55, 62
  relationship with Mao,
    129–30
  speech against capitalism, 18
  view of English, 7
Star Wars, 97, 170, 213
Strategic Arms Limitation
  Talks, 95, 164–6
Strategic Defence Initiative
  (SDI), 97, 170, 213
Strehla meeting, 1
Suez Canal, 76, 177–9, 180, 184
Summit conferences, 70–1, 87,
  132, 219–20

Supreme Soviet, 18
Sutterlin, Heinz, 234–5
SWAPO, 200
Syria, 175, 181
  Suez crisis, 177–9

Taiwan Strait Crisis, 129, 130
Tehran, Big Three meeting, 10
television, coverage of Vietnam,
  145
terrorist attacks 9/11, 252
Tet offensive, 141
Thatcher, Margaret
  anti-communist attitude,
    213–14
  criticism of USSR, 170
Tiananmen Square massacre,
  246–7
Tito, 24–5, 231
totalitarian states, 27
trade agreements, USA/
  USSR, 164
tram from Czechoslovakia,
  149–50
Treaty of Moscow, 158
Treaty of Warsaw, 158
Truman, Harry S.
  attitude to Stalin, 15, 16
  dropping of atomic bombs,
    17
  Korean War, 55, 57, 61
  support for Greece, 26–7
Truman Doctrine, 27
Turkey, US missile base, 122
Twin Towers, terrorist attacks,
  252
Two Thousand Word Manifesto,
  The, 152

U-2 spy planes, *86–7, 90, 238*
Ulbricht, Walter, *24*
UNITA, *197, 199, 200*
United Nations, *13*
   see also League of Nations
USA
   and Afghanistan, *190, 192*
   role in Africa, *196–7, 198–9,*
    201
   anti-war movements, *145*
   atomic threat, *66*
   and Chile, *205–7*
   and China, *51, 162–3*
   drugs problem, *145–6*
   economy post-war, *31*
   and El Salvador, *210*
   Embassy siege, Iran, *187*
   invasion of Grenada, *98*
   and Iran/Iraq war, *188–9*
   and Korean War, *55, 56–63*
   missile bases, *90, 122, 169*
   motives for détente, *160*
   mover in second Cold War,
    213–14
   and Nicaragua, *207–10*
   nuclear weapons, *84–5,*
    85–6, 87
   relationship with Shah of
    Iran, *186*
   reparation cessation, *37*
   response to SE Asia
    communism, *128–9*
   Sputnik, *88–9*
   spy techniques, *238–9*
   support for Chiang Kai-shek,
    50, 51, 128
   support for economic
    recovery in Europe, *28–31*
   support for Greek monarchy,
    26–7
   support for Israel, *174–6,*
    177–8, 179, 180–1, 182–3, 184
   technological education, *89*
   terrorist attacks 9/11, *252*
   and USSR, *163–4*
   as victor in Cold War, *252*
   Vietnam conflict, *66, 134–5,*
    138, 140–4, 145–6
   see also Carter; CIA;
    Eisenhower; Ford; Kennedy,
    John; Nixon; Obama;
    Reagan; Roosevelt; Truman
USSR
   action in Poland, *216*
   and Afghanistan, *189–92*
   and Africa, *196, 198, 200, 201*
   aid to Middle East, *72, 174*
   aid to nationalist revolutions,
    73
   aid to Vietnam, *144*
   aims for post-war Europe, *8*
   attitude to Latin America,
    204, 210
   buffer zone, *17–18*
   and change in Eastern Europe,
    222–4
   and China, *51, 128, 129–31*
   communist coup 1991, *247*
   dependence of West, *165–6*
   détente, *160, 169, 219–20*
   economic reform, *218*
   and Egypt, *72, 179, 181, 183,*
    184
   end, *248*
   glasnost, *218, 248*
   hot-line to Washington, *124*

USSR *(Contd)*
    KGB, *190, 236, 237–8, 239*
    missile bases, *113–23*
    nuclear weapons, *82–4, 88, 90*
    reduction in military force, *101*
    spies, *16–17, 234–5, 236, 237, 238–9, 242–4*
    support for Syria, *175, 181*
    treaty with Iraq, *180*
    and USA, *163–4*
    view of Marshall Plan, *29*
    see also Brezhnev; Gorbachev; Khrushchev; Stalin; Yeltsin

Velvet Revolution, *156, 227–8*
Vietcong, *134, 136, 137–8, 141, 143*
Vietminh, *132*
Vietnam
    conflict, *66*
    consequences of war, *144*
    creation, *132*
    films, *251*
    peace initiatives, *141, 142, 143*
    US non-communist support, *66*
    wartime resistance groups, *132*
    see also North Vietnam; South Vietnam
Vietnam veterans, rejection, *146*
Vietnamization policy, *142–3*

Walesa, Lech, *215*
war crimes trials, Nuremberg, *35*
Warsaw, 1944 massacre, *11*

Warsaw Defence Treaty, *42–3*
Warsaw Pact countries
    concern over Czechoslovakia, *152, 153*
    formation, *42–3*
    Hungary's wish to withdraw, *76, 78*
    Poland remains, *74*
Washington Summit, *220*
West Bank, *185*
West Germany
    Basic Treaty, *159*
    membership of NATO, *42*
    reunification with East Germany, *226–7*
    unification of Western sectors, *37–8*
western frontier, USSR, *21*
Western powers
    aims for post-war Europe, *7*
    effect of Russian spy operations, *16–17, 82, 236, 237*
    see also Britain; France; USA
'winds of change', *194–5*
World Trade Centre, terrorist attacks, *252*

Yalta meeting, Big Three, *12–15*
Yeltsin, Boris, *247, 248*
Yugoslavia
    British/USSR influence, *12*
    communism under Tito, *24–5, 231*
    ethnic conflict and division, *232*